W9-ADB-067

TECHNICAL COLLEGE OF THE LOWCOUNTRY
LEARNING RESOURCES CENTER
POST OFFICE BOX 1288
BEAUFORT, SOUTH CAROLINA 29901-1288

Bloom's Modern Critical Views

Bloom's Modern Critical Views

Bloom's Modern Critical Views

NATHANIEL HAWTHORNE
Updated Edition

Edited and with an introduction by
Harold Bloom
Sterling Professor of the Humanities
Yale University

CHELSEA HOUSE
PUBLISHERS
An imprint of Infobase Publishing

Bloom's Modern Critical Views: Nathaniel Hawthorne—Updated Edition

Copyright ©2007 Infobase Publishing

Introduction © 2007 by Harold Bloom

All rights reserved. No part of this publication may be reproduced or utilized in any form or by any means, electronic or mechanical, including photocopying, recording, or by any information storage or retrieval systems, without permission in writing from the publisher. For more information contact:

Chelsea House
An imprint of Infobase Publishing
132 West 31st Street
New York NY 10001

Library of Congress Cataloging-in-Publication Data
Nathaniel Hawthorne / Harold Bloom, editor. — Updated ed.
       p. cm — (Bloom's modern critical views)
    Includes bibliographical references and index.
    ISBN 0-7910-9315-8
  1. Hawthorne, Nathaniel, 1804–1864—Criticism and interpretation. I.
Bloom, Harold. II. Title. III. Series.
    PS1888.N295 2007
    813'.3—dc22   2006031067

Chelsea House books are available at special discounts when purchased in bulk quantities for businesses, associations, institutions, or sales promotions. Please call our Special Sales Department in New York at (212) 967-8800 or (800) 322-8755.

You can find Chelsea House on the World Wide Web at http://www.chelseahouse.com

Contributing Editor: Janyce Marson
Cover designed by Takeshi Takahashi
Cover photo © Library of Congress Prints and Photographs Division

Printed in the United States of America
Bang EJB 10 9 8 7 6 5 4 3 2 1

This book is printed on acid-free paper.

All links and web addresses were checked and verified to be correct at the time of publication. Because of the dynamic nature of the web, some addresses and links may have changed since publication and may no longer be valid.

Contents

Editor's Note

My Introduction considers Hawthorne in the context both of Emerson's influence upon *The Scarlet Letter* and of the ambivalent responses by Henry James to the influences upon *him* of both Emerson and Hawthorne. After interpreting Hester as an Emersonian heroine, I go on to analyze Hawthorne's superb final tale, "Feathertop."

Millicent Bell examines Hawthorne's three artist-heroes: Coverdale in *The Blithedale Romance*, Holgrave the writer in *The House of the Seven Gables*, and Kenyon the sculptor in *The Marble Faun*.

Hawthorne's own psychology is traced in *The House of the Seven Gables* by Frederick C. Crews, while Jane Donahue Eberwein examines "The Custom-House" sketch as a thematic introduction to *The Scarlet Letter*, as does David C. Cody.

The Blithedale Romance is approached biographically by Edwin Haviland Miller, after which Samuel Coale disputes the historicism of Sacvan Bercovich as a wholly satisfactory way into Hawthornian romance.

Michael Dunne studies the relationships between Romanticism and Hawthorne's tales, after which Joseph Flibbert considers Hawthorne's representation of Judge Pyncheon in *The House of the Seven Gables*.

The defensive critique of *The Scarlet Letter* by Henry James prompts Dan McCall's own account of the great novel, while David B. Kesterson reads *The Marble Faun's* representation of the Roman Carnival as a kind of an apocalypse.

In this volume's final essay, Richard Kopley uncovers the influence of the narrative poem "A Legend of Brittany," by Hawthorne's friend, James Russell Lowell, upon *The Scarlet Letter*.

HAROLD BLOOM

Introduction

I

Henry James's *Hawthorne* was published in December 1879, in London, in the English Men of Letters series. Unique among the thirty-nine volumes of that group, this was a critical study of an American by an American. Only Hawthorne seemed worthy of being an English man of letters, and only James seemed capable of being an American critic. Perhaps this context inhibited James, whose *Hawthorne* tends to be absurdly overpraised, or perhaps Hawthorne caused James to feel an anxiety that even George Eliot could not bring the self-exiled American to experience. Whatever the reason, James wrote a study that requires to be read between the lines, as here in its final paragraph:

> He was a beautiful, natural, original genius, and his life had been singularly exempt from worldly preoccupations and vulgar efforts. It had been as pure, as simple, as unsophisticated, as his work. He had lived primarily in his domestic affections, which were of the tenderest kind; and then—without eagerness, without pretension, but with a great deal of quiet devotion—in his charming art. His work will remain; it is too original and exquisite to pass away; among the men of imagination he will always have his niche. No one has had just that vision of life, and

no one has had a literary form that more successfully expressed his vision. He was not a moralist, and he was not simply a poet. The moralists are weightier, denser, richer, in a sense; the poets are more purely inconclusive and irresponsible. He combined in a singular degree the spontaneity of the imagination with a haunting care for moral problems. Man's conscience was his theme, but he saw it in the light of a creative fancy which added, out of its own substance, an interest, and, I may almost say, an importance.

Is *The Scarlet Letter* pure, simple, and unsophisticated? Is *The Marble Faun* a work neither moral nor poetic? Can we accurately assert that man's conscience, however lit by creative fancy, is Hawthorne's characteristic concern? James's vision of his American precursor is manifestly distorted by a need to misread creatively what may hover too close, indeed may shadow the narrative space that James requires for his own enterprise. In that space, something beyond shadowing troubles James. Isabel Archer has her clear affinities with Dorothea Brooke, yet her relation to Hester Prynne is even more familial, just as Millie Theale will have the lineage of *The Marble Faun*'s Hilda ineluctably marked upon her. James's representations of women are Hawthornian in ways subtly evasive yet finally unmistakable. Yet even this influence and its consequent ambivalences do not seem to be the prime unease that weakens James's *Hawthorne*. Rather, the critical monograph is more embarrassed than it can know by James's guilt at having abandoned the American destiny. Elsewhere, James wrote to some purpose about Emerson (though not so well as his brother William did), but in *Hawthorne* the figure of Emerson is unrecognizable and the dialectics of New England Transcendentalism are weakly abused:

> A biographer of Hawthorne might well regret that his hero had not been more mixed up with the reforming and free-thinking class, so that he might find a pretext for writing a chapter upon the state of Boston society forty years ago. A needful warrant for such regret should be, properly, that the biographer's own personal reminiscences should stretch back to that period and to the persons who animated it. This would be a guarantee of fulness of knowledge and, presumably, of kindness of tone. It is difficult to see, indeed, how the generation of which Hawthorne has given us, in *Blithedale*, a few portraits, should not, at this time of day, be spoken of very tenderly and sympathetically. If irony enter into the allusion, it should be of the lightest and gentlest.

Certainly, for a brief and imperfect chronicler of these things, a writer just touching them as he passes, and who has not the advantage of having been a contemporary, there is only one possible tone. The compiler of these pages, though his recollections date only from a later period, has a memory of a certain number of persons who had been intimately connected, as Hawthorne was not, with the agitations of that interesting time. Something of its interest adhered to them still—something of its aroma clung to their garments; there was something about them which seemed to say that when they were young and enthusiastic, they had been initiated into moral mysteries, they had played at a wonderful game. Their usual mark (it is true I can think of exceptions) was that they seemed excellently good. They appeared unstained by the world, unfamiliar with worldly desires and standards, and with those various forms of human depravity which flourish in some high phases of civilisation; inclined to simple and democratic ways, destitute of pretensions and affectations, of jealousies, of cynicisms, of snobbishness. This little epoch of fermentation has three or four drawbacks for the critics—drawbacks, however, that may be overlooked by a person for whom it has an interest of association. It bore, intellectually, the stamp of provincialism; it was a beginning without a fruition, a dawn without a noon; and it produced, with a single exception, no great talents. It produced a great deal of writing, but (always putting Hawthorne aside, as a contemporary but not a sharer) only one writer in whom the world at large has interested itself. The situation was summed up and transfigured in the admirable and exquisite Emerson. He expressed all that it contained, and a good deal more, doubtless, besides; he was the man of genius of the moment; he was the Transcendentalist *par excellence*. Emerson expressed, before all things, as was extremely natural at the hour and in the place, the value and importance of the individual, the duty of making the most of one's self, of living by one's own personal light, and carrying out one's own disposition. He reflected with beautiful irony upon the exquisite impudence of those institutions which claim to have appropriated the truth and to dole it out, in proportionate morsels, in exchange for a subscription. He talked about the beauty and dignity of life, and about every one who is born into the world being born to the whole, having an interest and a stake in the whole. He said "all that is clearly due to-day is not to lie," and a great many other things which it would be still easier to present in a ridiculous light. He insisted upon sincerity and independence and spontaneity, upon acting in harmony with one's nature, and not conforming and compromising for the sake of being more comfortable. He urged that a man should await his call, his finding the thing to do which he should really believe in doing, and not be urged by the world's opinion to do simply the world's work. "If no call should come for years, for centuries, then I know that the want of the Universe is the attestation of faith by my abstinence.... If I cannot work, at least I need not lie." The doctrine of the supremacy of the individual to himself, of his originality, and, as regards his own character, *unique* quality, must have had a great charm for people living in a society in which introspection—thanks to the want of other entertainment— played almost the part of a social resource.

The "admirable and exquisite Emerson" was "as sweet as barbed wire," to quote President Giamatti of Yale. Any reader of that great, grim, and most American of books, *The Conduct of Life*, ought to have known this. James's Emerson, dismissed here by the novelist as a provincial of real charm, had provoked the senior Henry James to an outburst of more authentic critical value: "O you man without a handle!" Hawthorne too, in a very different way, was a man without a handle, not less conscious and subtle an artist than the younger Henry James himself. *The Scarlet Letter*, in James's *Hawthorne*, is rightly called the novelist's masterpiece, but then is accused of "a want of reality and an abuse of the fanciful element—of a certain superficial symbolism." James was too good a reader to have indicted Hawthorne for "a want of reality," were it not that Hawthornian representation had begun too well the process of causing a Jamesian aspect of reality to appear.

II

Of the four principal figures in *The Scarlet Letter*, Pearl is at once the most surprising, and the largest intimation of Hawthorne's farthest imaginings. There is no indication that Hawthorne shared his friend Melville's deep interest in ancient Gnosticism, though esoteric heresies were clearly part of Hawthorne's abiding concern with witchcraft. The Gnostic *Gospel of Thomas* contains a remarkable mythic narrative, "The Hymn of the Pearl," that juxtaposes illuminatingly with the uncanny daughter of Hester Prynne and the Reverend Mr. Dimmesdale. In Gnostic symbolism, the pearl is identical with the spark or *pneuma* that is the ontological self of the adept who shares in the Gnosis, in the true knowing that surmounts mere faith. The pearl particularly represents what is best and oldest in the adept, because creation is the work of a mere demiurge, while the best part of us, that which is capable of knowing, was never made, but is one with the original Abyss, the Foremother and Forefather who is the true or alien God. When Hawthorne's Pearl passionately insists she was not made by God, we hear again the most ancient and challenging of all Western heresies:

> The old minister seated himself in an arm-chair, and made an effort to draw Pearl betwixt his knees. But the child, unaccustomed to the touch or familiarity of any but her mother, escaped through the open window and stood on the upper step, looking like a wild, tropical bird, of rich plumage, ready to take flight into the upper air. Mr. Wilson, not a little astonished at this outbreak,—for he was a grandfatherly sort of personage, and usually a vast favorite with children,—essayed, however, to proceed with the examination.
>
> "Pearl," said he, with great solemnity, "thou must take heed to instruction, that so, in due season, thou mayest wear in thy bosom the pearl of great price. Canst thou tell me, my child, who made thee?"
>
> Now Pearl knew well enough who made her; for Hester Prynne, the daughter of a pious home, very soon after her talk with the child about her Heavenly Father, had begun to inform her of those truths which the human spirit, at whatever stage of immaturity, imbibes with such eager interest. Pearl, therefore, so large were the attainments of her three years' lifetime, could have borne a fair examination in the New England Primer, or the first column of the Westminster Catechism, although unacquainted with the outward form of either of those celebrated works. But that perversity, which all children have more or less of, and of which little Pearl had a tenfold portion, now, at the most inopportune moment, took thorough possession of her, and closed her lips, or impelled her to speak words amiss. After putting her finger in her mouth, with many ungracious refusals to answer good Mr. Wilson's question, the child finally announced that she had not been made at all, but had been plucked by her mother off the bush of wild roses, that grew by the prison-door.

That Pearl, elf-child, is the romance's prime knower no reader would doubt. The subtlest relation in Hawthorne's sinuously ambiguous romance is not that between Chillingworth and Dimmesdale, let alone the inadequate ghost of the love between Hester and Dimmesdale. It is the ambivalent and persuasive mother-daughter complex in which Hester is saved both from suicidal despair and from the potential of becoming the prophetess of a feminist religion only by the extraordinary return in her daughter of everything she herself has repressed. I will venture the speculation that both Hester and Pearl are intense representations of two very different aspects of Emersonianism, Hester being a prime instance of Emerson's American religion of self-reliance, while Pearl emerges from a deeper stratum of Emerson, from the Orphism and Gnosticism that mark the sage's first anarchic influx of power and knowledge, when he celebrated his own version of what he called, following the Swedenborgians, the terrible freedom or newness. Emerson, Hawthorne's Concord walking companion, is generally judged by scholars and critics to be antithetical to Hawthorne. I doubt that judgment, since manifestly Hawthorne does not prefer the pathetic Dimmesdale and the mock-satanic Chillingworth to the self-reliant Hester and the daemonic Pearl. Henry James, like T. S. Eliot, considered Emerson to be deficient in a sense of sin, a sense obsessive in Dimmesdale and Chillingworth, alien to Pearl, and highly dialectical in Hester.

In the Gnostic mode of Pearl, the young Emerson indeed affirmed: "My heart did never counsel me to sin. . . ./ I never taught it what it teaches me." This is the adept of Orphic mysteries who also wrote: "It is God in you that responds to God without, or affirms his own words trembling on the lips of another," words that "sound to you as old as yourself." The direct precursor to *The Scarlet Letter*'s Pearl is a famous moment in Emerson's "Self-Reliance," an essay surely known to Hawthorne:

> I remember an answer which when quite young I was prompted to make to a valued adviser who was wont to importune me with the dear old doctrines of the church. On my saying, "What have I to do with the sacredness of traditions, if I live wholly from within?" my friend suggested,—"But these impulses may be from below, not from above." I replied, "They do not seem to me to be such; but if I am the Devil's child, I will live then from the Devil."

Call this Pearl's implicit credo, since her positive declaration is: "I have no Heavenly Father!" Even as Pearl embodies Emerson's most anarchic, antinomian strain, Hester incarnates the central impulse of "Self-Reliance." This is the emphasis of chapter 13 of the romance, "Another View of Hester," which eloquently tells us: "The scarlet letter had not done its office." In effect, Hawthorne presents her as Emerson's American precursor, and as the forerunner also of movements still working themselves through among us:

> Much of the marble coldness of Hester's impression was to be attributed to the circumstance that her life had turned, in a great measure, from passion and feeling, to thought. Standing alone in the world,—alone, as to any dependence on society, and with little Pearl to be guided and protected,—alone, and hopeless of retrieving her position, even had she not scorned to consider it desirable,—she cast away the fragments of a broken chain. The world's law was no law for her mind. It was an age in which the human intellect, newly emancipated, had taken a more active and a wider range than for many centuries before. Men of the sword had overthrown nobles and kings. Men bolder than these had overthrown and rearranged—not actually, but within the sphere of theory, which was their most real abode—the whole system of ancient prejudice, wherewith was linked much of ancient principle. Hester Prynne imbibed this spirit. She assumed a freedom of speculation, then common enough on the other side of the Atlantic, but which our forefathers, had they known of it, would have held to be a deadlier crime than that stigmatized by the scarlet letter. In her lonesome cottage, by the sea-shore, thoughts visited her, such as dared to enter no other dwelling in New England; shadowy guests, that would have been as perilous as demons to their entertainer, could they have been seen so much as knocking at her door.
>
> It is remarkable, that persons who speculate the most boldly often conform with the most perfect quietude to the external regulations of society. The thought suffices them, without investing itself in the flesh and blood of action. So it seemed to be with Hester. Yet, had little Pearl never come to her from the spiritual world, it might have been far otherwise. Then, she might have come down to us in history, hand in hand with Ann Hutchinson, as the foundress of a religious sect. She might, in one of her phases, have been a prophetess. She might, and not improbably would, have suffered death from the stern tribunals of the period, for attempting to undermine the foundations of the Puritan establishment. But, in the education of her child, the mother's enthusiasm of thought had something to wreak itself upon. Providence, in the person of this little girl, had assigned to Hester's charge the germ and blossom of womanhood, to be

cherished and developed amid a host of difficulties. Every thing was against her. The world was hostile. The child's own nature had something wrong in it, which continually betokened that she had been born amiss,—the effluence of her mother's lawless passion,—and often impelled Hester to ask, in bitterness of heart, whether it were for ill or good that the poor little creature had been born at all.

Indeed, the same dark question often rose into her mind, with reference to the whole race of womanhood. Was existence worth accepting, even to the happiest among them? As concerned her own individual existence, she had long ago decided in the negative, and dismissed the point as settled. A tendency to speculation, though it may keep woman quiet, as it does man, yet makes her sad. She discerns, it may be, such a hopeless task before her. As a first step, the whole system of society is to be torn down, and built up anew. Then, the very nature of the opposite sex, or its long hereditary habit, which has become like nature, is to be essentially modified, before woman can be allowed to assume what seems a fair and suitable position. Finally, all other difficulties being obviated, woman cannot take advantage of these preliminary reforms, until she herself shall have undergone a still mightier change; in which, perhaps, the ethereal essence, wherein she has her truest life, will be found to have evaporated. A woman never overcomes these problems by any exercise of thought. They are not to be solved, or only in one way. If her heart chance to come uppermost, they vanish. Thus, Hester Prynne, whose heart had lost its regular and healthy throb, wandered without a clew in the dark labyrinth of mind; now turned aside by an insurmountable precipice; now starting back from a deep chasm. There was wild and ghastly scenery all around her, and a home and comfort nowhere. At times, a fearful doubt strove to possess her soul, whether it were not better to send Pearl at once to heaven, and go herself to such futurity as Eternal Justice should provide.

Only the emanation of Pearl from the spiritual world has saved Hester from the martyrdom of a prophetess, which is Hawthorne's most cunning irony, since without Pearl his romance would have been transformed into a tragedy. That may be our loss aesthetically, since every reader of *The Scarlet Letter* comes to feel a great regret at Hester's unfulfilled potential. Something in us wants her to be a greater heretic even than Ann Hutchinson. Certainly we sense an unwritten book in her, a story that Hawthorne did not choose to write. But what he has written marks the true beginning of American prose fiction, the absolute point of origin from which we can trace the sequence that goes from Melville and James to Faulkner and Pynchon and that domesticates great narrative art in America.

III

Hawthorne's highest achievement is not in *The Scarlet Letter* and *The Marble Faun*, distinguished as they are, but in the best of his tales and sketches. The last of these, the extraordinary "Feathertop," subtitled "A Moralized Legend," is as uncanny a story as Kafka's "Country Doctor" or "Hunter Gracchus," and has about it the dark aura of Hawthorne's valediction, his farewell to his own art. In its extraordinary strength at representing an order of reality that intersects our own, neither identical with the mundane nor quite transcending the way things are, "Feathertop" may be without rivals in our language.

Mother Rigby, a formidable witch, sets out to create "as lifelike a scarecrow as ever was seen," and being weary of making hobgoblins, determines to give us "something fine, beautiful, and splendid." An authentic forerunner of Picasso as sculptor, the witch chooses her materials with bravura:

The most important item of all, probably, although it made so little show, was a certain broomstick, on which Mother Rigby had taken many an airy gallop at midnight, and which now served the scarecrow by way of a spinal column, or, as the unlearned phrase it, a backbone. One of its arms was a disabled flail, which used to be wielded by Goodman Rigby, before his spouse worried him out of this troublesome world; the other, if I mistake not, was composed of the pudding-stick and a broken rung of a chair, tied loosely together at the elbow. As for its legs, the right was a hoe-handle, and the left, an undistinguished and miscellaneous stick from the wood-pile. Its lungs, stomach, and other affairs of that kind, were nothing better than a meal-bag stuffed with straw. Thus, we have made out the skeleton and entire corporosity of the scarecrow, with the exception of its head; and this was admirably supplied by a somewhat withered and shrivelled pumpkin in which Mother Rigby cut two holes for the eyes and a slit for the mouth, leaving a bluish-colored knob, in the middle, to pass for a nose. It was really quite a respectable face.

Gaudily attired, the scarecrow so charms its demiurgic creator ("The more Mother Rigby looked, the better she was pleased") that she emulates Jehovah directly, and decides to breathe life into the new Adam by thrusting her own pipe into his mouth. Once vivified, Mother Rigby's creature is urged by her to emulate Milton's Adam: "Step forth! Thou hast the world before thee!" Hawthorne does not allow us to doubt the self-critique involved, as all romance is deliciously mocked:

> In obedience to Mother Rigby's word, and extending its arm as if to reach her outstretched hand, the figure made a step forward—a kind of hitch and jerk, however, rather than a step—then tottered, and almost lost its balance. What could the witch expect? It was nothing, after all, but a scarecrow, stuck upon two sticks. But the strong-willed old beldam scowled, and beckoned, and flung the energy of her purpose so forcibly at this poor combination of rotten wood, and musty straw, and ragged garments, that it was compelled to show itself a man, in spite of the reality of things. So it stept into the bar of sunshine. There it stood—poor devil of a contrivance that it was!—with only the thinnest vesture of human similitude about it, through which was evident the stiff, ricketty, incongruous, faded, tattered, good-for-nothing patchwork of its substance, ready to sink in a heap upon the floor, as conscious of its own unworthiness to be erect. Shall I confess the truth? At its present point of vivification, the scarecrow reminds me of some of the lukewarm and abortive characters, composed of heterogeneous materials, used for the thousandth time, and never worth using, with which romance-writers (and myself, no doubt, among the rest) have so over-peopled the world of fiction.

But the critique surpasses mere writers and attacks the greatest of romancers, Jehovah himself, as Mother Rigby deliberately frightens her pathetic creature into speech. Now fully humanized, he is named Feathertop by his creator, endowed with wealth, and sent forth into the world to woo the beautiful Polly, daughter of the worshipful Judge Gookin. There is only the one catch; poor Feathertop must keep puffing at his pipe, or he will dwindle again to the elements that compose him. All goes splendidly; Feathertop is a social triumph, and well along to seducing the delicious Polly, when he is betrayed by glances in a mirror:

By and by, Feathertop paused, and throwing himself into an imposing attitude, seemed to summon the fair girl to survey his figure, and resist him longer, if she could. His star, his embroidery, his buckles, glowed, at that instant, with unutterable splendor; the picturesque hues of his attire took a richer depth of coloring; there was a gleam and polish over his whole presence, betokening the perfect witchery of well-ordered manners. The maiden raised her eyes, and suffered them to linger upon her companion with a bashful and admiring gaze. Then, as if desirous of judging what value her own simple comeliness might have, side by side with so much brilliancy, she cast a glance towards the full-length looking-glass, in front of which they happened to be standing. It was one of the truest plates in the world, and incapable of flattery. No sooner did the images, therein reflected, meet Polly's eye, than she shrieked, shrank from the stranger's side, gazed at him, for a moment, in the wildest dismay, and sank insensible upon the floor. Feathertop, likewise, had looked towards the mirror, and there beheld, not the glittering mockery of his outside show, but a picture of the sordid patchwork of his real composition, stript of all witchcraft.

Fleeing back to his mother, Feathertop abandons existence in despair of his reality, and flings the pipe away in a kind of suicide. His epitaph is spoken by a curiously softened Mother Rigby, as though experience had rendered her a more maternal demiurge:

"Poor Feathertop!" she continued. "I could easily give him another chance, and send him forth again to-morrow. But, no! his feelings are too tender; his sensibilities too deep. He seems to have too much heart to bustle for his own advantage, in such an empty and heartless world. Well, well! I'll make a scarecrow of him, after all. 'Tis an innocent and a useful vocation, and will suit my darling well; and if each of his human brethren had as fit a one, 'twould be the better for mankind; and as for this pipe of tobacco, I need it more than he!"

Gentle and whimsical as this is, it may be Hawthorne's darkest irony. The witch is more merciful than the remorseless Jehovah, who always does send us forth again, into a world that cannot sustain us. Feathertop is closer to most of us than we are to Hester Prynne. That final dismissal of heroism is Hawthorne's ultimate legacy, glowing on still in the romances of Nathanael West and Thomas Pynchon.

MILLICENT BELL

The Artists of the Novels:
Coverdale, Holgrave, Kenyon

The artist-hero appears in three of Hawthorne's four novels. Coverdale the poet, Holgrave the story writer and photographer, and Kenyon the sculptor represent Hawthorne's most mature formulations of the artistic character. It will be seen that these three artists are direct developments of the narrator-artist Oberon, of the sketches, and still act as authorial witnesses. This is most clearly true of Miles Coverdale in *The Blithedale Romance*, which alone among Hawthorne's longer fictional works is written in the first person. Both Holgrave and Kenyon, however, retain some of the narrator's function in their respective novels, and we observe the action and the other characters from viewpoints fairly close to theirs. As a result, we get more intense inner pictures of these artist-personalities than we do of the surrounding personages; they are Hawthorne's most "psychological" characters.

Miles Coverdale is the most fully explored character in *The Blithedale Romance*, though he takes no real part in the growth of the action. He is not merely the narrator of the story, for it sometimes seems that the story itself exists as much to show us the nature of the storyteller as for its own sake. It is against the action that we judge Coverdale, measuring him in turn by Hollingsworth's idealism, Zenobia's intensity, and Priscilla's innocence.

From *Hawthorne's View of the Artist*, pp. 151–172. © 1962 by the State University of New York.

In *The Blithedale Romance* the artist is viewed in terms of progressive self-disclosure. Coverdale comes to Blithedale with the finest of romantic notions about his worth as a poet. On his first evening at Blithedale he declares:

> I ... hope now to produce something that shall really deserve to be called poetry,—true, strong, natural, and sweet, as is the life which we are going to lead, something that shall have the notes of birds twittering through it, or a strain like the wind-anthems in the woods, as the case may be (V, 336).

But when the story he relates is at an end, Coverdale admits himself to be a failure both in life and art. He has lost a sense of purpose.

> As for poetry, I have given it up, notwithstanding that Dr. Griswold—as the reader, of course, knows—has placed me at a fair elevation among our minor minstrelsy, on the strength of my pretty little volume, published ten years ago.... I lack a purpose.... I by no means wish to die. Yet were there any cause, in this whole chaos of human struggle worth a sane man's dying for, and which my death would benefit, then—provided, however, the effort did not involve an unreasonable amount of trouble—methinks I might be bold to offer up my life. If Kossuth, for example, would pitch the battlefield of Hungarian rights within an easy ride of my abode, and choose a mild, sunny morning, after breakfast, for the conflict, Miles Coverdale would gladly be his man, for one brave rush upon the levelled bayonets. Further than that, I should be loath to pledge myself (V, 599).

Coverdale traverses the course from illusion to cynicism as the drama of his Blithedale companions reveals his own ineffectual role in life. More and more he finds himself involved in the part of a voyeur; like the narrator of "Sights from a Steeple," he observes his fellow Blithedalers from a sort of crow's-nest elevated above the pains and ardors of normal men and women. Indeed, it does not take him long to find a literal eyrie to symbolize his detached interest in his neighbors. In the wood adjacent to Blithedale he discovers "a kind of leafy cave, high upward into the air, among the midmost branches of a white-pine tree ... a perfect nest for Robinson Crusoe or King Charles!" (V, 431). And from this natural turret he is wont to peep upon the oblivious companions of his Blithedale adventure.

... my position was lofty enough to serve as an observatory, not for starry investigations, but for those sublunary matters in which lay a lore as infinite as that of the planets. Through one loophole I saw the river lapsing calmly onward, while in the meadow, near its brink, a few of the brethren were digging peat for our winter's fuel. On the interior cart-road of our farm, I discerned Hollingsworth, with a yoke of oxen hitched to a drag of stones.... The harsh tones of his voice, shouting to the sluggish steers, made me sensible, even at such a distance, that he was ill at ease.... "Mankind, in Hollingsworth's opinion," thought I, "is but another yoke of oxen, as stubborn, stupid, and sluggish as our old Brown and Bright. He vituperates us aloud, and curses us in his heart, and will begin to prick us with the goad stick by and by.... At my height above the earth the whole matter looks ridiculous!" (V, 432–33)

Seeing his friend Hollingsworth from this height, he is unmoved by his philanthropic schemes—and that is well enough. But his hidden vantage point gives him also a detached perspective of Priscilla, whom he spots at a window in the farmhouse. To a passing bird he sends an imaginary message:

"Tell her ... that her fragile thread of life has inextricably knotted itself with other and tougher threads, and most likely it will be broken. Tell her that Zenobia will not be long her friend. Say that Hollingsworth's heart is on fire with his own purpose, but icy for all human affection; and that, if she has given him her love, it is like casting a flower into a sepulchre. And say that if any mortal really cares for her, it is myself; and not even I, for her realities,— poor little seamstress, as Zenobia rightly called her!—but for the fancy-work with which I have idly decked her out!" (V, 433–34)

It is the fiery Zenobia who first becomes aware of the peculiar nature of Coverdale's observation. One day, as she feels his speculative glance, she declares:

"Mr. Coverdale ... I have been exposed to a great deal of eyeshot in the few years of my mixing in the world, but never, I think, to precisely such glances as you are in the habit of favoring me with. I seem to interest you very much; and yet—or else a woman's instinct is for once deceived—I cannot reckon you as an admirer. What are you seeking to discover in me?" (V, 373–74)

He is always fingering and teasing the sensibilities of his friends—trying to make them give up their secrets. As he slyly questions Priscilla, for example, he reflects, "No doubt it was a kind of sacrilege in me to attempt to come within her maidenly mystery; but, as she appeared to be tossed aside by her other friends, or carelessly let fall, like a flower which they had done with, I could not resist the impulse to take just one peep beneath her folded petals" (V, 463). He feels the prompting of curiosity before all other emotions. After terminating his interview in the woods with the detestable Westervelt, he reminds himself that he might have learned something from this diabolic personage: "I could not help regretting that I had so preëmptorily broken off the interview, while the stranger seemed inclined to continue it. His evident knowledge of matters affecting my three friends might have led to disclosures or inferences that would perhaps have been serviceable" (V, 429). Later, in his attempt to discover more about the role of Hollingsworth in the lives of the two women, he irritates Zenobia into an outburst of scorn:

> "Why do you bring up his name at every turn? ... You know not what you do! It is dangerous, sir, believe me, to tamper thus with earnest human passions, out of your mere idleness, and for your sport. I will endure it no longer!" (V, 514)

Precisely this curious species of interest bars Coverdale from the confidence of his three friends. As he prepares to leave the farm for his holiday in Boston, Zenobia tells him:

> "Do you know, Mr. Coverdale, that I have been several times on the point of making you my confidant, for lack of a better and wiser one? But you are too young to be my father confessor; and you would not thank me for treating you like one of those good little handmaidens who share the bosom secrets of a tragedy-queen."
>
> "I would, at least, be loyal and faithful," answered I, "and would counsel you with an honest purpose, if not wisely."
>
> "Yes," said Zenobia, "you would be only too wise, too honest. Honesty and wisdom are such a delightful pastime, at another's expense!"
>
> "Ah, Zenobia," I exclaimed, "if you would but let me speak!"
>
> "By no means," she replied, "especially when you have just resumed the whole series of social conventionalism, together with that strait-bodied coat. I would as lief open my heart to a lawyer or to a clergyman!" (V, 482)

A very similar scene takes place, as we shall see, in *The Marble Faun*, when Miriam considers, then rejects, Kenyon as a confidant.

When Coverdale reaches the city he finds that the drama which has been absorbing him has shifted conveniently to an apartment whose windows face his hotel room. As he stands behind his curtain watching the figures of Westervelt, Zenobia, and Priscilla across the intervening space, he reminds one of his prototype in the sketch "Sunday at Home." He muses:

> ... there seemed something fatal in the coincidence that had borne me to this one spot, of all others in a great city, and transfixed me there, and compelled me again to waste my already wearied sympathies on affairs which were none of mine, and persons who cared little for me. It irritated my nerves; it affected me with a kind of heart-sickness. After the effort which it cost me to fling them off,—after consummating my escape, as I thought, from these goblins of flesh and blood, and pausing to revive myself with a breath or two of an atmosphere in which they should have no share,—it was a positive despair, to find the same figures arraying themselves before me, and presenting their old problem in a shape that made it more insoluble than ever (V, 498–99).

The fatality of which Coverdale speaks is psychologically nothing but his own compulsion to watch and analyze the lives of others—as Hawthorne felt the artist must. From this obsession, indeed, he cannot escape.

Coverdale soon begins to feel that his detached curiosity is immoral and inhuman, as Hawthorne's artists generally do discover. He admits quite early:

> It is not, I apprehend, a healthy kind of mental occupation, to devote ourselves too exclusively to the study of individual men and women. If the person under examination be one's self, the result is pretty certain to be diseased action of the heart, almost before we can snatch a second glance. Or, if we take the freedom to put a friend under our microscope, we thereby insulate him from many of his true relations, magnify his peculiarities, inevitably tear him into parts, and, of course, patch him together very clumsily again (V, 398).

As he leaves Blithedale for Boston, he reflects:

I was full of idle and shapeless regrets. The thought impressed itself upon me that I had left duties unperformed. With the power, perhaps, to act in the place of destiny and avert misfortune from my friends, I had resigned them to their fate. That cold tendency, between instinct and intellect, which made me pry with a speculative interest into people's passions and impulses, appeared to have gone far towards unhumanizing my heart (V, 495).

Zenobia gives Coverdale a still more cutting account of his own character:

"I have long recognized you as a sort of transcendental Yankee, with all the native propensity of your countrymen to investigate matters that come within their range, but rendered almost poetical, in your case, by the refined methods which you adopt for its gratification" (V, 505).

Coverdale pleads that "an uncertain sense of some duty to perform" brings his mind to dwell upon his friends, but Zenobia hisses derisively,

"Oh, this stale excuse of duty! ... I have often heard it before from those who sought to interfere with me, and I know precisely what it signifies. Bigotry; self-conceit; an insolent curiosity; a meddlesome temper; a cold-blooded criticism, founded on a shallow interpretation of half-perceptions; a monstrous scepticism in regard to any conscience or any wisdom, except one's own; a most irreverent propensity to thrust Providence aside, and substitute one's self in its awful place,—out of these, and other motives as miserable as these, comes your idea of duty! But beware, sir! With all your fancied acuteness, you step blindfold into these affairs. For any mischief that may follow your interference, I hold you responsible!" (V, 514–15)

Coverdale finds himself separated from those who most interest him, "excluded from everybody's confidence, and attaining no further, by my most earnest study, than to an uncertain sense of something hidden from me" (V, 518). He returns sadly to Blithedale.

Hollingsworth, Zenobia, Priscilla! They glided mistily before me, as I walked. Sometimes, in my solitude, I laughed with the bitterness of self-scorn, remembering how unreservedly I had given up my heart and soul to interests that were not mine.... It was both sad and dangerous, I whispered to myself, to be in too close affinity with the passions, the errors, and the misfortunes of individuals who stood within a circle of their own, into which, if I stept at all, it must be as an intruder, and at a peril that I could not estimate (V, 552–53).

Zenobia's last talk with him before her suicide contains the final taunt: "Is it you, Miles Coverdale? ... Ah, I perceive what you are about! You are turning this whole affair into a ballad. Pray let me hear as many stanzas as you happen to have ready" (V, 572).

The Blithedale Romance includes, then, among its fundamental themes, the bankruptcy of the transcendental artist as a human participant. As Coverdale discovers that the idealism of the Blithedalers does not succeed in its aim of ennobling life—"the clods of earth, which we so constantly belabored and turned over and over, were never etherealized into thought" (V, 394)—he also discovers that the artist's egotism is a fatal deformity which separates him from his brother men. He may not love or be loved. Coverdale's final declaration that he has all along been in love with Priscilla does not carry conviction. In his psychologizing interest in her affairs, his own emotions would seem to have been absorbed. She, in her turn, never thinks of "Mr. Coverdale" as a lover at all. One must admit that Coverdale cuts rather a poor figure in his own tale.

One suspects, really, that he has loved Zenobia. This may be supposed not merely because of the obvious fascination her personality has exercised upon him—he has, after all, also been interested in his other two friends, Hollingsworth and Priscilla. But Zenobia is plainly one of Hawthorne's magnetic ladies of experience, resembling Beatrice Rappaccini even to the flower with which she is associated—a woman beautiful, mysteriously tainted, and fated to death. Thus, as I have noted before, she represents the allure and the penalty of the artist's forbidden knowledge. He would, indeed, save himself by loving the modest Priscilla, the blond young priestess of innocence. Such was the rescue of the Village Uncle, as we have seen, and such will be the redemption of Holgrave and of Kenyon, the artist-heroes of Hawthorne's two later novels. But, with the rather matter-of-fact realism that distinguishes this work above any others by Hawthorne, the story does not permit this recovery to Coverdale. He will go on, one supposes, being that cursed thing, a writer.

The House of the Seven Gables is, we have noted, a story steeped in the variegated symbolism of the Gothic romance, and Holgrave, the artist with the wizard eye, is, to begin with, a symbol of the menacing qualities attributed to the Gothic, Faustian intellectual. His descent from the wizard of colonial times, Matthew Maule, is a deliberate metaphor. Holgrave, like his ancestor, possesses an acuity concerning the inner workings of the soul which seems somehow illicit and dangerous, and which is represented in his skill as a mesmerist. But Holgrave also exists on the realist level suggested by his appearance not under the Maule name, but under a new, ancestorless one. Throughout the novel we are made aware of the double nature of this Maule-Holgrave. As Holgrave, he is a young man of varied though commonplace experience, given to numerous intellectual enthusiasms, who takes portraits by means of the newfangled daguerreotype and writes stories for current magazines—in other words, an American artist of the eighteen-forties. The Maule element acts, as occult material generally does in Hawthorne's work, to bring into the discourse the moral viewpoint of an older tradition in which men were burnt at the stake for witchcraft and in which knowledge that was not moral knowledge was considered the Devil's art.

Some of the Maule characteristics which Holgrave inherits may be considered characterizations of the Romantic-Gothic view of the artist's temperament.

> So long as any of the race were to be found, they had been marked out from other men—not strikingly, nor as with a sharp line, but with an effect that was felt rather than spoken of—by an hereditary character of reserve. Their companions, or those who endeavored to become such, grew conscious of a circle round about the Maules, within the sanctity or the spell of which, in spite of an exterior of sufficient frankness and good-fellowship, it was impossible for any man to step. It was this indefinable peculiarity, perhaps, that, by insulating them from human aid, kept them always so unfortunate in life. It certainly operated to prolong in their case, and to confirm to them as their only inheritance, those feelings of repugnance and superstitious terror with which the people of the town, even after awakening from their frenzy, continued to regard the memory of the reputed witches. The mantle, or rather the ragged cloak, of old Matthew Maule, had fallen upon his children. They were half believed to inherit mysterious attributes; the family eye was said to possess strange power. Among other good-for-nothing properties and privileges, one was especially assigned them—that of exercising an influence over people's dreams (III, 41–42).

Here we see the traits that are the now quite familiar lineaments of Hawthorne's portrait of the artist. The reserved personality, with its suggestion of an inner fastness inaccessible to others; the penalty of a solitary doom; the impression of mystic attributes and strange power; the ability especially to move the nonrational half of man's nature, the world of dream and imagination—these might as easily have been distinguished in the painter-hero of "The Prophetic Pictures."

Now what has such a somber complex to do with Holgrave, the Yankee jack-of-all-trades, who had been a strolling schoolmaster, a lecturer on mesmerism, a salesman in a village store, a district schoolmaster, the editor of a country newspaper, and who "had subsequently traveled New England and the Middle States as a peddler, in the employment of a Connecticut manufactory of Cologne water and other essences" (III, 212). He is, to begin with, an *artist*—a writer and a daguerreotype portraitist. His name, he tells Phoebe, with some pique at her ignorance of it, "has figured ... on the covers of Graham and Godey, making as respectable an appearance, for aught I could see, as any of the canonized bead-roll with which it was associated" (III, 223); the story of Alice Pyncheon, which forms Chapter XIII of *The House of the Seven Gables*, is said to be one of his compositions. As a photographer, he has as keen an interest in the disclosure of the secret springs of personality as he already possesses as a story writer. He praises the daguerreotype for its truth-telling power:

> There is a wonderful insight in Heaven's broad and simple sunshine. While we give it credit only for depicting the merest surface, it actually brings out the secret character with a truth that no painter would venture upon, even could he detect it (III, 116).

Consequently his portrait of Judge Pyncheon reveals that smiling hypocrite's inner nature and shows Holgrave to be possessed of the hereditary Maule clairvoyance in the guise of artistic perception.

But, like his forebears, Holgrave is insulated from the flow of human sympathy. Phoebe thinks his hardly an affectionate nature.

> He was too calm and cool an observer. Phoebe felt his eye, often; his heart, seldom or never. He took a certain kind of interest in Hepzibah and her brother, and in Phoebe herself. He studied them attentively, and allowed no slightest circumstances of their individualities to escape him. He was ready to do them whatever good he might; but after all, he never exactly made common cause with them, nor gave any reliable evidence that he loved

them better in proportion as he knew them more. In his relations with them, he seemed to be in quest of mental food, not heart-sustenance. Phoebe could not conceive what interested him so much in her friends and herself, intellectually, since he cared nothing for them, or, comparatively, so little, as objects of human affection (III, 213).

As Miles Coverdale was fascinated by the riddle of Hollingsworth, Zenobia, and Priscilla, so Holgrave is drawn by the mystery of the House of the Seven Gables, where he pursues studies, he tells Phoebe, not in books, but of another sort (III, 221). Particularly does the enigmatic history of Clifford Pyncheon intrigue him. "Had I your opportunities," he says to Phoebe another time, "no scruples would prevent me from fathoming Clifford to the full depth of my plummet-line!" (III, 214). She in turn later asks him frankly whether he wishes good or ill to Hepzibah and her brother. He answers:

"Undoubtedly ... I do feel an interest in this antiquated, poverty-stricken old maiden lady, and this degraded and shattered gentleman, this abortive lover of the beautiful. A kindly interest, too, helpless old children that they are! But you have no conception of what a different kind of heart mine is from your own. It is not my impulse, as regards these two individuals, either to help or hinder; but to look on, to analyze, to explain matters to myself, and to comprehend the drama which, for almost two hundred years, has been dragging its slow length over the ground where you and I now tread. If permitted to witness the close, I doubt not to derive a moral satisfaction from it, go matters how they may."

But Phoebe protests:

"I wish you would speak more plainly ... and above all, that you would feel more like a Christian and a human being! How is it possible to see people in distress, without desiring, more than anything else, to help and comfort them? You talk as if this old house were a theatre; and you seem to look at Hepzibah's and Clifford's misfortunes, and those of generations before them, as a tragedy, such as I have seen acted in the hall of a country hotel, only the present one appears to be played exclusively for your amusement. I do not like this. The play costs the performers too much, and the audience is too cold-hearted" (III, 258–59).

But the Maule element does not finally prevail in Holgrave's character. He refrains from exercising his mesmerist skill over Phoebe, and appears to give up his intellectual quest, finally, for love of her. Now Phoebe is one of Hawthorne's most charming heroines—simple, natural, unintellectual. She is the very embodiment of Heart. Her presence in the Pyncheon household makes a home of the cold, old mansion and in praise of her quality Hawthorne writes:

> She was real! Holding her hand, you felt something; a tender something; a substance, and a warm one; and so long as you should feel its grasp, soft as it was, you might be certain that your place was good in the whole sympathetic chain of human nature (III, 171).

This sympathetic chain is precisely what Hawthorne's intellectuals are always in danger of letting slip from their grasp. Ethan Brand, it may be recalled, having cultivated his mental powers beyond the eminence of the philosophers of the earth, was said to have "lost his hold of the magnetic chain of humanity" (III, 495). Phoebe places Holgrave's hand upon it again. Her closest cousin in Hawthorne's fiction is probably Susan, in "The Village Uncle," who leads her artist-husband to renounce his obsessions of solitary achievement for "chaste and warm affections, humble wishes, and honest toil for some useful end ..."

Holgrave's destiny is undoubtedly that of the Village Uncle. It is true that we are not specifically told that he will toss aside pen and camera. But we are made to realize that he will surrender the wilder ideas of his youth concerning the possibility of human perfectibility.

> He would still have faith in man's brightening destiny, and perhaps love him all the better, as he should recognize his helplessness in his own behalf; and the haughty faith, with which he began life, would be well bartered for a far humbler one at its close, in discerning that man's best effort accomplishes a kind of dream, while God is the sole worker of realities (III, 216).

Phoebe fears that Holgrave will lead her out of her own quiet path, but he assures her that, on the contrary, she will lead him.

> The world owes all its onward impulses to men ill at ease. The happy man inevitably confines himself within ancient limits. I have a presentiment that, hereafter, it will be my lot to set out

trees, to make fences,—perhaps, even, in due time, to build a
house for another generation,—in a word, to conform myself to
laws, and the peaceful practice of society (III, 363).

Mrs. Hawthorne liked the ending of *The House of the Seven Gables* in
which the estranged artist-personality is reconciled to normal, everyday life,
the conservative pulse of health, through his marriage to Phoebe. It is
certainly a more comfortable ending than that of *The Scarlet Letter*, which
seems to have sent her to bed with a headache.[1] But it must be admitted that
we are left with the impression that Holgrave will never be quite as
interesting a man as he promised to be at our first encounter with him. He
has broken his magician's staff.

There are so many art-objects in *The Marble Faun*, so many discussions
on matters of aesthetic taste, and so many artists in background and
foreground, that one would expect Hawthorne's view of the artist to receive
profoundest expression here. This is not quite the case. Yet despite the large
amount of adventitious guidebook observation, *The Marble Faun* does
contain much valuable material reflecting Hawthorne's view of artistic
questions. In previous chapters we have already observed the transcendental
aestheticism so prominent in Chapter XV, "An Aesthetic Company," and the
abundant use in this novel of symbolically magical works of art. In addition,
the story itself concerns the fate of the artist as represented by most of the
chief characters.

Like *The Blithedale Romance* and *The House of the Seven Gables*, *The
Marble Faun* contains an artist-observer, whose prospects of happiness and
relations to the lives of others constitute just such a problem as we have seen
confronting Coverdale and Holgrave. Kenyon is a less intricately developed
character than these previous examples of the artist's nature, and his choice
between the warmth of life and the ideal service of art is of less dramatic
importance in the book as a whole. Yet he is worth our close attention as
Hawthorne's last portrait of an artist.

The very fact that Kenyon is not presented as an idiosyncratic member
of society, but as the representative citizen of an art colony, tends to make his
relations with the other characters less difficult. He is a more trusted friend of
Miriam, Donatello, and Hilda than is Coverdale of Zenobia, Hollingsworth,
and Priscilla. He is actually able to help his friends to solve their problems,
and he succeeds in winning happiness himself by winning the love of his
Puritan sweetheart, as Coverdale does not. In this he resembles Holgrave,
who by gaining Phoebe achieves the norm and all the hearthside joys that
belong to it, although to begin with Holgrave's peril is greater than Kenyon's.

Yet Kenyon contains all the traits—indicated less darkly, perhaps—which characterize Hawthorne's artists. It would seem that he himself believes that natural feeling is incompatible with intellectual development, for he explains that Donatello possesses in abundance those emotional qualities which Miriam must find lacking in herself—and which, by implication, Kenyon likewise misses—"the wholesome gush of natural feeling, the honest affection, the simple joy, the fulness of contentment with what he loves.... True, she may call him a simpleton. It is a necessity of the case; for a man loses the capacity for this kind of affection, in proportion as he cultivates and refines himself" (VI, 129). At a crucial moment of desperate need, Miriam rejects Kenyon's counsel because she senses some central failure of sympathy in his cool nature. First appealing to him passionately for help, she suddenly draws back.

> "Ah, I shall hate you!" cried she, echoing the thought which he had not spoken; she was half choked with the gush of passion that was thus turned back upon her. "You are as cold and pitiless as your own marble."
> "No; but full of sympathy, God knows!" replied he...."
> "Keep your sympathy, then, for sorrows that admit of such solace," said she, making a strong effort to compose herself. "As for my griefs, I know how to manage them. It was all a mistake: you can do nothing for me unless you petrify me into a marble companion for your Cleopatra there ..." (VI, 155-56).

It is interesting to note how closely this conversation parallels the colloquy between Zenobia and Coverdale, previously quoted. But Zenobia rejects Miles Coverdale's interest to the last, jeering at his protestations even as she goes to her death. Miriam, on the other hand, finally accepts the assistance of Kenyon in regaining Donatello's trust, assenting to the plan he formulates by which she is able to meet her unhappy lover by the statue of Pope Julius in Perugia. And eventually both she and Donatello put their problem before this friend.

> "Speak!" said Miriam. "We confide in you."
> "Speak!" said Donatello. "You are true and upright (VI, 368).

Kenyon has the artist's gift of discernment. Piece by piece he puts together the tragic story of Miriam and Donatello's crime before they tell him anything about it. Witnessing the curious attitude of Miriam at the bier of the dead Capuchin, his nerves suddenly signal alarm.

Kenyon, as befitted the professor of an imaginative art, was endowed with an exceedingly quick sensibility, which was apt to give him intimations of the true state of matters that lay beyond his actual vision. There was a whisper in his ear: it said, "Hush!" (VI, 221)

His intuitive understanding is, of course, illustrated most strongly in his art itself. His bust of Donatello has the same sort of divined truth as Holgrave's daguerreotype of Judge Pyncheon, and is almost as prescient as the "prophetic pictures." It is Kenyon's aim to exhibit his friend's essential nature, his most personal characteristics.

These it was his difficult office to bring out from their depths, and interpret them to all men, showing them what they could not discern for themselves, yet must be compelled to recognize at a glance, on the surface of a block of marble (VI, 312).

He is unable to accomplish satisfactory results until he surrenders to the nonrational forces of his nature and becomes a "medium."

Hopeless of a good result, Kenyon gave up all preconceptions about the character of his subject and let his hands work uncontrolled with the clay, somewhat as a spiritual medium while holding a pen, yields it to an unseen guidance other than that of her own will. Now and then he fancied that this plan was destined to be the successful one. A skill and insight beyond his consciousness seemed occasionally to take up the task. The mystery, the miracle, of imbuing an inanimate substance with thought, feeling, and all the intangible attributes of the soul, appeared on the verge of being wrought. And now, as he flattered himself, the true image of his friend was about to emerge from the facile material, bringing with it more of Donatello's character than the keenest observer could detect at any one moment in the face of the original (VI, 313).

This piece of sculpture, as it progresses, is truly a "living" work of art, a magic statue, assuming in succession the representation of Donatello's past and future development as a moral being. Working in exasperated frenzy the sculptor suddenly comes upon the Donatello who had hurled Miriam's persecutor from the Tarpeian Rock:

> By some accidental handling of the clay, entirely independent of his own will, Kenyon had given the countenance a distorted and violent look, combining animal fierceness with intelligent hatred. Had Hilda, or had Miriam, seen the bust, with the expression which it had now assumed, they might have recognized Donatello's face as they beheld it at that terrible moment when he held his victim over the edge of the precipice (VI, 314).

The repentant Donatello tells the sculptor to chisel that look in eternal marble, but Kenyon urges that whatever guilt weighs upon his friend's heart can be expiated by good deeds, and changes the expression to one prophetic of the new Donatello.

> They now left the sculptor's temporary studio, without observing that his last accidental touches, with which he hurriedly effaced the look of deadly rage, had given the bust a higher and sweeter expression that it had hitherto worn—for here were still the features of the antique Faun, but now illuminated with a higher meaning, such as the old marble never bore (VI, 315–16).

The "transformation," to which Hawthorne's English title for the book referred, has taken place. The Faun of Praxiteles has come alive in the living man and in the "living" statue of Kenyon. When, much later, Hilda sees the bust, she remarks on its resemblance to the faun, and says of the new quality of its expression that

> "It has an effect as if I could see this countenance gradually brightening while I look at it. It gives the impression of a growing intellectual power and moral sense. Donatello's face used to evince little more than a genial, pleasurable sort of vivacity, and capability of enjoyment. But, here, a soul is being breathed into him; it is the Faun, but advancing towards a state of higher development" (VI, 433).

But to Kenyon the desires of the heart prove stronger than even the wonder-working power of art. When Hilda suddenly disappears from Rome he realizes his need of her, and his mind can contain no other interest. Not even the ageless beauty of an ancient statue which Donatello has unearthed can move him now. "Ah Miriam," he exclaims impatiently, "I cannot respond to you.... Imagination and the love of art have both died out of me" (VI, 483).

"So Kenyon won the gentle Hilda's shy affection, and her consent to be his bride" (VI, 520–21). With this fairy-tale consummation ends the story of Hawthorne's artist. "The mind wanders wild and wide," Kenyon declares, "and so lonely as I live and work, I have neither pole-star above nor light of cottage-windows here below to bring me home. Were you my guide, my counsellor, my inmost friend, with that white wisdom which clothes you as a celestial garment, all would go well. O Hilda, guide me home" (VI, 520). Despite her unearthly purity, we suspect that Hilda is doing the office of Susan of Swampscott for the Village Uncle. Kenyon's children, one imagines, will be cautioned not to whittle woodshavings, lest they fall into perilous ways.

Perhaps we should here add a word about Hawthorne's artist-heroines in two of the novels—Zenobia, the writer, in *The Blithedale Romance*, and Miriam, the painter, in *The Marble Faun*. Strangely similar, these two women are the most tragically blighted of all Hawthorne's dark heroines, less vernal than Beatrice Rappaccini, less triumphant in expiation than Hester Prynne. All four women, of course, are intellectuals—Hester becomes an audacious thinker and Beatrice is reputed to have absorbed her father's learning along with the poison that has infiltrated her system. But Zenobia and Miriam are, like Coverdale and Kenyon, the men who observe them, dedicated to the perilous service of art itself. And art has somehow made them unhappy, distorted their femininity, as Hawthorne understood the quality, and doomed one, at least, to tragic death. I say "art" had done this—but, of course, Hawthorne really suggests that some unspecified experience, some moral taint, had already touched and altered Zenobia and Miriam before we meet them in the stories. Only in the case of Hester has he clearly explained his dark heroine's sins as somehow sexual; for the others we have only vague hints. And in the case of his artist-heroines, it is possible that the aim and life of art bear a direct relationship to sin. Just as Zenobia and Miriam symbolize the dark marriage with experience which is offered to the artist who is a man, so, in themselves, they are also examples of the penalty of the life of art.

Of Zenobia's activities as a writer, we see and hear little, though indeed we see more of her art than we do of Coverdale's, for the inset-story of Chapter XIII, "The Silvery Veil," is a narrative extemporized by her before an audience of Blithedalers. But we get a much more detailed picture of Miriam's performances as an artist, and, indeed, her works of art have a symbolic function to play in the narrative. Miriam's studio, the habitation of a character who is both artist and "dark lady" of experience, is the shadowy source of art-objects obscurely and dangerously prophetic. When Donatello visits her she tells him: "We artists purposely exclude sunshine, and all but a partial light, because we think it necessary to put ourselves at odds with Nature before trying to imitate her" (VI, 57). She thus identifies herself for us as an artist whose sources of power are darker and more hidden than those present in the sunny workshop of the woodcarver Drowne. Donatello is alarmed by a glimpse of a wooden lay figure, who appeared to be "a woman with long dark hair, who threw up her arms with a wild gesture of tragic despair" (VI, 58), and though reassured that she is only a pliable mannikin (or that, symbolically, the artist's imagination is the obedient subject of his will) he is shaken by the impression that "her arms moved, as if beckoning me to help her in some direful peril"—a clear prophecy, we know, of a scene of crime that he and Miriam will soon enact. And insistently prophetic as well are the artist's own sketches—one of Jael, driving the nail through the temple of Sisera, which seemed to Donatello to have the force of a "bloody confession" (VI, 60), another of Judith with the head of Holofernes"—"over and over again ... the idea of woman, acting the part of a revengeful mischief towards man" (VI, 61). Of these, she herself confesses an unwilled origin: "They are ugly things that stole out of my mind; not things that I created, but things that haunt me" (VI, 61).

Surely this is a mischief-making art—not only prophetic but actually suggestive to the beholder—and arising from an uncanny and plainly unheavenly source. It does not surprise us, even without the extra moral mystery to scent out in Miriam's background, that she suffers the lonely estrangement of the artist of the "prophetic pictures." During the visit just described, she shows Donatello other products of her pencil and brush: sketches and paintings of such themes as a maiden's first love, an infant's first shoe, and so on. But always she had included in these scenes of homely happiness a melancholy, watching figure curiously resembling herself. It would seem to be Miriam's acknowledgment that from such happy scenes she was forever excluded.

What love, the love of Donatello, will do to Miriam's art after the long period of penance is past Hawthorne does not tell us. In the face of the greater moral mystery of the transformed faun and his destiny, Hawthorne has lost interest in Miriam's vocation as an artist. But her character and her story as we do see it already suggest the reason why, like Kenyon, she too falls in love with a simple and uncorrupt soul who feels no need to rival divine creation with his wits. It is quite understandable that the pure Hilda is not really an artist but a copyist of rare skill, wonderfully sympathetic and wonderfully adept at catching the life of art created at such cost by darker spirits.

NOTE

1. Stewart, *Nathaniel Hawthorne*, pp. 113, 95.

FREDERICK C. CREWS

Homely Witchcraft

"A thought may be present to the mind, so distinctly that no utterance could make it more so; and two minds may be conscious of the same thought, in which one or both take the profoundest interest; but as long as it remains unspoken, their familiar talk flows quietly over the hidden idea, as a rivulet may sparkle and dimple over something sunken in its bed. But, speak the word; and it is like bringing up a drowned body out of the deepest pool of the rivulet, which has been aware of the horrible secret all along, in spite of its smiling surface."
                                        —HAWTHORNE, *The Marble Faun*

Anyone who is following Hawthorne's romances in order must review his methodology when he reaches *The House of the Seven Gables* (1851). From this book through *The Blithedale Romance*, *The Marble Faun*, and the four romances that remained unfinished, Hawthorne's fictional world is beset with incongruities. Characters sincerely explain their motives, apparently with Hawthorne's concurrence, and then reveal quite opposite motives that are never discussed. They sometimes raise the social and moral questions that came to preoccupy Hester Prynne, but instead of answering those questions they bend all efforts to not thinking about them any more; and when they succeed in this blackout Hawthorne seems relieved. Relief, indeed, is the desired end-point of each romance—not a solution to its

From *The Sins of the Fathers: Hawthorne's Psychological Themes*, pp. 171–193. © 1966 by Frederick C. Crews.

thematic issues but oblivion to them. As we suggested at the start of the previous chapter, it is Hawthorne himself and not his characters for whom this oblivion can be understood as meaningful. No wonder the characters are so inarticulate when they try to explain why they feel troubled; the trouble lies more in their meaning for Hawthorne than in their somewhat flimsy literal dilemmas. The critic must decide whether to go on trying to explain the characters' reticences and oddities without referring to this private symbolism. Once committed to the seemingly unexceptionable premise that Hawthorne and his late characters consciously know what they are doing, the critic is helpless to account for an art that becomes progressively more cryptic, bizarre, and self-defeating.

The problem is, to be sure, relatively inconspicuous in *The House of the Seven Gables*, which can engage the reader successfully either in its love story, its picturesque Salem history, its Yankee humor, its romantic legend, its modern realism, its melodrama, or even its few moments of Gothic terror. Only when he tries to find aesthetic order in these motley effects does the critic begin to see that there is something fundamentally contradictory in Hawthorne's romance. Why does the announced moral purpose of showing that "the wrong-doing of one generation lives into the successive ones, and ... becomes a pure and uncontrollable mischief" (III, 14) get dissolved in the "dear home-loveliness and satisfaction" that Sophia Hawthorne discerned in the final pages? Is it because Hawthorne's true intention was comic and sentimental all along? But if so, how do we account for the primitive intensity with which both Hawthorne and his "good" characters seem to despise and fear the villain of the story, Judge Jaffrey Pyncheon? Why is Holgrave, the daguerreotypist, author, and social radical, represented as being both self-sufficient and in desperate need of marriage to the busy little conformist, Phoebe Pyncheon? Why does the mere death of Jaffrey Pyncheon, rather than any conscious moral penance, free the modern Pyncheons from the real or metaphorical curse that has dogged their family for two centuries? Why does Hawthorne feel obliged to dwell whimsically, but at disconcerting length, on a number of largely trivial symbols—a house, an elm, a well, a spring, a mirror, some posies, a garden, some hens, some bees? Why must he apologize over and over for being tedious or inconsistent in tone? Why does he use his plot for an extensive yet partly covert review of all the scandals and weaknesses in his own family history? And why, in his avowed attempt at writing a popular romance, does he give such prominence to two characters, Hepzibah and Clifford Pyncheon, for whom nearly all the possibilities of life are already exhausted?

In order to take a sufficiently inclusive view of *The House of the Seven Gables* we must both examine and look beyond Hawthorne's surface emphasis. The book is not a diabolical exercise in deceit; Hawthorne means, or would like to mean, what he says about his characters and their doings. But his deeper hints of characterization, his imagery, and the direction of his plot all bespeak an overriding concern with an unstated theme. The ending, which strikes the modern reader as morally complacent, is in fact psychologically urgent, an ingeniously ambiguous gesture of expiation for a dominant idea that has been warping the book's direction. When the obsessed Holgrave, the character who most nearly resembles Hawthorne-as-artist, swears to Phoebe that he has already turned conservative for her sake, he is making a declaration on behalf of the entire romance. *The House of the Seven Gables* "turns conservative" as a way of evading its deepest implications—the same fantasy-implications we have noted elsewhere.

Looking forward to Hawthorne's creative breakdown as well as backward to the tales mentioned in Chapter 9, we shall argue that on its autobiographical level *The House of the Seven Gables* is "about" the risks of artistic imagination, which are simply the risks of seizure by unconscious wishes. Roughly the same debate between fantasy and inhibition recurs in each of the late romances, and always with the same outcome. Since forbidden thoughts inevitably smirk through the best efforts at conventionality, the whole enterprise of fiction must be symbolically renounced—or, in the case of the four abortive romances, quite literally renounced. We shall be able to show that those last plots are not broken off because Hawthorne became sick or weary or morally confused, but because they too frankly embody the theme which is barely kept under control in the book at hand.

In one respect it is generally agreed that this romance has an autobiographical significance. The Pyncheon forebears, whose history opens the plot and is resumed at several points, are unmistakable representatives of the Hathornes; hence the mixture of nostalgia and resentment in their portrayal. Hawthorne's customary charges against his ancestors—of religious hypocrisy, social tyranny, and moral abuse—are leveled against the Pyncheons, and specific family shames such as the Salem witch hangings are exploited for the announced theme of inherited guilt. The decline of the Pyncheons is half-seriously attributed to a curse which is closely modeled on one that the accused witch Sarah Good supposedly laid upon John Hathorne (really upon Nicholas Noyes). And the disinherited modern Pyncheons resemble Hawthorne in regretting the gradual loss of the authority under which their family's historic crimes were perpetrated. In this light it is significant that the plot works toward a symbolic expiation and a reversal of bad fortune for the sympathetic Pyncheons. Hawthorne can laugh at the worthless "eastern claims" of the Pyncheon-Hathornes, but his satire is blunted by the fact that Hepzibah and Clifford come into easy circumstances, while the "guilty" remnant of Puritan days, the arch-villain Jaffrey Pyncheon, is conveniently and mysteriously put to death. The providential ending, in other words, amounts to a wishful settling of old scores on Hawthorne's part.[1]

The very fact that Jaffrey Pyncheon *is* a villain—one who is treated even less generously than Roger Chillingworth—deserves pondering in view of the meaning of ancestral tyrants throughout Hawthorne's fiction. Jaffrey is a slightly attenuated reincarnation of the original Colonel Pyncheon, the family's father; and the entire romance prior to his death is oppressed with a sense of fierce authority and inhibition. Jaffrey's effect on his cousins is exactly that of Colonel Pyncheon's portrait, which, with its "stern, immitigable features," acts as "the Evil Genius of his family," ensuring that "no good thoughts or purposes could ever spring up and blossom" (III, 36) under his gaze. By now we might feel entitled to surmise from such phrases that Jaffrey's role in *The House of the Seven Gables* is paternal, and that the two sets of characters who survive him are symbolically his children. There is in fact more than sufficient evidence for this reading. At present, however, let us rest content with the observation that Jaffrey's death is the central event of the plot, enabling one couple to have a euphoric escape and another couple to marry and become rich. Nor should we omit the effect of Jaffrey's death on Hawthorne himself. Whether or not Jaffrey is recognized as a father figure, the reader must surely acknowledge the clogged passion, the vindictive pleasure, expressed in that extraordinary chapter (18) which is given over to a fearful taunting of Jaffrey's corpse.

A mixture of awe and hatred is discernible through the entire rendering of Judge Pyncheon. His villainy is separated from his conscience by layers of self-esteem and public honor which seem to impress Hawthorne despite his moral disapproval of them. For Hawthorne as for Clifford and Hepzibah, Jaffrey is an imminent presence, an unspecified threat, rather than an active criminal. While he is alive his specific guilt can only be suggested in an elaborate, highly tentative metaphor. In some forgotten nook of the "stately edifice" of an important man's character, says Hawthorne,

> may lie a corpse, half decayed, and still decaying, and diffusing its death-scent all through the palace! The inhabitant will not be conscious of it, for it has long been his daily breath! Neither will the visitors, for they smell only the rich odors which the master sedulously scatters through the palace ... Now and then, perchance, comes in a seer, before whose sadly gifted eye the whole structure melts into thin air, leaving only the hidden nook,

the bolted closet, ... or the deadly hole under the pavement, and the decaying corpse within. Here, then, we are to seek the true emblem of the man's character, and of the deed which gives whatever reality it possesses to his life. And, beneath the show of a marble palace, that pool of stagnant water, foul with many impurities, and, perhaps, tinged with blood,—that secret abomination, above which, possibly, he may say his prayers, without remembering it,—is this man's miserable soul! (III, 274)

Hawthorne makes it sufficiently clear that Jaffrey's case is being described here, yet the deviousness and Gothic gruesomeness of the accusation show a reluctance to approach the matter very closely. The metaphor, in declaring that only the sadly gifted eye of the seer can perceive Jaffrey's real nature, encourages us to look for repressed guilt or be left with specious appearances; yet Hawthorne himself is less willing than formerly to explain the nature and operation of that guilt. Even in death Jaffrey remains inscrutable and terrifying, resistant to the autopsy of motives that Hawthorne does not yet feel ready to undertake.

We do, of course, finally learn the exact circumstances that make Hawthorne "almost venture to say ... that a daily guilt might have been acted by [Jaffrey], continually renewed ... without his necessarily and at every moment being aware of it" (III, 273). Jaffrey has robbed his uncle, named Clifford; his uncle, witnessing the deed, has consequently died of shock; and Jaffrey has framed his cousin, young Clifford Pyncheon, for this supposed murder. Thus the ex-convict Clifford is, in the sense of Hawthorne's metaphor, Jaffrey's "corpse"—or, to use another word that is much emphasized, his "ghost." In this light the manner of Jaffrey's own death becomes ironically appropriate. As Alfred H. Marks persuasively argues, Hawthorne implies that Jaffrey's mysterious death is caused by the unexpected sight of the "ghost" Clifford Pyncheon.[2] It is likely that Jaffrey dies in the same way as his uncle. A Clifford, in this event, has caused the death of Jaffrey after Jaffrey has caused the death of a Clifford—a symmetry of justice reminiscent of "Roger Malvin's Burial."

To mention "Roger Malvin's Burial," however, is to measure the distance Hawthorne has traveled from the early 1830's. Jaffrey's guilt, unlike Reuben Bourne's, is never rendered in terms of observable behavior; at the moment of his death he is as imposing and impenetrable as ever. It would seem that Hawthorne is more anxious to avoid him than to understand him. Surely it is meaningful that Jaffrey dies offstage through no one's intention, and is only gingerly approached in death by the morbidly scornful narrator. We are nearing the strange world of the unfinished romances, where figures of authority receive sudden outbursts of unexplained authorial hatred and are savagely killed, not by their antagonists, but by "innocent" mischances of plotting. Filial obsession, in other words, is beginning to destroy objective characterization and moral interest.[3]

Yet in a cryptic way *The House of the Seven Gables* deals extensively with moral and psychological affairs. Its "necromancies," we are told, may one day find their true meaning within "modern psychology" (III, 42). In various ways Hawthorne allows us to see the entire historical, social, and symbolic framework of the romance as pertaining to the question of individual guilt. The focal symbol of the House is endowed from the opening page with "a human countenance" (III, 17), and the struggle for possession of it follows familiar Hawthornian lines. The falsely accused wizard Matthew Maule has not been simply executed by his enemy, Colonel Pyncheon; he has been incorporated into the subsequent life of the House. The new structure "would include the home of the dead and buried wizard, and would thus afford the ghost of the latter a kind of privilege to haunt its new apartments..." (III, 21). Like the more strictly figurative "ruined wall" of *The Scarlet Letter*, the Pyncheon estate embodies a mental condition in which an uneasy re-enactment of guilt will be made necessary by the effort to avoid responsibility for that guilt. For all its political and social ramifications, the Maule-Pyncheon antagonism is chiefly a metaphor of imperfect repression.[4]

This imperfect repression is the agent of all the ironic justice in *The House of the Seven Gables*. Every tyrant is psychologically at the mercy of his victim; or, as Hawthorne puts it in his notebook, "All slavery is reciprocal" (*American Notebooks*, p. 107). The rule is first applied to the original Colonel Pyncheon, who dies while inaugurating the House he has built on the executed Matthew Maule's property. It is clear that the Colonel's "curse" of susceptibility to sudden death is nothing other than his guilt toward Maule. The pattern is repeated for Gervayse Pyncheon in the story told by Holgrave; this Pyncheon's greed makes him tacitly co-operate when the second Matthew Maule, supposedly in exchange for a valuable document, takes mesmeric control over his daughter and subsequently causes her death. And if Marks's theory is correct, Jaffrey Pyncheon is similarly enslaved to the oppressed Clifford, who is able to cause Jaffrey's death merely by entering his field of vision. In all these cases it is bad conscience, rather than arbitrary plotting on Hawthorne's part, that has exacted punishment for abuses of power.

It is not possible, however, to say that perfect justice is done. If the authoritarian characters suffer from a secret *malaise* and eventually come to grief, they nevertheless have their full stomachs and public dignity for compensation; revenge is sudden and therefore incomplete. The meek victims, by contrast, are in continual misery (if they survive at all) until the reversal occurs, and even then they retain their internalized sense of persecution. Hepzibah and Clifford, who are presented as figures of infantile innocence, are more pathetic in trying to enjoy their freedom after Jaffrey's death than in their former state of intimidation. "For, what other dungeon is so dark as one's own heart! What jailer so inexorable as one's self!" (III, 204). These sentences, applied to two characters who have done nothing wrong and indeed have been virtually incapable of feeling temptation, may remind us that Hawthorne's focus is not on moral guilt but on a broader phenomenon of psychological tyranny. The very prominence of Hepzibah and Clifford in the plot, along with the somewhat ponderous emphasis on the wasting-away of the Pyncheon energies from generation to generation, suggests that impotence rather than guilt may be Hawthorne's true theme.

I mean the term *impotence* in both a social and sexual sense. It is implied that in some way the Pyncheons have become effete by continuing to deny the claims of the vigorous and plebeian Maules. We could say that a failure of adaptation to modern democratic conditions has left the Pyncheons socially and economically powerless. Clearly, however, this failure has a sexual dimension. Not the least of the Maules' secret privileges is to "haunt ... the chambers into which future bridegrooms were to lead their brides" (III, 21f.)—a fairly direct reference to some interference with normal sexuality. Just as denial of the earthy Maule element in society leads eventually to a loss of social power, so the same denial in emotional nature— symbolized by refusal to intermarry with the Maule line—leads to a loss of sexual power. Hepzibah and Clifford are the embodied result of these denials, as we shall see.

The conjunction of the sexual and social themes is best illustrated in Holgrave's legend of Alice Pyncheon. The aristocratic Alice, who "deemed herself conscious of a power—combined of beauty, high, unsullied purity, and the preservative force of womanhood—that could make her sphere impenetrable" (III, 242), is in effect seduced by the second Matthew Maule. The language of the entire episode is transparently sexual, and Alice is drawn not merely by mesmeric prowess but by "the remarkable comeliness, strength, and energy of Maule's figure" (III, 240). The outcome of this seduction, however, is not a union of any sort. Having been socially insulted by Alice's arrogant father, Maule uses his sexual mastery only to demonstrate sadistic control over Alice. "A power that she little dreamed of had laid its grasp upon her maiden soul. A will, most unlike her own, constrained her to do its grotesque and fantastic bidding" (III, 249).

This is to say that Maule is perversely toying with Alice's unladylike susceptibility to his erotic appeal, much as the other Maules exploit the

Pyncheons' unpaid debt to them. The purpose is exactly opposite to healthy fulfillment, as the final event of Alice's life makes especially clear. The still-virginal Alice, who "would have deemed it sin to marry" because she is "so lost from self-control" (III, 250), is hypnotically summoned to attend Matthew Maule's wedding to a laborer's daughter. Alice's former "purity" and her class-consciousness—they are really a single fastidiousness—are thus successfully flouted; she is spurned and mocked by a man who supposedly had no claim on her interest. Significantly, the only "penetration" of Alice's "sphere" occurs on the way home from this wedding, when a fatal dose of consumption makes its entry into "her thinly sheltered bosom" (III, 250). Alice becomes a romantic prototype of the later, more realistically inhibited Pyncheons who find themselves removed from the possibility of sexual fulfillment. The warfare between repression and the repressed will end only with the marriage of a Pyncheon to a Maule, and this will occur only after the chief impediment to both social and sexual democracy is removed.

What is that impediment? In Alice Pyncheon's case it is a father who imposes his elite pretensions on her, prevents her from considering marriage to a workingman, and half-willingly barters her away for a greedy purpose of his own. Each detail recalls the peculiarly unhealthy situation of Beatrice Rappaccini. When we turn to the modern Pyncheon "children," Hepzibah and Clifford, we find that the role of Gervayse Pyncheon or Dr. Rappaccini is played by cousin Jaffrey. Jaffrey is after the very same document that Gervayse Pyncheon was, and he too has made a "child"—the childlike Clifford—pay for his own criminality. Most strikingly, Jaffrey has hoarded to himself the dwindling sum of Pyncheon eroticism. Though he is not completely immune to the family enervation (see III, 148f.), Jaffrey is still characterized by "a kind of fleshly effulgence" (III, 144) and by "brutish ... animal instincts" (III, 368). In his hypocritical gesture of family affection toward Phoebe, "the man, the sex, somehow or other, was entirely too prominent..." (III, 146). And it is suggested more than once that Jaffrey, like his first Puritan ancestor, "had fallen into certain transgressions to which men of his great animal development, whatever their faith or principles, must continue liable ..." (III, 151). We begin to understand that the theory of Pyncheon decline—a decline that seems to apply only to real or metaphorical children—is inseparable from the recurrence in each generation of a licentious and selfish male Pyncheon—a caricature of the Freudian child's imagined father.

Two lines of a familiar triangle are thus discernible as an underlying configuration in *The House of the Seven Gables*: an overbearing, terrifying, and guilty "father" is matched against innocent but emotionally withered "children." The third line, which we could infer equally well from

Hawthorne's previous work or from psychoanalytic doctrine, should be incest fear—the fantasy-terror which goes into the very idea of an all-forbidding and self-indulging Jaffrey Pyncheon. The Oedipal villain, in other words, is an embodied idea of paternal punishment for thoughts of incest, and the form actually taken by such punishment is impotence.

As it happens, *The House of the Seven Gables* abounds in ambiguous innuendo about both incest and impotence. Thus, for example, Holgrave uses the Pyncheons to illustrate a caution against too prolonged a family dynasty: "in their brief New England pedigree, there has been time enough to infect them all with one kind of lunacy or another!" (III, 222). What cannot quite be uttered about human inbreeding can be said of the family chickens, who are explicit emblems of their owners (see III, 184): "It was evident that the race had degenerated, like many a noble race besides, in consequence of too strict a watchfulness to keep it pure" (III, 113). Whether incest has been literally committed is as open a question for the Pyncheons as it was for the Mannings (see p. 36f. above); the real significance of the incest hints lies in their connection to the other Oedipal features of the total work. Those features do not encourage us to look for evidence of actual incest, but on the contrary for the emotional starvation that ensues from a morbid dread of incest. And this is exactly what we find in the decrepit siblings, Hepzibah and Clifford.

Hepzibah is of course a classic old maid, and Hawthorne keeps the sexual implications of her state before our minds. He introduces her in mock-erotic terms ("Far from us be the indecorum of assisting, even in imagination, at a maiden lady's toilet!" [III, 46]), and he repeatedly characterizes her feelings as those of an aged virgin. He also supplies us with what might be an etiological suggestion as to why Hepzibah has remained virginal. Unlike the other modern Pyncheons, she willingly submits herself to the imposing portrait of the first Colonel Pyncheon: "She, in fact, felt a reverence for the pictured visage, of which only a far-descended and time-stricken virgin could be susceptible" (III, 50). The father of the Pyncheon dynasty has acquired some of the affection that would normally be reserved for a husband. And this admittedly dim suggestion of incestuous feeling is greatly heightened by Hepzibah's secret and tender absorption in another portrait, whose subject might well have been "an early lover of Miss Hepzibah" (III, 48)—but is in truth her brother Clifford as a young man!

Clifford in turn is effeminate and attached to the image of his mother. His physical traits alone are emphatically revealing: "full, tender lips, and beautiful eyes" (III, 48), a face "almost too soft and gentle for a man's" (III, 117), "thin delicate fingers" (III, 174), and so on. His portrait not only shows "feminine traits, moulded inseparably with those of the other sex"; it also makes one think inevitably "of the original as resembling his mother, and she a lovely and lovable woman, with perhaps some beautiful infirmity of character..." (III, 80). And later we hear of Clifford's dreams, "in which he invariably played the part of a child, or a very young man. So vivid were they ... that he once held a dispute with his sister as to the particular figure or print of a chintz morning-dress, which he had seen their mother wear, in the dream of the preceding night" (III, 205). Clifford's dream-memory turns out to be exact.

If Clifford's mother is his dream, I find it significant that Jaffrey, who is blamed for his passage directly "from a boy into an old and broken man" (III, 205), is called his "nightmare" (III, 299, 371). Here again the strictest Freudian expectations are fulfilled. The melodramatic villainy of the "father" is blamed for a failure of manhood whose sources are clearly temperamental, and which antedates that villainy. The power of intimidation which Jaffrey has come to symbolize is explained by the manner of Clifford's brief release from it at Jaffrey's death. In a wild exhilaration that contrasts sharply with Hepzibah's more anxious response, Clifford simultaneously tosses off Oedipal rivalry, the Puritan past, and moral restraint; they are all revealed to be emotionally identical. Rocketing to an unknown modern destination on a railroad train that is leaving Jaffrey's corpse ever farther behind, the timid eunuch Clifford suddenly becomes a universal Eros. By means of the telegraph, he predicts excitedly, "Lovers, day by day,—hour by hour, if so often moved to do it,—might send their heart-throbs from Maine to Florida, with some such words as these, 'I love you forever!'—'My heart runs over with love!'—'I love you more than I can!' and, again, at the next message, 'I have lived an hour longer, and love you twice as much!'" (III, 313). This is the Clifford who feared to venture outside his home while Jaffrey lived.

Clifford is perhaps the supreme example in Hawthorne's fiction of a man whose feelings have become polarized between an exquisite aestheticism and frustrated sensuality. His worship of the beautiful and his hypersensitivity are matched by his huge appetite for food and his rather prurient titillation in the company of the developing virgin, Phoebe. Though his interest in her is described as chaste, Hawthorne adds that

> He was a man, it is true, and recognized her as a woman.... He took unfailing note of every charm that appertained to her sex, and saw the ripeness of her lips, and the virginal development of her bosom. All her little womanly ways, budding out of her like blossoms on a young fruit-tree, had their effect on him, and sometimes caused his very heart to tingle with the keenest thrills of pleasure. At such moments,—for the effect was seldom more

than momentary,—the half-torpid man would be full of
harmonious life, just as a long-silent harp is full of sound, when
the musician's fingers sweep across it. (III, 171f.)

Significantly, Phoebe's company enables Clifford to retreat more easily into
a state of childhood (see III, 180)—one in which his "gentle and voluptuous
emotion" (III, 48) need meet no challenges from mature sexual reality.

To understand why Phoebe produces just this effect on Clifford, it is
now necessary to consider her general symbolic role in the romance. It is, of
course, a redemptive role, though by no means a theological one. To the
social and psychological decadence of the House she brings one supreme
virtue that has thus far been lacking: "There was no morbidness in Phoebe"
(III, 166). Her function is to dispense symbolic sunshine (note her name)
where hereditary gloom prevailed before. This is very obvious; but as always
in Hawthorne's serious work, the banal theme is rooted in psychological
relationships of considerable subtlety.

On the patent level Phoebe represents a kind of innocent energy and
prettiness, a domestic competence unhindered by any brooding over the
meaning of things. Her Pyncheon blood endows her marriage to Holgrave-
Maule with familial symbolism, but in fact she is antithetical to most of the
Pyncheon traits, and her effect on the ancestral property is to cancel or
reverse many of its dark implications. Thus in the Pyncheon garden,
"unctuous with nearly two hundred years of vegetable decay" (III, 93), she
discovers a perfect rose, with "not a speck of blight or mildew in it" (III, 137).
This "nice girl" and "cheerful little body" (III, 96, 97) aligns herself with all
the symbols of persisting purity amid the general collapse—with the singing
birds and above all with the unpolluted fountain in the garden. She is even
able to neutralize the suggestive implications of her very bedroom, where
"the joy of bridal nights had throbbed itself away." Hawthorne assures us that
"a person of delicate instinct would have known at once that it was now a
maiden's bedchamber, and had been purified of all former evil and sorrow by
her sweet breath and happy thoughts. Her dreams of the past night, being
such cheerful ones, had exorcised the gloom, and now haunted the chamber
in its stead" (III, 95).

Now, this passage shows us Phoebe's chief part in the romance, which
is not simply to stand for innocence but to refute or "exorcise" sexual
cynicism. Hepzibah and Clifford, after all, are innocent enough; but
Phoebe's purity has thematic weight because she is seen at the brink of
womanhood. Hawthorne deliberately puts her within a sexual perspective in
order to declare her exempt from erotic inclinations. She dreams, but
cheerfully; she has "brisk impulses" (III, 209), but they urge her to hike in

the countryside; her "ordinary little toils," unlike Hester Prynne's, do not register unfulfilled desire but merely "perfect health" (III, 167). She is even observed by Clifford at the moment of recognizing the existence of her emergent sexual appeal, yet she pays for this recognition with nothing more than a maidenly blush and a slight modification of her forthrightness (see III, 263).

Phoebe's role is epitomized at one point in a striking oxymoron. In neutralizing the morbidity of her surroundings she is said to wield a "homely witchcraft" (III, 94)—that is, a marriage of spiritual power and tidy domesticity. In Hawthorne's usual world this is unthinkable; one can be either a conventional nobody or a moral outlaw with a special potency of spirit. The "limit-loving" (III, 161) Phoebe, in contrast, derives her power of exorcism precisely from her ignorant conventionality—indeed, from her unwillingness to face unpleasant truths. This is especially apparent in her relations with Clifford: "whatever was morbid in his mind and experience she ignored; and thereby kept their intercourse healthy ..." (III, 173). So, too, she innocently evades the lecherous Jaffrey's kiss (see III, 145) and fails to confirm Hepzibah's original fears that she will be a rival for Clifford's love (see III, 91, 98). When she finally confesses that her sentiments toward Hepzibah and Clifford have been maternal (see III, 258), this exemption from sexuality takes on an Oedipal significance. Despite her youth Phoebe stands in the place of an ideal parent, a selfless breadwinner and moral guide who can replace the tyrannical parent of guilty fantasy.

The real test of this role is provided by Holgrave, whose interest in Phoebe is necessarily amorous. Like Jaffrey, he is both haunting and haunted. As a Maule he owns the mesmeric power which seduces and destroys, yet this power leaves him prone to self-destructive monomania. By marrying Phoebe after virtually hypnotizing her and then allowing her to go free after all, he offers a model of self-restraint from the morbid "experimentation" upon womankind that is so tempting for Hawthornian males generally. He and Phoebe together—he having renounced his unconscious, she scarcely having noticed hers—finally embody a contradictory but necessary vision of mature love combined with indefinitely protracted childhood.

It is noteworthy that Hawthorne strains verisimilitude in order to work Holgrave into his concern for fathers and sons. Without any apparent reason the resourceful and independent daguerreotypist is oppressed by the figure of Jaffrey Pyncheon in death. As he tells Phoebe,

"The presence of yonder dead man threw a great black shadow over everything; he made the universe, so far as my perception could reach, a scene of guilt and of retribution more dreadful than the guilt. The sense of it took away my youth. I never hoped to feel young again! The world looked strange, wild, evil, hostile; my past life, so lonesome and dreary; my future, a shapeless gloom, which I must mould into gloomy shapes! But, Phoebe, you crossed the threshold; and hope, warmth, and joy came in with you!" (III, 362)

Here the theme of patricidal guilt, again as in "Roger Malvin's Burial," is being stretched to include a wholly symbolic father who has not been murdered at all. Holgrave's fear of "retribution" has no basis in stated motives, yet it reminds us that his view of society and history has been metaphorically Oedipal. The cruel world in his estimate is "that gray-bearded and wrinkled profligate, decrepit, without being venerable" (III, 215); and the tyranny of the past is "just as if a young giant were compelled to waste all his strength in carrying about the corpse of the old giant, his grandfather, who died a long while ago, and only needs to be decently buried" (III, 219). Jaffrey's death thus satisfies a patricidal strain in Holgrave's nature—a fact which is corroborated by his "unmotivated" anxiety before Jaffrey's corpse.

The best indication that the "happy" outcome of *The House of the Seven Gables* was not cathartic for its contriver is an omnipresent uneasiness about the propriety, the honesty, and the quality of fictive art. From the defensively humble Preface onward Hawthorne seems to despair of sustaining the picturesque effects which he simultaneously equates with artistic value and denigrates as trickery. The ending to his plot confirms his pessimism: modern ordinariness triumphs over a compulsive and romantic addiction to the past. To a certain extent this pattern is put to good comic use; in the world of homely witchcraft the only ghosts are "the ghosts of departed cook-maids" (III, 124), and Maule's well is no more bewitched than "an old lady's cup of tea" (III, 120). Especially in his treatment of Hepzibah, who resembles him in trying to sell to "a different set of customers" such traditional wares as "sugar figures, with no strong resemblance to the humanity of any epoch ..." (III, 53), Hawthorne manages to take a whimsical view of his artistic plight. Like her creator in his post-college years, Hepzibah, "by secluding herself from society, has lost all true relation with it" (III, 257f.) and must now try to "flash forth on the world's astonished gaze at once" (III, 57). And yet her failure to do so—her bondage to an anachronistic stock-in-trade—has a desperate autobiographical meaning for Hawthorne. He as well as Hepzibah, if they are to stay in business at all, must follow the cynical advice on modern salesmanship offered by the earthbound Yankee, Uncle Venner:

"Put on a bright face for your customers, and smile pleasantly as you hand them what they ask for! A stale article, if you dip it in a good, warm, sunny smile, will go off better than a fresh one that you've scowled upon" (III, 87).[5]

If Hepzibah illustrates the futility of Hawthornian art in the nineteenth century, Clifford and Holgrave may be said to illustrate the flaws and dangers of the artistic temperament. Clifford, the artist *manqué*, is both squeamish and vicariously sensual, both "ideal" and secretly voracious. At times he is merely irritable and dull, but occasionally his fantasy is given symbolic rein, as when he blows artistic bubbles to be pricked by unappreciative passers-by (see III, 206f.). In either capacity, however, he remains enveloped in a robe of moonshine, "which he hugged about his person, and seldom let realities pierce through" (III, 205). Thus he is an extreme version of the withdrawn Hawthornian artist, and it is not difficult to see what he has withdrawn from. His "images of women," says Hawthorne, "had more and more lost their warmth and substance, and been frozen, like the pictures of secluded artists, into the chillest ideality" (III, 170). As usual, ideality and coldness toward women are the same thing, and are associated with "secluded artists." Only Phoebe, the embodied negation of all unpleasant fantasies about women, can persuade Clifford that "the world was no longer a delusion."[6]

Similarly, Phoebe aids Holgrave in restraining his tendency to be an "all-observant" (III, 189) peeper. His interest in his companions has essentially been an author's overview of his characters, and at one point he actually makes a literary work out of Pyncheon history. Alice Pyncheon's legend and the circumstances of its narration sum up everything Hawthorne has to say about the secret meaning of art. The legend itself, says Holgrave, "has taken hold of my mind with the strangest tenacity of clutch ..." and he is telling it "as one method of throwing it off" (III, 223). Authorship, including the intention to publish the work in a magazine, is presented as a way of mastering obsession. Yet Holgrave has a more immediate purpose as well, to impress Phoebe with his talent. The covert eroticism of the story is evidently communicated to its listener, for at the end she "leaned slightly towards [Holgrave], and seemed almost to regulate her breath by his":

> A veil was beginning to be muffled about her, in which she could behold only him, and live only in his thoughts and emotions. His glance, as he fastened it on the young girl, grew involuntarily more concentrated; in his attitude there was the consciousness of power, investing his hardly mature figure with a dignity that did not belong to its physical manifestation. It was evident that, with but one wave of his hand and a corresponding effort of his will, he could complete his mastery over Phoebe's yet free and virgin

spirit: he could establish an influence over this good, pure, and simple child, as dangerous, and perhaps as disastrous, as that which the carpenter of his legend had acquired and exercised over the ill-fated Alice. (III, 252f.)

The thinly euphemistic nature of this scene presumably enabled its first readers to ignore, or at least to perceive indistinctly, the implication that cheery little Phoebe is endowed with sexual desire. She unconsciously welcomes her seducer, and he "involuntarily" tightens his hold on her. This hold has been won through the mesmeric power of art, and motivated not simply by desire but by the prying and rapacious tendency which in Hawthorne's harsh view constitutes the artistic character. That tendency must be "cured," at least in symbolism, if a satisfactory resolution is to be reached. And thus Holgrave obligingly steps out of his Maule identity and reforms both himself and the spirit of the romance. He relaxes his spell over Phoebe and allows her deliberate obtuseness to have the final say: "But for this short life of ours, one would like a house and a moderate garden-spot of one's own" (III, 188). At the end, though the revitalized Pyncheon chickens have begun "an indefatigable process of egg-laying" (III, 372), art has been tacitly set aside and forgotten.

The logic of this conclusion is impeccable. If the image of Jaffrey Pyncheon in death makes Holgrave's future appear to be "a shapeless gloom, which I must mould into gloomy shapes," and if Phoebe alone can erase that image from his mind, then marriage to Phoebe obviates the need for moulding further "gloomy shapes." To become free of anxiety is to lose all reason for creativity. For Holgrave it cannot matter that Phoebe is in fact a tissue of symbolic contradictions: motherly child, sisterly bride, fertile and prolific virgin. It is Hawthorne for whom this subtle compromise is finally meaningful. And in a broader sense the incongruities of his plot—the yoking together of ancestral guilt, of maladaptation to modern reality, and of a villain's death which produces unholy erotic glee and a therapeutic marriage—find their rationale in Hawthorne's struggle to disbelieve that the world is indeed "a scene of guilt and of retribution more dreadful than the guilt." Not Holgrave but Hawthorne, who called his wife Phoebe, has set Phoebe-ism as the steep ransom from obsession. And it is Hawthorne, ultimately, who with secret and wistful irony measures the consequence of this surrender for his own later career. "The world owes all its onward impulses to men ill at ease," he has Holgrave tell Phoebe with great truthfulness; and shortly thereafter Holgrave adds, "If we love one another, the moment has room for nothing more" (III, 363).

NOTES

1. It is also noteworthy that Clifford Pyncheon has been imprisoned for a crime resembling the White murder case—a page of recent history that Hawthorne found particularly shameful—but is later vindicated by the discovery that no murder took place at all. See note 8 on p. 37 above.

2. See "Who Killed Judge Pyncheon? The Role of the Imagination in *The House of the Seven Gables*," *PMLA*, LXXI (June 1956), 355–69.

3. The privacy of Hawthorne's filial concern may be gauged from another piece of veiled family biography. Jaffrey's death is immediately, we might almost say causally, followed by the death by cholera, in a foreign port, of his last direct heir. Hawthorne's own father died of a fever (first reported to be cholera) in Surinam—a fact that could hardly have been generally known to readers of *The House of the Seven Gables*. Thus Hawthorne stamps a paternal significance on Judge Pyncheon not for any instructive purpose, but because that is what secret fantasy demands.

4. Note, for example, that the hereditary mesmeric power of the Maules, who are said to dominate the Pyncheons in "the topsy-turvy commonwealth of sleep" (III, 42), directly depends on the Pyncheons' continuing bad conscience. Holgrave, the last of the Maules, tells us this (III, 64), and Hawthorne himself speculates "whether each inheritor of the property—conscious of wrong, and failing to rectify it—did not commit anew the great guilt of his ancestor, and incur all its original responsibilities" (III, 34).

5. The Hawthorne–Hepzibah parallel can be carried further. In her devotion to the past Hepzibah is said by Holgrave to be "peopling the world with ugly shapes, which you will soon find to be as unreal as the giants and ogres of a child's story-book" (III, 62). The prediction comes true: Hepzibah and Clifford eventually "bade a final farewell to the abode of their forefathers, with hardly more emotion than if they had made it their arrangement to return thither at tea-time" (III, 877). While this is pleasant for Hepzibah, from Hawthorne's point of view it is entirely too easy. He is committed as an artist to the realm of picturesque ancestral guilt which even Hepzibah finds outdated and indeed imaginary.

6. One of Hawthorne's miniature allegories of art is especially revealing in this connection. Clifford finds himself aesthetically delighted by an organ-grinder's puppets, until he notices the lewd and greedy monkey who is collecting coins. He is especially struck by the monkey's "wrinkled and abominable little visage" and his "thick tail curling out into preposterous prolixity from beneath his tartans" (III, 197). This tail, "too enormous to be decently concealed," betokens a "deviltry of nature" that is particularly offensive to Clifford-as-artist; for the monkey is seizing pennies on behalf of a parody of art. Clifford "had taken childish delight in the music, and smiled, too, at the figures which it set in motion. But, after looking a while at the long-tailed imp, he was so shocked by his horrible ugliness, spiritual as well as physical, that he actually began to shed tears ..." (III, 198). Clifford weeps for his own secret feeling that the aesthetic realm is polluted by greed and lust.

JANE DONAHUE EBERWEIN

"The Scribbler of Bygone Days": Perceptions of Time in Hawthorne's "Custom-House"

"The Custom-House" sketch, it is generally acknowledged, serves many purposes. It allows Hawthorne to court the reader's favor by recalling earlier confidences in *Mosses From an Old Manse* and by capitalizing on the publicity which attended his dismissal from the Salem appointment. It provides a forum for his discussion of romance. It links *The Scarlet Letter* with other stories in the volume he originally planned. And it provides a genial introduction to Hester's story.[1] The sketch serves yet another purpose for the modern reader, alerting him to a characteristic but often ignored quality of Hawthorne's historical fiction: his curiously elongated sense of time. Close attention to the temporal sequence of the sketch itself, ranging backward from the author's immediate situation to the middle decades of the seventeenth century, reveals an idiosyncratic grasp of time which may illumine *The Scarlet Letter* itself and other examples of Hawthorne's historical fiction.[2] If one follows the time scheme of "The Custom-House" attentively, filling in dates and estimating gaps of years, one discovers that the romancer evokes a sense of ancient history even while dealing with contemporary events, thereby allowing colonial experience to fade into immemorial tradition so distant as to be beyond reach of historian or novelist—accessible only to the artist of mythic, timeless imagination.

From *The Nathaniel Hawthorne Journal* 1977, ed. C.E. Frazer Clark, Jr., pp. 239–247. © 1980 by Bruccoli Clark Publishers, Inc.

The Scarlet Letter was published in 1850; Hawthorne had been fired from his Salem position in 1849. When he actually wrote "The Custom-House," then, he was at most a year distant from his experiences there. Yet, he reports, that life "lies like a dream behind me,"[3] and only a few of the merchants he knew there linger even faintly in his memory. Soon, he expects, Salem itself will be forgotten as well, transformed by brief separation into "an overgrown village in cloudland" (44). If a year can do such irreparable damage to memory, the reader stands forewarned that time possesses extraordinary powers of mutation and erosion within the narrative as a whole.

Consider the men to whom Hawthorne introduces us as Custom-House employees. "A patriarchal body of veterans" (12), most are described in imagery of extreme decrepitude. They crawl out of hibernation only "to bore one another with the several thousandth repetition of old sea-stories, and mouldy jokes, that had grown to be pass-words and countersigns among them" (14). Those called out for special attention serve as barely-living links with supposedly remote periods of American history. The old Inspector, for instance, is introduced as "a man of fourscore years, or thereabouts" (16) and holds a sinecure preserved for him by his father, a Revolutionary colonel. His wholly sensate memory, however, offers no useful link with the past, recalling nothing more significant than the tragedy of a peculiarly tough roast goose.

The old General, a trifle more youthful at about "threescore years and ten" (20), somehow seems even older, perhaps because repeated references to Ticonderoga obscure the fact that his military glory has been won in the second war with England and in later service on the frontier. A veteran of the War of 1812, it may be useful to remember, was about as far distanced from Hawthorne in age as World War II veterans from today's young adults—senior, certainly, but not unimaginably ancient nor particularly rare. Yet this historic worthy, like the Inspector, evokes images of the past without providing a truly living connection with it: "He seemed away from us, although we saw him but a few yards off; remote, though we passed close beside his chair; unattainable, though we might have stretched forth our hands and touched his own" (23). His silent withdrawal into memories isolates him in time, making his past inaccessible.

Papers and records, too, fail to bridge the gap between past and present, serving instead to augment Hawthorne's illusion of extended time. As colonial records had been carried off to Halifax during the Revolution, official papers stored in the Custom-House dated from the 1780s at the earliest—a maximum period of seventy years. Yet there are piles of documents, now just rubbish, recording Salem trade and the rise of prominent families "from the petty and obscure beginnings of their traffic, at periods generally much posterior to the Revolution, upward to what their children look upon as long-established rank" (28–29). The vessels have now "foundered at sea or rotted at the wharves"; their owners, long dead, moulder beneath mossy tombstones with indecipherable inscriptions. Somehow, Hawthorne induces the reader to believe that such devastation could naturally occur in a time span comparable to that which divides our decade from the beginning years of our century.

Having been eased into the assumption that documents yellow and gravestones erode within fifty or sixty years, the reader is prepared for reflection on Mr. Surveyor Pue, Hawthorne's almost-forgotten predecessor. Dead for about eighty years, Pue has gained brief recent attention as the victim of an archaeological study. His remains, dug up in the graveyard of St. Peter's Church, include only an imperfect skeleton, a few bits of clothing, and "a wig of majestic frizzle"—in much better condition than the skull it once adorned. This ghostly introduction to the former surveyor encourages one to think of him as far more distant in time than chronology suggests and relegates his antiquarian researches to the category of ancient history or folklore. The nature of his study, preserved on a few sheets of yellow parchment, reinforces this sense, as Pue's inquiry consisted of interviews with the most aged citizens of his pre-Revolutionary Salem. These withered elders recalled their childhood observations of Hester Prynne as "a very old, but not decrepit woman, of a stately and solemn aspect" (32). None, of course, remembered the young woman of Hawthorne's story. No chain of human historical remembrance links her with her romancer.

That one connection, the scarlet A itself, has survived all this devastation is surely remarkable and lends force to the suggestion of preternatural qualities associated with the letter. Can the reader be surprised to learn, however, that the needlework itself demonstrates its origin in the immemorial past and that the stitch "gives evidence of a now forgotten art, not to be recovered even by the process of picking out the threads" (31)?

By elongating his perspective on time so that a few decades seem like a century and the Revolution stands as the dividing line between historical epochs, Hawthorne gives to seventeenth-century Boston the fantastic air of unreality which other romancers found in medieval legends. Everything about "The Custom-House" suggests layers of age, so that the reader can hardly be amazed to find the prisonhouse already weatherworn in the opening scene of *The Scarlet Letter*, set only about twelve years after the settlement of Boston. Many Americans, of course, have been quick to agree with Hawthorne that colonial experience or even the nearer past must remain inaccessible to the modern citizen; in general, such people have emphasized youth and the appeal of the future. "The Custom-House," however, illustrates Hawthorne's rejection of this alternative by his portrayal of youth.

The overwhelming impression is one of age. The few young people appear weak. The "smart young clerk," for instance, aspires to mercantile eminence "when he had better be sailing mimic boats upon a mill-pond" (6). The "outward-bound sailor" sets to sea "in quest of a protection" (6). There are, we hear, young and capable men among the Custom-House employees, but their energies are wasted in a life of dependence, and they fade into insignificance beside the Inspector and the General. Even Hawthorne's self-portrait contributes to this debasement of youth. Stressing his harmlessness and ineffectiveness as a federal officer, he presents himself as a figure of fun and readily acknowledges the decline of family ability from the early Puritan generations to his own. He no more than his venerable colleagues enjoys a useable past; his literary career means nothing to his associates and little even to himself in his changed situation. And the Transcendentalists with whom he has just been associated at Brook Farm and in Concord, those proclaimers of new life and fresh vision, fade into dream more rapidly than the ancients. "Even the old Inspector," he confesses, "was desirable, as a change of diet, to a man who had known Alcott" (25).

The immediate future summons no images to the author's eye. All he knows is that things will be different for him and his children. There will be changes, but of some unspecified kind. He seems most at ease when looking toward a future as distant and as dimly conjectured as the history he recalls in "The Custom-House." The sketch ends, in fact, with the hope that "the great-grandchildren of the present race may sometimes think kindly of the scribbler of bygone days, when the antiquary of days to come, among the sites memorable in the town's history, shall point out the locality of THE TOWN-PUMP!" (45). When one translates this hope into approximate dates and realizes that he hopes that the children of the nineteen-thirties and forties may remember him as kindly, though as distantly, as his own children might conceive of Mr. Surveyor Pue, one perceives how radically he has managed to distort normal perceptions of time. The irony gains greater impact, of course, by his assumption that he will be remembered, if at all, for the slight, sentimental accomplishment of a minor sketch, not for the substantial though tragic achievement of *The Scarlet Letter* itself.

When the present and future seem so nebulous, the past exerts the only force imaginable. As there is no direct intellectual or psychological connection with colonial history, no accessible chain of human memory, art offers the single hope for recapturing the spiritual realities of early New England, when moral and even physical qualities were more vigorously developed, though recalled now only by occasional artifacts: a pump, a tombstone, a frizzled wig, an embroidered letter.

The idea that the past is intellectually lost because time rots all connections emerges from imagery which steadily confronts the reader with pictures of decay. Salem itself has long been in decline from its brief prominence as a thriving seaport. Some of its houses have sunk down "covered half-way to the eaves by the accumulation of new soil" (10), and serve as emblems for the obscurity of Hawthorne's own family. He writes frequently of death, developing the guillotine image at length as a metaphor for his political demise. He even thinks of subtitling his book "the POSTHUMOUS PAPERS OF A DECAPITATED SURVEYOR" (43). He refers at one point to the spasms of a cholera victim after death (39). The cheerfulness of old men reminds him of "the phosphorescent glow of decaying wood" (16). The most common pattern of imagery, however, is probably that of physical decay in the grave. Like the author's ancestors, most of the Inspector's many children have long since returned to dust (17), and the old gourmand still recalls "dinners, every guest at which, except himself, had long been food for worms" (19). Repeated references to Mr. Surveyor Pue's immortal wig only emphasize the paradox of his mouldered body and tenuous fame.

"But the past was not dead" (27), we are told, though the present seems moribund, and Hawthorne's previous achievements as an author still occasionally revive ambitions for continued imaginative activity—work which attempts to revitalize the historical figures whom he can dimly picture in the "tarnished mirror" (34) of his imagination. As one should realize from the famous passage in "The Custom-House" which celebrates moonlight and mirrored revelations of a familiar room as the best stimuli of romantic imagination, this tarnished mirror may well represent the ideal opportunity for the historical writer. Having been at pains to undermine any sense of familiarity with early New England, Hawthorne succeeds in translating seventeenth-century Boston into that hypnogogic area between dream and reality where he can shape it into the characteristic forms of his fiction.

Yet he was, in fact, remarkably true to the temporal perceptions of the Puritans themselves. They, too, had exaggerated the time span between generations and evoked belief in long tradition where most of us discern only novelty. The similarity is nowhere more evident than in the *Magnalia Christi Americana*, written in the last few years of the seventeenth century and published at the beginning of the next. In his epic history of New England Congregationalism, Cotton Mather recorded a sequence of events from 1620 which suggested vast reaches of time, substantially different eras, and a general pattern of declining force from generation to generation. Mather would have found nothing odd in Hawthorne's statement that Hester Prynne "had flourished during a period between the early days of Massachusetts and the close of the seventeenth century" (32). Like Hawthorne, he showed concern about the fading of past influences; there is even a quality of desperation in his effort to record events and recall people before their memories might lose all constructive force. Even in so short a time, however, he had lost all information about some of the founding ministers beyond knowledge of their names and parishes. His history attempted to provide that connecting link of human memory that Hawthorne claimed to have lost with Hester's generation. Again like Hawthorne, Mather felt no confidence in the future (secular future, anyway), admitting uncertainty even about the continued existence of the New England experiment. A similar sense of time may be found even in Bradford's *History of Plymouth Plantation*, in which understanding between the founders and their children already presents a problem.[4]

A characteristic sense of time seems to have been part of Hawthorne's legacy from the frowning Puritan ancestors he sketches in "The Custom-House." A shared distrust of linear sequence asserts itself in his sustained assault on ordinary chronology. And, despite his genial nineteenth-century bows to the idea of progress, he shows little convincing faith in steady historical improvement. His examples of progress in *The Scarlet Letter* itself can all be read ironically: lessened respect for authority, decreasing capacity for merriment, and the diminished robustness of women. All, in fact, give evidence of the decline of which the early Puritans accused their posterity. Not even Hawthorne's awareness of his ancestors' sins need be taken as proof of moral progress. The difference, after all, between hanging a man for selling his soul to the devil and satirizing him for never having had a soul at all may be a better argument for diminishing force over the centuries than for moral ascent. Despite a history of lessened energy, however, there is no consistent pattern of decline from generation to generation; there is, instead, an extended period of mediocrity, broken at times by bursts of achievement—in Hawthorne's family the distinction of the first two generations and his own achievement as a writer, which he knows to be significant despite its conflict with seventeenth-century Salem values. With no consistent pattern of progress nor decline, the sketch questions the relevance of linear time.

Somewhat more comfortable with cyclic patterns of history, Hawthorne summarizes the repetitive experience of his family for almost two centuries:

> "From father to son, for above a hundred years, they followed the
> sea; a gray-headed shipmaster, in each generation, retiring from

the quarter-deck to the homestead, while a boy of fourteen took the hereditary place before the mast, confronting the salt spray and the gale, which had blustered against his sire and grandsire. The boy, also, in due time, passed from the forecastle to the cabin, spent a tempestuous manhood, and returned from his world-wanderings, to grow old, and die, and mingle his dust with the natal earth." (10–11)

His own choice of vocation has broken this cycle, however, and the births of his children in other towns make the disruption permanent. This monotonous temporal cyclic pattern cannot be reestablished once lost. On the other hand, he shares with the Puritans an allegorical interest in spiritually important events which recur at irregular but significant intervals. The parallel between his discovery of Hester Prynne and Surveyor Pue's provides a good example of this phenomenon, offering a meaningful historical link within the otherwise mechanical rotation of political office. It is the quality of repeated experiences that matters, not the frequency of repetition.

Hawthorne's time sense proves to be, not linear nor even cyclic in any systematic sense, but eschatological, like that of the early Puritans. Time has meaning in terms of eternity but little relevance to past or future. Consequently, those events which provide spiritual illumination possess a kind of imaginative immortality, a partaking in eternity, while events detached from eternal values, even if seemingly more important, sink into oblivion. Hawthorne reminds us occasionally that his fellow-workers in the Custom-House have sunk into such a death-in-life, describing them once as "These old gentlemen—seated, like Matthew, at the receipt of custom, but not very liable to be summoned thence, like him, for apostolic errands" (7) and warning that "Neither the front nor the back entrance of the Custom-House opens on the road to Paradise" (13). He worries about his own fate unless called out of the chronology of daily life and record-keeping to be forced into that more significant dimension of time where it intersects eternity.

This inherently Puritan perspective on time which sees eternity in an instant of apparently minor experience and sees value in events in proportion to the spiritual enlightenment they offer helps to clarify Hawthorne's anomalous uses of time in *The Scarlet Letter* itself. It may explain why the prison is so weather-stained and prematurely old, while the rose-bush remains fresh and blooming. Perhaps it may suggest as well why Hester could wait a year at most for her husband before turning to someone else, but could wait seven years for Dimmesdale and then assume that a past experience, frozen in time, could be recovered at will and even reenacted in some hazily projected future. Even Chillingworth's age may be taken as a measure or sign of his submission to conventional time. Something similar is true of Dimmesdale, who, though born and educated in England and, therefore, counted with the first generation of ministers, exhibits the frailty and loss of force which Hawthorne found in his own family after the decline of original Puritan vigor.[5] Hester, by contrast, retains vitality by living perpetually in the one occasion which had, for her, a spiritually stimulating effect. When Chillingworth and Dimmesdale submit to linear time, looking either to the past for vengeance or the future for relief, they are appropriately transformed: Chillingworth withers while Dimmesdale seems ever more disembodied.

And, of course, Hawthorne frequently reminds the reader that his characters are finally to be judged elsewhere and that their tragedy must be perceived in eschatological terms (which may conceivably transform it into a comedy, even for Chillingworth). When Hester is buried beside her lover's grave, already "an old and sunken one" (264), she eludes the researches of antiquarians like Pue and the curiosity of nineteenth-century seamstresses bewildered by her embroidery. Her story is accessible only to the romancer with a time sense like her own, who can intuit the eternal significance of an hour in the woods and another on the scaffold.

NOTES

1. Some recent useful studies of "The Custom-House" include: John E. Becker, *Hawthorne's Historical Allegory: An Examination of the American Conscience* (Port Washington, N.Y.: Kennikat Press, 1971), pp. 61–87; C. E. Frazer Clark, Jr., "Posthumous Papers of a Decapitated Surveyor: *The Scarlet Letter* in the Salem Press," *SNNTS* 2:4 (1970), 395–419; James M. Cox, "The Scarlet Letter Through the Old Manse and the Custom House," *VQR* 51:3 (1975), 432–447; Paul J. Eakin, "Hawthorne's Imagination and the Structure of 'The Custom-House'," *AL* 43 (1971), 346–358; Clifford C. Huffman, "History in Hawthorne's 'Custom-House'," *ClioW* 2 (1973), 161–169; Donald D. Kummings, "'The Custom-House' and the Conditions of Fiction in America," *CEA* 33:3 (1971), 15–18; John E. McCall, "The Design of Hawthorne's 'Custom-House'," *NCF* 21 (1967), 349–358; David H. Stouck, "The Surveyor of the Custom-House: A Narrator for *The Scarlet Letter*," *CentR* 15 (1971), 309–329; and Marshall Van Deusen, "Narrative Tone in 'The Custom-House' and *The Scarlet Letter*," *NCF* 21:1 (1966), 61–71.

2. Studies dealing with Hawthorne's sense of time in his historical fiction include: Margaret V. Allen, "Imagination and History in Hawthorne's 'Legends of the Province House'," *AL* 43 (1971), 432–437; Jane Donahue Eberwein, "Temporal Perspective in 'The Legends of the Province House'," *ATQ* 14 (1972), 41–45; and Leo B. Levy, "'Time's Portraiture': Hawthorne's Theory of History," *NHJ* 1 (1971), pp. 192–200.

3. *The Scarlet Letter*, Centenary Edition, vol. 1 (Columbus: Ohio State University Press, 1962), p. 44. All my references are to this edition and will be annotated in the text.

4. A perceptive inquiry into relationships between characteristic patterns of American literature, including Hawthorne's fiction, and a time sense influenced by Puritan conversion theology may be found in John F. Lynen's essay, "The Design of Puritan Experience," *Theories of American Literature*, ed. Donald M. Kartiganer and Malcolm A. Griffith (New York: The Macmillan Co., 1972), pp. 302–323.

5. Michael D. Bell, "The Young Minister and the Puritan Fathers: A Note on History in *The Scarlet Letter*," *NHJ* 1 (1971), pp. 159–168.

DAVID C. CODY

"The Dead Live Again": Hawthorne's Palingenic Art

In creating the character Oberon, the melancholy protagonist of "The Devil in Manuscript," Nathaniel Hawthorne was clearly sketching a portrait of an earlier and a younger self confronted by a pervasive sense of artistic failure that must, at times, have threatened to overwhelm him. At a crucial point in the story, brooding over the emblematic fire that has consumed the manuscripts of his abortive stories, Oberon laments that "it has annihilated the creations of long nights and days, which I could no more reproduce, in their first glow and freshness, than cause ashes and whitened bones to rise up and live."[1] References to the revival of such "ashes and whitened bones" occur with unusual frequency in Hawthorne's work, nearly always in conjunction with his attempts to characterize his creative impulses, thwarted or otherwise. In this paper I would like to comment both on his sources for the image itself and on the ways he employs it—particularly in "The Custom-House"—as a metaphor for his own creative (or, in this case, re-creative) process.

Hawthorne saw the ability to make the "dead live again," as the painter in "The Prophetic Pictures" has it—the capacity to recall them "to their old scenes," and give "their gray shadows the lustre of a better life, at once earthly and immortal"—as a prerogative of the true literary artist (9:179). It

From *ESQ*, vol. 35, no. 1 (1st Quarter 1989), pp. 23–42. © 1989 by the Board of Regents of Washington State University Press.

is this ability to recall "the fleeting moments of History," to "call up the multiform and many-colored Past before the spectator, and show him the ghosts of his forefathers," that links the Hawthornean artist of "Main-street" with the necromantic adepts and virtuosi (the Witch of Endor, Agrippa, Paracelsus, Bacon, and Faustus, for example) of history and of legend (11:336).[2] "The Prophetic Pictures" and "Main-street" are, of course, only two of a number of stories and sketches—"The Hollow of the Three Hills," "An Old Woman's Tale," "The Haunted Mind," "Alice Doane's Appeal," "Fancy's Show Box," "Doctor Heidegger's Experiment," "The Gray Champion," and "Night Sketches" come readily to mind—that betray his fascination with reviving the past.

Hawthorne knew from his own experience how difficult such a process could be. The narrator of "Edward Fane's Rosebud," for example, acknowledges that "there is hardly a more difficult exercise of fancy, than, while gazing at a figure of melancholy age, to re-create its youth," but nevertheless asks his readers to attempt to "take one of these doleful creatures, and set fancy resolutely at work to brighten the dim eye, and darken the silvery locks, and paint the ashen-cheek with rose-color, and repair the shrunken and crazy form, till a dewy maiden shall be seen in the old matron's elbow-chair" (9:179). His own "exercise of fancy" fails because the harsh reality of things overwhelms him: "Alas!" he confesses, "the charm will not work. In spite of fancy's most potent spell, I can see only an old dame cowering over the fire, a picture of decay and desolation" (9:464–65). Hawthorne was also well aware of, and troubled by, the morally ambiguous nature of such attempts, and a number of his stories and sketches reflect his ambivalent sense of his own function. In the deceptively didactic "Dr. Heidegger's Experiment," for example—a story that is closely related to "Edward Fane's Rosebud"—he created a self-portrait of the artist as manipulative quack. The apparently ingenuous Heidegger, capable only of the illusory revival of the past, is an egoist, a player of Faustian "merry jests" whose preliminary experiment with the rejuvenated "rose of fifty summers" anticipates his equally successful duping of his aged guests. The story itself is a commentary on Hawthorne's frustrated relationship with his own audience, a relationship that is portrayed as being similarly manipulative and deceptive. Both the failures and the ambiguous successes of the Hawthornean artist, then, reflect their creator's preoccupation with a difficult creative process predicated upon attempts to revive a seemingly dead past—a preoccupation shared, as we shall see, by the Surveyor of "The Custom-House," whose account of the genesis of *The Scarlet Letter* is a personal myth of re-creation.

Although (or perhaps because) clues to his sense of the ways in which his creative process functioned abound in Hawthorne's work, an incident in

"The Birth-mark" (1843) provides us with a relevant *point d'appui*. At one point in the story Aylmer, that "eminent proficient in every branch of natural philosophy" (10:35), seeks to amuse his wife Georgiana by putting "in practice some of the light and playful secrets, which science had taught him among its profounder lore" (10:44). One such "secret" is revealed in an "abortive" preliminary experiment that is clearly meant to foreshadow the larger experiment that will result in the death of Georgiana herself. Aylmer bids his wife to

> cast her eyes upon a vessel, containing a quantity of earth. She did so, with little interest at first, but was soon startled, to perceive the germ of a plant, shooting upward from the soil. Then came the slender stalk—the leaves gradually unfolded themselves—and amid them was a perfect and lovely flower.
>
> "It is magical!" cried Georgiana, "I dare not touch it."
>
> "Nay, pluck it," answered Aylmer, "pluck it, and inhale its brief perfume while you may. The flower will wither in a few moments, and leave nothing save its brown seed-vessels—but thence may be perpetuated a race as ephemeral as itself."
>
> But Georgiana had no sooner touched the flower than the whole plant suffered a blight, its leaves turning coal-black, as if by the agency of fire.
>
> "There was too powerful a stimulus," said Aylmer thoughtfully. (10:45)

Aylmer is experimenting with "Palingenesis," a process involving the careful heating, usually in a hermetically sealed glass, of the ashes of a plant or animal mingled with a mysterious powder. If the experiment were successful, a ghostly image of the dead object would be revived. Partly chemical, partly magical, and wholly imaginary—and related, however faintly, to the alchemical process itself—palingenesis fascinated seventeenth-century natural philosophers, both in England and on the Continent, not least because it seemed to have a basis in Scripture. As we shall see, it also appeared to provide an apparently rational basis both for practical necromancy and for a later pseudo-scientific theory of apparitions.

The result of Aylmer's preliminary experiment anticipates the result of his final experiment upon his wife: she too will be fatally "blighted" because the obsessive experimenter continues to employ "too powerful a stimulus." The blight that afflicts the plant, however, also suggests the destructive influence that both aesthetic pressures and "reality" tended to have upon the shadowy and ephemeral "pale blooms" of Hawthornean art. Hawthorne destroyed much of his own work, especially during the relatively solitary years of his literary apprenticeship, and Aylmer's experiments may be interpreted as metaphoric or symbolic explorations of the dangers inherent in the artist's obsessive search for perfection in art. The palingenic process may function, then, as a metaphor for the creative process—just as Henry James would later refer to a "deep well of unconscious cerebration,"[3] and describe his own creative process in terms of a "crucible of [the] imagination" (230).

Or so, at any rate, an examination of the sources that may lie behind Hawthorne's description of Aylmer's experiment would seem to suggest. Possible sources for the account are, characteristically, many and varied. Several critics have noted Hawthorne's familiarity with Isaac D'Israeli's *Curiosities of Literature* (1791–1834), which contains, as we shall see, a detailed description of the phenomenon.[4] He would also have been familiar with the passage in Sir Thomas Browne's *Religio Medici* (1642) in which Browne suggests that "at the last day"

> our estranged and divided ashes shall unite again; that our separated dust, after so many pilgrimages and transformations into the parts of minerals, plants, animals, elements, shall, at the voice of God, return into their primitive shapes, and join again to make up their primary and predestinate forms.[5]

This "return" was to be accomplished, of course, by palingenic means, and Browne's belief in the practicability of the process led him to suggest that it provided an experimental proof of the possibility of resurrection in the body:

> A plant or vegetable consumed to ashes to a contemplative and school-philosopher seems utterly destroyed, and the form to have taken his leave for ever; but to a sensible artist the forms are not perished, but withdrawn into their incombustible part, where they lie secure from the action of that devouring element. This is made good by experience, which can from the ashes of a plant revive the plant, and from its cinders recall it into its stalk and leaves again.[6]

Browne was not alone in his optimism, and neither was he the first to suggest that the Deity himself might be a practicing palingenesist. In the passage quoted above, in fact, he might very well have been recalling the famous lines of John Donne from a sermon preached at St. Paul's in 1626, in which he maintained that "God that knowes in which Boxe of his Cabinet all this seed Pearle lies, in what corner of the world every atome, every graine of every mans dust sleeps, shall recollect that dust, and then recompact that body, and then re-inanimate that man, and that is the accomplishment of all."[7] Browne would also have been familiar with the detailed discussion of the palingenic process that had appeared in Sir Kenelm Digby's *A Discourse Concerning the Vegetation of Plants*, which, though unpublished until 1669, was available to Browne in manuscript. Digby notes that "Quercetanus"—one Joseph Duchesne, "the famous Physician of King *Henry* the fourth"—

> telleth us a wonderful story of a *Polonian* Doctor that showed him a dozen glasses Hermetically Sealed, in each of which was a different Plant; for example, a Rose in one, a Tulip in another, a Clove-Gilly-flower in a third; adso [sic] of the rest. When he offered these Glasses to your first view, you saw nothing in them but a heap of Ashes in the bottom. As soon as he held some gentle heate under any of them, presently there arose out of the Ashes, the Idaea of a Flower; the Flower and the Stalk spread abroad to the due height and just dimensions of such a Flower, and had perfect Colour, Shape, Magnitude, and all other accidents, as if it were really that very Flower. But when ever you drew the heate from it, as the Glasse and the enclosed Aire and matter grew to cool by degrees, so would this flower sink down little by little, till at length it would bury it self in its bed of Ashes.[8]

Like Browne and Donne, Digby goes on to suggest that palingenesis provides a means by which human bodies, after death, might be physically resurrected.

During the later seventeenth century the process itself became something of a commonplace. In his *The Vanity of Dogmatizing* (1661), for example, Joseph Glanvill could make a casual reference to the "artificial *resurrection* of *Plants* from their *ashes*, which *Chymists* are so well acquainted with."[9] At the same time, however, fewer authors were willing to insist on the reality of the process—and we might note in passing that none of the advocates cited above claimed to have witnessed a palingenic revival at first hand (though we have Browne's comment that the reality of the process "is made good by experience"). Most often, of course, the evidence is circumstantial: Browne writes on the authority of his friend Digby, who had his "facts" from "Quercetanus," who had his, in turn, from "a *Polonian* Doctor." In his meditative "The Resurrection," however, Jeremy Taylor permitted himself to doubt: "I will not now insist," he writes, "upon the story of the rising bones seen every year in Egypt, nor the pretense of the chemists, that they from the ashes of flowers can reproduce from the same materials the same beauties in color and figure."[10] Cotton Mather, credulous enough in other matters, also professed skepticism in his *Magnalia Christi Americana* (1702), in a passage that nevertheless displays, as Barton Levi St. Armand notes, "Puritan rhetoric at its most voluble and voluminous":

> If such a renowned chymist as Quercetanus, with a whole tribe of "labourers in the fire," since that learned man, find it no easie thing to make the common part of mankind believe that they can take a *plant* in its most vigorous consistence, and after a due *maceration, fermentation*, and *separation*, extract the *salt* of that plant, which, as it were, in a *chaos*, invisibly reserves the *form* of the whole, with its vital principle; and, that keeping the salt in a *glass* hermetically sealed, they can, by applying a *soft fire* to the glass, make the *vegetable* rise by little and by little out of its *ashes*, to surprize the spectators with a notable illustration of that *resurrection*, in the faith wherefor the Jews, returning from the graves of their friends, pluck up the grass from the earth, using the words of the Scripture thereupon, "Your bones shall flourish like an herb:" 'tis likely, that all the observations of such writers as the incomparable Borellus, will find it hard enough to produce our belief that the *essential salts of animals* may be so prepared and preserved, that an ingenious man may have the whole *ark* of Noah in his own study, and raise the fine *shape* of an animal out of its ashes at his pleasure: and that, by the like method from the *essential salts of human dust*, a philosopher may, without any criminal necromancy, call up the *shape* of any *dead* ancestor from the dust whereinto his body had been incinerated. The resurrection of the dead will be as just, as great an article of our *creed*, although the *relations* of these learned men should pass for incredible romances: but yet there is an anticipation of that blessed resurrection, carrying in it some resemblance of these curiosities, which is performed, when we do in a *book*, as in a *glass*, reserve the history of our departed friends; and by bringing our *warm affections* unto such a history, we revive, as it were, out of their *ashes*, the true *shape* of those friends, and bring to a fresh view what was memorable and inimitable in them.[11]

Even as the palingenic process gradually came to be viewed with greater skepticism, it continued to intrigue the gentlemanly antiquary with whom it had always been associated. [One of the defining characteristics of

Samuel Butler's satirical "An Antiquary" (written ca. 1667–69, but first published in 1759) is that he "fetches things out of Dust and Ruins, like the Fable of the chemical Plant raised out of its own Ashes."][12] In 1832, an anonymous review of various works concerned with the "Philosophy of Apparitions" appeared in *The Quarterly Review*, in which its author noted that "Some of the ancient philosophers"

> did attempt to assign a physical cause for the supposed reappearance of the dead; and our modern alchymists continued to invest that explanation with all the solemnity of truth.... the alchymists of the seventeenth century ... conceived that by the processes of *Palingenesy*, as it was called, they could reproduce the rose, or any other plant, from its ashes. The saline residuum of the flower, mixed with a *certain* substance, was exposed to a gentle heat, and from the midst of its ashes there arose, in all its native beauty, the stem, the leaves, and the corolla of the plant. In this fanciful result, which the alchymists declare that they obtained, Kircher speedily discovered what he thought was the real origin of apparitions.... [believing that after death] the saline particles of the human body, liberated by decomposition, were exhaled from its earthly tenement, and resumed, in a shadowy outline, the same position which they had held in the living frame.[13]

"This explanation of ghosts," we are told, "was in perfect harmony with the speculations of the age," and "the chemical magician experienced no difficulty in extricating phantoms from the soil of the churchyard, or in causing the shade of the executed felon to hover above his pounded bones." The review also contains an entertaining abstract (from the '*Miscellanea Curiosa*') of an account of spontaneous palingenic necromancy:

> 'A malefactor was executed, of whose body a grave physician got possession, for the purpose of dissection. After disposing of the other parts of the body, he ordered his assistant to pulverize part of the cranium, which was a remedy at that time admitted in dispensatories. The powder was left in a paper on the table of the museum, where the assistant slept; about midnight he was awakened by a noise in the room, which obliged him to rise immediately. The noise continued about the table without any visible agent; and at length he traced it to the powder, in the midst of which he now beheld, to his unspeakable dismay, a small head, with open eyes staring at him; presently two branches

approached, which formed into arms and hands; then the ribs became visible, which were soon clothed with muscles and integuments; next the lower extremities sprouted out, and when they appeared perfect the puppet (for his size was small) raised himself on his feet; instantly his clothes came upon him, and he appeared in the very cloak he wore at his execution. The affrighted spectator, who stood hitherto mumbling his prayers with great application, now thought of nothing but making his escape from the revived ruffian; but this was impossible, for the apparition placed himself in his way, and, after diverse fierce looks and threatening gestures, opened the door and went out.'[14]

His duty as Sir Thomas Browne's editor in the 1835–36 edition of his *Works*, as well as his own fascination with antiquarian lore, led Simon Wilkin to quote the following excerpt from Isaac D'Israeli's *Curiosities of Literature* as a gloss on Browne's description of the process, quoted above:

Never was a philosophical imagination more beautiful than that exquisite *Palingenesis*, as it has been termed from the Greek, or a regeneration; or rather, the apparitions of animals and plants. Schott, Kircher, Gaffarel, Borelli, Digby, and the whole of that admirable school [Mather's "whole tribe of labourer's in the fire"], discovered in the ashes of plants their primitive forms, which were again raised up by the force of heat. Nothing, they say, perishes in nature; all is but a continuation, or a revival. The semina of resurrection are concealed in extinct bodies, as in the blood of man; the ashes of roses will again revive into roses, though smaller and paler than if they had been planted: unsubstantial and unodoriferous, they are not roses which grew on rose-trees, but their delicate apparitions; and, like apparitions, they are seen but for a moment! The process of the *Palingenesis*, this picture of immortality, is described. These philosophers having burnt a flower, by calcination disengaged the salts from its ashes, and deposited them in a glass phial; a chemical mixture acted on it, till in the fermentation they assumed a bluish and spectral hue. This dust, thus excited by heat, shoots upwards into its primitive forms; by sympathy the parts unite, and while each is returning to its destined place, we see distinctly the stalk, the leaves, and the flower arise: it is the pale spectre of a flower coming slowly forth from its ashes. The heat passes away, the magical scene declines, till the whole matter again precipitates itself into the chaos at the bottom. This vegetable phoenix lies thus concealed in its cold ashes, till the presence of heat produced this resurrection—as in its absence it returns to its death. Thus the dead naturally revive; and a corpse may give out its shadowy reanimation, when not too deeply buried in the earth.[15]

Similar references to palingenesis as a "philosophical imagination" or poetical conceit, though rare, continued to appear during Hawthorne's lifetime. His old friend Longfellow, for example, in a letter dated 20 March 1859, wrote that "Spring always reminds me of the *Palingenesis*, or re-creation, of the old alchemists, who believed that form is indestructible and that out of the ashes of a rose the rose itself could be reconstructed."[16] Later, during the same month (June 1864) in which he wrote the brief poem "Hawthorne," a moving tribute to his dead friend, Longfellow penned "Palingenesis," a poem that invokes the palingenic process in conjunction with the traditional *carpe florem* motif that manifested itself so frequently (and so ambiguously) in Hawthorne's best work:

> There was an old belief that in the embers
> Of all things their primordial form exists,
>   And cunning alchemists
> Could re-create the rose with all its members
> From its own ashes, but without the bloom,
>   Without the lost perfume.
>
> Ah me! what wonder-working, occult science
> Can from the ashes in our hearts once more
>   The rose of youth restore?
> What craft of alchemy can bid defiance
> To time and change, and for a single hour
>   Renew this phantom-flower?[17]

Clearly, then, palingenesis was still being evoked in Hawthorne's day, if only as a quaintly imaginative conceit. It is also clear that Hawthorne was acquainted with a number of authors who employed the concept in their work, either as fact or as metaphor, and that he did in fact draw upon a received tradition of palingenic lore. At the very least, he had access to the relevant commentaries by Browne, Mather, and D'Israeli, all of which appear in works he withdrew at various times from the Salem Athenaeum. What is most interesting, however, is the use to which Hawthorne would put this inherited palingenic tradition. His own descriptions of his creative process suggest that he became a practicing palingenesist himself. But his was palingenesis of a peculiarly literary sort, for he worked not with the ashes of the dead, as his seventeenth-century precursors had done, but with old newspapers, aged books, and yellowed manuscripts—the ephemerae, the rubbish, the evocative detritus of history, that served him in place of the "ashes" of the Past. In calling up the "multiform and many-colored Past" before the spectator in order to "show him the ghosts of his forefathers," then, he was not merely adopting the familiar guises of the Showman or the sportively Gothic necromancer, but also playing the palingenic adept.

As we have seen, Cotton Mather suggests that although the "relations" of the seventeenth-century alchemists concerning the anticipated palingenic revival of the dead might be "incredible romances," an "anticipation of that blessed resurrection" is nevertheless possible "when we do in a *book*, as in a *glass*, reserve the history of our departed friends." His suggestion that "by bringing our *warm affections* unto such a history, we revive, as it were, out of their *ashes*, the true *shape* of those friends, and bring to a fresh view what was memorable and inimitable in them" employs the palingenic process not only as a metaphor for the function of memory itself—in this case, in the memorial act of writing a biography, a merging of private memory and public history— but also as a means of characterizing the ideal sympathetic interaction between a reader (the "kind and apprehensive friend" invoked by Hawthorne in "The Custom-House") and the literary text itself, which "contains" the "ashes" of the dead. In Mather's conceit, the book itself substitutes for the palingenesist's hermetically sealed vessel containing the ashes of the dead, and the reader's "warm affections"—the emotional responses that are the psychological equivalent of the "soft fire" required for the palingenic process—permit the revival of dead friends in their "true shape."

Hawthorne, however, would employ palingenesis not as a way to characterize reading but as a metaphor for the imaginative process itself, which permitted him to recall "the ghosts of his forefathers" to "life." His mind itself became the vessel within which the ashes of the Past, like the palingenic powder made from the pulverized cranium of the executed criminal of the *Quarterly Review* essay, might be revived by the "gentle heate" of his "fancy." His use of this sort of palingenic imagery is most insistent in "The Custom-House," in which Hawthorne-as-Surveyor attempts to revive the Past from what, in "The Devil in Manuscript," he had referred to as "ashes and whitened bones"—the words and artifacts, the ephemeral literary and historical documents that permitted him to reconstruct environments and personalities. Earlier Hawthornean narrators had anticipated the Surveyor's use of the "ashes" of the Past. One recalls, for example, the obscure newspaper article that provided the germ for "Wakefield," and the "little dingy half-sheets" of newspapers, "yellow and time-stained, of a coarse fabric, and imprinted with a rude old type," that permit the narrator of "Old News" (1835) to "picture forth the personage, who, above ninety years ago, held it, wet from the press, and steaming, before the fire" (11:32). In "The Old Manse," similarly, "a few old newspapers, and still older almanacs" are sufficient to reproduce to the "mental eye" of Hawthorne's narrator "the epochs when they had issued from the press, with a distinctness that was altogether unaccountable" (10:20). The yellowing letters in "A Book of Autographs" (1844), penned by "soldiers and statesmen of the Revolution," make "profitable reading in a quiet afternoon, and in a mood withdrawn from too intimate relation with the present time" because in contemplating and analyzing them we can "glide backward some three-quarters of a century, and surround ourselves with the ominous sublimity of circumstance that then frowned upon the writers" (11:359).[18] Such documents, then, recall Mather's suggestion that careful reading was a process permitting the reader to "bring to a fresh view what was memorable and inimitable" in his dead friends. The letters become

> magic scrolls, if read in the right spirit. The roll of the drum and the fanfare of the trumpet is latent in some of them; and in others, an echo of the oratory that resounded in the old halls of the Continental Congress, at Philadelphia; or the words may come to us as with the living utterance of one of those illustrious men, speaking face to face, in friendly communion. Strange, that the mere identity of paper and ink should be so powerful. (1:359)

A suitably sympathetic reader, bringing imagination, erudition, and sympathy to bear upon such letters, may therefore be able—magically, as it were—to recall or re-create the Past itself. A letter from Franklin to his wife is admirably suited to the process, for in "this conjugal epistle, brief and unimportant as it is," the narrator discovers

> the elements that summon up the past, and enable us to create anew the man, his connexions, and circumstances. We can see the sage in his London lodgings—with his wig cast aside, and replaced by a velvet cap—penning this very letter; and then can step across the Atlantic, and behold its reception by the elderly, but still comely Madame Franklin. (1:365)

Like "Main-street," then, "A Book of Autographs" may be read as a preliminary version of the crucial revelatory experience in the later

"Custom-House" essay, for it is his discovery of the Scarlet Letter—at once character, missive, icon, and surrepticious autograph—that permits the famous Surveyor to successfully evoke the buried Past. Given his qualified insistence that he is only the "editor" of a newly discovered manuscript, his task is to re-discover "the elements that summon up the past," the facts that will enable him to "create anew" the facts in the case (the "connexions, and circumstances") of Hester Prynne. To use Mather's phrase, his task is to "revive, as it were, out of their *ashes*, the true *shapes*" of Hester Prynne, Roger Chillingworth, and Arthur Dimmesdale, "and bring to a fresh view what was memorable and inimitable in them."

If this metaphorically palingenic revival is to succeed, however, the Surveyor himself must first be recalled to imaginative life. He is a man of letters who has (temporarily, at least) ceased to be a "writer of tolerably poor tales and essays," and become instead "a tolerably good Surveyor of the Customs" (1:38).[19] He finds nothing very remarkable to survey in the decaying port of Salem, however, and in his guise as heir of the *Spectator*, the *Rambler*, and the *Idler* he spends a great deal of his time in observing the somnolent and ennervated Customs of the denizens of the Custom-House itself, which figures here as a latter-day Castle of Indolence. By his own account he has become an Artist of the Inert, a sort of intellectually comatose Owen Warland, cocooned and embalmed in a sophorific bureaucracy. Surrounded by fellow officers of "long continuance" who have lost "the capability of self-support," he fears that his will be a similar fate, for he senses that his own intellectual and creative powers are fading. Because he has become a mere "Surveyor" of life rather than a partaker in it, that is, he is gradually losing the artist's capacity to read, to interpret, to be "sympathetic."

Even in this torpid state, however, he attempts, on a memorably rainy afternoon, to summon up the ghost of Salem itself, as it had appeared during its eighteenth-century heyday. "Poking and burrowing into the heaped-up rubbish in the corner" of a large unfinished room in the Custom-House, surrounded by "bundles of official documents" and "musty papers" (1:28), glancing about him "with the saddened, weary, half-reluctant interest which we bestow on the corpse of dead activity," he exerts his "fancy, sluggish with little use, to raise up from these dry bones an image of the old town's brighter aspect, when India was a new region, and only Salem knew the way thither" (1:29). Just as the narrator of "Edward Fane's Rosebud" found himself unable to "re-create" the youthful image of the "figure of melancholy age," this tentative attempt at imaginative palingenesis fails, because the Surveyor's lethargic fancy will not permit a successful revival of an "image" of the Past. His very failure, however, prefigures another and a much more significant attempt, for he informs us that "I chanced to lay my hand on a small package, carefully done up in a piece of ancient yellow parchment.... There was something about it that quickened an instinctive curiosity, and made me undo the faded red tape, that tied up the package, with the sense that a treasure would here be brought to light" (1:29). Here Hawthorne, recalling his own fruitless searches for a literary Great Carbuncle in the attic of the Old Manse, also conforms to a pattern long established by literary and antiquarian precursors of the fortuitous discovery of the lost treasure: we recall the narrator of the "General Preface" of *Waverly*, coming upon his own "long-lost manuscript" in "an old writing-desk" as he searches for some fishing-tackle; the similar discovery by Irving's Seth Handaside—in the saddle-bag of the vanished Diedrich Knickerbocker—of the "large bundle of blotted paper" that is the manuscript of *A History of New York*; and the emergence of *The Old Curiosity Shop* and *Barnaby Rudge* from the "piles of dusty paper" in "the bottom of the old dark closet" of Master Humphrey's clock.

Like Scott's narrator, Irving's Knickerbocker, and Hawthorne's Surveyor, Dickens's Humphrey and his antiquarian friends are palingenic virtuosi, "alchemists," as Dickens has it, "who would extract the essence of perpetual youth from dust and ashes." They are—and it is a phrase more Hawthornean than Dickensian—men of "secluded habits with something of a cloud upon [their] early fortunes, whose enthusiasm nevertheless has not cooled with age, whose spirit of romance is not yet quenched, who are content to ramble through the world in a pleasant dream, rather than ever waken again to its harsh realities." Their "objects of search" include the "Spirits of past times," although they differ from "most philosophers"—as Master Humphrey himself, echoing Hotspur, will suggest—in that they "can ensure their coming at our command."[20] It was precisely this power, this certainty, that Hawthorne himself sought with such peculiar avidity, and it is this power that his Surveyor, when we first encounter him, so conspicuously lacks.

The passing reference to the crucial Chaucerian "quickening" that will initiate the palingenic revival of his own dormant "fancy" immediately precedes the Surveyor's realization that the package is an inheritance from his "respected predecessor" Mr. Surveyor Pue, who has himself been recently unearthed. He too becomes a "text" that our Surveyor will subject to "interpretation"—there is a typically ghoulish Hawthornean irony in the fact that the package containing the Scarlet Letter is done up in "a piece of ancient yellow parchment," for parchment is, after all, dried skin. His descendant remembers reading a newspaper account of "the digging up of his remains in the little grave-yard of St. Peter's Church, during the renewal of that edifice." Nothing remains of Pue "save an imperfect skeleton, and some fragments of apparel, and a wig of majestic frizzle; which, unlike the head that it once adorned, was in very satisfactory preservation," and these poor fragments do not suffice, initially at least, to enable our palingenic Surveyor to raise up a satisfactory image of his ancestor (1:30). In certain "documents," however, preserved in the same "heap of Custom-House lumber"—not official papers, but items "of a private nature, or, at least, written in his private capacity, and apparently with his own hand"—he discovers "more traces of Mr. Pue's mental part, and the internal operations of his head, than the frizzled wig had contained of the venerable skull itself" (1:30). These literary remains are much more significant than any "ashes and whitened bones" could be, for they permit the Surveyor to commence his own literary version of the palingenic revival, just as the "magic scrolls" of "A Book of Autographs" enabled a previous narrator/medium to "create [Benjamin Franklin] anew." Recorded upon a "small roll of dingy paper" made up of "several foolscap sheets," they reveal "many particulars respecting the life and conversation of one Hester Prynne."[21] The Surveyor confesses that he is "strangely interested" by this "ornamental article," and tells us that his eyes "fastened themselves upon the old scarlet letter, and would not be turned aside. Certainly, there was some deep meaning in it, most worthy of interpretation, and which, as it were, streamed forth from the mystic symbol, subtly communicating itself to my sensibilities, but evading the analysis of my mind" (1:31).

It was this imminent encounter that he had anticipated when, at his most torpid, he reminded himself that "Once in a great while, the thoughts, that had seemed so vital and so active, yet had been put to rest so quietly, revived again" (1:27). His overt reference to the palingenic process—when he attempts to "raise up" from the "dry bones" of his Salem "an image of the old town's brighter aspect"—only hints, however, at the surrepticious but pervasive presence of the process as an underlying metaphor in "The Custom-House," in which it is the touch of the Scarlet Letter, more than the fact of his political "decapitation," that recalls the Surveyor to intellectual, spiritual, and imaginative life—just as in the romance itself Hester's "womanly" nature, latent in her even when it seems to have been lost forever, emerges when she encounters Dimmesdale in the forest. Placing the letter upon his breast, the Surveyor experiences "a sensation not altogether physical, yet almost so, as of burning heat; and as if the letter were not of red cloth, but red-hot iron" (1:32). This almost-physical "sensation," charged as it is with a variety of cultural and historical meanings, also suggests an intensification of the alchemical fires necessary for the alchemical Great Work, and recalls as well the *"soft fire"* or "gentle heate" of the palingenic process itself. Mather's "warm affections" acquire a peculiar intensity here, for the Letter is a repository of human passion, and even of human identity. The Surveyor's intellectual torpor is such that only an encounter of this intensity will serve as a stimulus to renewed creativity (and we are reminded once more of D'Israeli's description of the palingenically revived flower: "This vegetable phoenix lies thus concealed in its cold ashes, till the presence of heat produces this resurrection—in its absence it returns to its death"). The revival, then, is two-fold and mutually beneficial, for it is only when the Surveyor's dormant fancy—the phoenix slumbering in the ashes—is recalled to life that Hester's long-lost story can be told.

The Surveyor is now able to revive the apparition of Mr. Surveyor Pue himself, and with "his own ghostly hand, the obscurely seen, but majestic, figure," a whimsical version of Hamlet's father's ghost, imparts to his heir "the scarlet symbol, and the little roll of explanatory manuscript," reminding him "with his own ghostly voice" of his "filial duty and reverence towards him,—who might reasonably regard himself as my official ancestor,—to bring his mouldy and moth-eaten lucubrations before the public" (1:33). It is from Pue that the Surveyor inherits his role as the conveyor of the living secrets of the dead past, a role for which he had already begun to position himself—conflating, for example, the roles of author and priest—in the preface to *Mosses from an Old Manse*. Like Pue, he must function here in his "private capacity": both auditor and confessor, his appointed task is to interpret and convey to others the "deep meaning" inherent in the "mystic symbol." Pue's account of the facts in the case of Hester Prynne, contained in a half-dozen sheets of foolscap, must be "embroidered" and intensified (just as Hester herself had elaborated her letter with flourishes of gold thread) if the attempt to convey the "deep meaning ... most worthy of interpretation" is to succeed. Revived, the Surveyor is capable of all that his imaginative and spiritual lethargy had made him incapable of: most significantly, he is now capable of absorbing and transmitting the latent psychic energy—the passion, guilt, love—with which Hester herself had originally imbued the emblem. He is charged, quite literally (both by the letter itself and by the ghostly Pue) with the task of re-embodying the Past, and in his hands its "ashes"—a "small roll of dingy paper" and a "rag of Scarlet Cloth"—will blossom as *The Scarlet Letter*. In a very real sense, then, the Surveyor's encounter with the talismanic Scarlet Letter represents an idealized encounter with the (perhaps blighted) ghosts of a seemingly-dead Past—embodied, as it were, in the "brown seed-vessels" of Aylmer's palingenic flower—which, brought within the charged field of Hawthorne's imagination, could return to the semblance at least of life. *The Scarlet Letter* is, in this sense at least, a palingenic bloom, and in "The Custom-House" itself palingenesis becomes a metaphor for the creative process that permitted Hawthorne to control the "elements that summon up the past," and "create anew" for his readers the crucial "connexions, and circumstances" that shaped the lives that had been touched by the Scarlet Letter.

NOTES

1. Nathaniel Hawthorne, "The Devil in Manuscript," in *The Snow-Image; Uncollected Tales*, vol. 11 of *The Centenary Edition of the Works of Nathaniel Hawthorne*, ed. William Charvat, et al., 20 vols. (Columbus: Ohio State Univ. Press, 1962–88), 336. All further references to Hawthorne's fiction are to this edition and are cited parenthetically by volume and page number.

2. "Main-street" serves Hawthorne as what Michael Colacurcio refers to as "a sort of finger exercise in preparation for the symphonic form of *The Scarlet Letter*" (*The Province of Piety* [Cambridge: Harvard Univ. Press, 1984], 32). I will argue here that "A Book of Autographs" is a similar "finger exercise."

3. Henry James, *The Art of the Novel*, ed. Richard P. Blackmur (New York: Charles Scribner's Sons, 1934), 23.

4. Most notably Alfred S. Reid, who comments on Hawthorne's familiarity with Digby's description of the process in his "Hawthorne's Humanism: 'The Birthmark' and Sir Kenelm Digby," in *American Literature* 38 (1966): 337–51.

5. Browne, *Religio Medici*, vol. 2 in *Sir Thomas Browne's Works* (London: William Pickering, 1835–36), 68–69. For discussions of the nature and extent of Hawthorne's debt to Browne and of his use of this edition, see David C. Cody's "Invited Guests At Hawthorne's 'Christmas Banquet': Sir Thomas Browne and Jeremy Taylor," *Modern Language Studies* 11.1 (Winter 1980–81): 17–26, and his "'Of Oddities and Strangenesses': Hawthorne's Debt to Sir Thomas Browne," *The Nathaniel Hawthorne Review* 14.2 (Fall 1988): 10–14.

6. Browne, *Religio Medici*, 69.

7. John Donne, "Sermon 21, The First Sermon upon this Text, Preached at S. Pauls, in the Evening, Upon Easter-day, 1626." *80 Sermons* (London: Richard Royston, 1640).

8. Sir Kenelm Digby, *A Discourse concerning the Vegetation of Plants* (London: Printed by J. C. for John Dakins near the Vine Tavern in Holborn, 1661), 225–27.

9. Joseph Glanvill, *The Vanity of Dogmatizing* (New York: Columbia Univ. Press, 1931), 47. (A Facsimile of the edition of 1661).

10. Jeremy Taylor, "The Resurrection," in *Selections From the Works of Jeremy Taylor* (Boston: Little Brown & Co., 1864), 243. Hawthorne might very well have seen this in Taylor's *Discourses on Various Subjects* (Boston: 1816, 3 v.), for as Marion Kesselring notes in her *Hawthorne's Reading 1828–1850* (New York: New York Public Library, 1949), Hawthorne withdrew individual volumes of this edition from the Salem Athenaeum in 1826 (v. 1), 1828 (2), 1829 (3, ?), and 1831 (1).

11. Cotton Mather, *Magnolia Christi Americana* (London: Printed for Thomas Parkhust, at the Bible and Three Crowns in Cheapside, 1702), 165. I am indebted to Professor Barton Levi St. Armand, who quotes this passage in his "The Source for Lovecraft's Knowledge of Borellus in *The Case of Charles Dexter Ward*" (*Nyctalops*, no. 13, May 1977), for bringing it to my attention. Kesselring notes that Hawthorne withdrew this edition of the *Magnalia* from the Salem Athenaeum in 1827 and again in 1828.

12. Samuel Butler, *Characters* (Cleveland: Press of Case Western Reserve Univ., 1970), 76.

13. "Philosophy of Apparitions," *The Quarterly Review* (1832): 289–91. Kesselring points out that Hawthorne withdrew this volume from the Salem Athenaeum on 1 June 1834.

14. "Philosophy of Apparitions," 290–91.

15. Kesselring notes that Hawthorne withdrew volumes of the 1823 edition of D'Israeli's *Curiosities of Literature* (published in six volumes between 1791 and 1834) from the Salem Athenaeum on several occasions in 1833. As I have suggested, however, he would also have found the pertinent passage quoted in its entirety in Wilkin's note to Browne's *Religio Medici*, 69–70.

16. Longfellow to Frances Farrer, Cambridge, 20, March 1859, *The Letters of Henry Wadsworth Longfellow*, vol. 4, ed. Andrew Hilen (Cambridge: The Belknap Press of Harvard Univ. Press, 1972), 126.

17. Henry Wadsworth Longfellow, "Palingenesis," in *The Complete Poetical Works* (Boston: Houghton Mifflin, 1917), 369.

18. It is worth noting that in his *The Sacred Game* (Cambridge: Cambridge Univ. Press, 1985), Albert J. von Frank arrives at a similar conclusion from a different perspective: "In Hawthorne's complaints about the elusiveness or unavailability of materials," he writes, "one sees the effect of the provincial conviction that all transmission involves loss and distortion, that all reports arriving across time and space are suspect, their images decayed and attenuated" (83). He goes on to suggest that Hawthorne saw himself as rescuing stories from history by means of the "constructive re-creation of the [decayed] object by the imagination" (89).

19. Relevant recent discussions of "The Custom-House" may be found in Larzer Ziff, "The Ethical Dimension of 'The Custom House,'" in *Nathaniel Hawthorne: Modern Critical Views*, ed. Harold Bloom (New York: Chelsea House Publishers, 1986); Michael Davitt Bell, "Arts of Deception: Hawthorne, 'Romance,' and *The Scarlet Letter*," David Van Leer, "Hester's Labyrinth: Transcendental Rhetoric in Puritan Boston," and Michael J. Colacurcio, "The Woman's Own Choice: Sex, Metaphor, and the Puritan 'Sources' of *The Scarlet Letter*," all in *New Essays on the Scarlet Letter*, ed. Michael J. Colacurcio (New York: Cambridge Univ. Press, 1985); Richard H. Brodhead, "Hawthorne by Moonlight," and Norman Bryson, "Hawthorne's Illegible Letter," in *The Scarlet Letter: Modern Critical Interpretations*, ed. Harold Bloom (New York: Chelsea House Publishers, 1986); and Nina Baym's *The Scarlet Letter: A Reading* (Boston: Twayne Publishers, 1986).

20. Sir Walter Scott, *Waverly*, in vol. 1 of *The Waverly Novels*, 5 vols. (Edinburgh: Charles and Adam Black, 1891), 5. The quotations from *A History of New York* appear in Irving's *History, Tales and Sketches* (New York: The Library of America, 1983), 376; those from Dickens's work appear in the Appendix to *The Old Curiosity Shop* (Harmondsworth: Penguin Books, 1977), 678.

21. It is worth noting that these documents, comprising a "reasonably complete explanation of the whole affair" (1:32), accompany the "certain affair of fine red cloth, much worn and faded" (1:31). The same word, that is, is employed to characterize both the letter and the description of the "doings and sufferings" of Hester Prynne, as though the Surveyor wishes to emphasize that both artifacts/texts—the roll of "dingy paper" and the faded Letter itself—communicate the same (twice-told) story. It may also be worth noting that the word "affair" itself contains a verbal echo of the letter "A," and so functions, like many of the other descriptive terms that accompany it ("faded," "greatly frayed," and "defaced," for example) as a deliberate and characteristically subtle bit of Hawthornean literary embroidery.

EDWIN HAVILAND MILLER

Intercourse with the World:
The Blithedale Romance

After completing *A Wonder-Book* in the summer of 1851, Hawthorne began to search for a subject for another large-scale romance. Of one thing he was certain when he wrote to Bridge on July 22: "Should it be a romance, I mean to put an extra touch of the devil into it; for I doubt whether the public will stand two quiet books in succession, without my losing ground." Somehow two days later he knew in broad outlines the subject matter of his next work—"some of my experiences and observations at Brook Farm." About that time he borrowed some of Fourier's writings from Caroline Tappan's library and began apparently to do some background reading which had no influence at all upon the romance, Hawthorne evidencing here as elsewhere little interest in ideas or ideology: his subject as always was the family and human dysfunctioning. The narrator, Miles Coverdale, meditates on his life twelve years earlier at Blithedale, a utopian settlement on the order of Brook Farm.[1]

Blithedale provides a pastoral setting for the exploding emotions and destructive interactions of four characters—two half-sisters, Zenobia and Priscilla, one a feminist and the other a seamstress; Hollingsworth, a former blacksmith and now a monomaniacal believer in the reform of prisons; and Coverdale, a bachelor and author of mediocre poetry. All are in flight from the discontents of urban and industrial life—at least such is their

From *Salem Is My Dwelling Place: A Life of Nathaniel Hawthorne*, pp. 366–376. © 1991 by the University of Iowa.

rationalization—although actually they make "a voyage through chaos" because of turmoils traceable, as one would expect in Hawthorne's writings, more to familial than to social sources. They dream, vaguely, that they can transform Blithedale into a communal Eden, ridding themselves of their emotional and intellectual burdens. They are blowing philanthropic bubbles, feigning faith in a collective solution of individual problems. Not surprisingly, Blithedale quickly becomes a "broken bubble."

In the preface to the romance Hawthorne, anticipating objections, insists that he "has ventured to make free with his old, and affectionately remembered home at *Brook Farm*" and that the characters "are entirely fictitious." Such disclaimers are useless, people believing what they wish, and false, authors inevitably drawing more extensively upon personal experience than they usually care to acknowledge. Emerson, who knew Brook Farm at secondhand as an infrequent visitor and lecturer, objected to Hawthorne's "ghastly and untrue account of that community" and vowed, according to one contemporary commentator, "to give what I think the true account of it." Emerson could hardly have been expected to embrace Hawthorne's awareness that "truth" is often perception mislabeled or wish-fulfillment, nor was he perhaps responsive to Hawthorne's depiction of the communal experiment as a kind of masquerade or drama constructed upon illusion and self-deception.[2]

From the beginning *The Blithedale Romance* achieved notoriety because the characterization of Zenobia was construed as an unsympathetic portrait of Margaret Fuller. Emerson protested that no one "could recognize her rich and brilliant genius under the dismal mark ... in that disagreeable story."[3]

Zenobia is not a literal portrait of Margaret Fuller, whose physical plainness is specifically attributed in the romance to Priscilla. Zenobia's erotic presence recalled Fuller as well as Mary Silsbee Sparks; her involvement in mesmerism is probably traceable to Elizabeth Peabody's attempt to have Una play medium; and her death reenacts an episode that took place on July 9, 1845, the third anniversary of the Hawthornes' marriage. The nineteen-year-old superintendent of a district school, Martha Hunt, "depressed and miserable for want of sympathy," Hawthorne wrote in his notebook, drowned herself in the Concord River not far from the Manse. Ellery Channing came to the Manse to borrow Hawthorne's boat and, joined by General Joshua Butterick and an unidentified "young man in a blue frock," set out to find the body. Hawthorne steered while the others dragged with long hooks and hay-rakes in the slow-moving water. Suddenly the young man in blue drew up the corpse and held the rigid body from the side of the boat while Hawthorne guided the boat toward shore. The pole had penetrated the heart, and the young woman's blood poured forth from her nose as she lay on the bank. The women who were summoned to lay out the body did not know how to arrange "that rigidly distorted figure into the decent quiet of the coffin." "I never saw nor imagined a spectacle of such perfect horror," Hawthorne commented.[4]

Because of Hawthorne's technical innovation, the new romance posed difficulties for some readers. Miles Coverdale is what we now describe as an unreliable narrator; that is, events and characters are refracted through his consciousness with inevitable distortions in perceptions which are not subject to correction since he is the sole source of information. To complicate matters, Coverdale indulges in self-mockery, only to confess, "I exaggerate my own defects." Although he at times appears passive and ineffectual, his aggressive nature is revealed usually during crises and, above all, in his control of his tale: the participants in the story underestimate his art, his insights, and his inner resources.

Like other great works produced in that extraordinary decade—*Moby-Dick*, "Song of Myself," and *Walden*—*The Blithedale Romance* cannot be confined in the usual literary rubric. Hence it has disappointed readers like Henry James, who found it flawed and inconsistent as satire, although Hawthorne had no intention of accepting such a limitation upon his authorial freedom. Because Hawthorne did not resolve mysteries and ambiguities, there will never be a consensus in the critical interpretation of the romance, which may be a strength or a weakness but which was clearly Hawthorne's design.

Responses to *The Blithedale Romance* are, then, divergent. Robert Browning admired it above Hawthorne's other romances. Hawthorne inquired in his notebook: "I wonder why. I hope I showed as much pleasure at his praise as he did at mine; for I was glad to see how pleasantly it moved him." Mark Van Doren, ordinarily a sympathetic commentator, was outraged. "Few poorer novels have been produced by a first-rate talent," he dogmatized. Zenobia's "tragedy is trash ... Coverdale is an ass." Maybe so, although one could, and in modesty should, assume that Hawthorne knew what he was about.

The Blithedale Romance is perhaps the most complex of the four great romances. If it is not more "hell-fired" than *The Scarlet Letter*, it sounds in its desperateness and ennui more ominous chords of disintegration and futility. Everything is fluid, and values are in doubt. Things are not what they seem, for *The Blithedale Romance* is theater. The actors group and regroup in a carefully structured series of confrontations. They speak their minds but veil their meanings. Present behavior is predetermined by past hurts and deprivations. The characters journey to a utopian setting, mouthing great expectations, but, as it turns out, make a "voyage through chaos," which is little different from what they left behind. Hawthorne leads us to stereotype the characters and to misread the events. The seeming strong fall, and the seeming weak survive. Hollingsworth, a man of Michelangelesque proportions and a fierce advocate of prison reform in order to ameliorate the world's ills, and Zenobia, who at various times is likened to Pandora, Eve, and Eros, tower over the others, only to collapse in self-destructive combat. Priscilla and Coverdale endure, the one in the role of mother-wife and the other as author of the romance. They are not heroic: they are maimed and passive survivors content to hold the fragments together, resigned to human limitations.

The characters come to the communal farm not to give but to receive. They expect the collective to fill needs and voids, to free them of despair and depression. Hollingsworth is ready to exploit the naïveté of the Blithedalers and further his own social-engineering scheme by taking over their property. Zenobia, the exotic hothouse flower in her hair mocking the simplicity of the Blithedale agrarian life and the purity of its ideal, needs shelter from an existence in which all relationships, familial, social, and sexual, have failed to provide either gratification or security. Priscilla is in flight from Westervelt, who through hypnosis markets her as the veiled lady. She seeks to find in Zenobia a half-sister who will fulfill her fantasy of a fairy princess, restore the broken family, and salvage her damaged self-image. Coverdale, "a devoted epicure of my own emotions," leaves his "cosey-pair of bachelor rooms" to collect experiences for his novel. He does not want to involve himself in the group more than necessary. Like the others he is free but trapped. "I hopped and fluttered, like a bird with a string about its tail," he writes, "gyrating round a small circumference, and keeping up a restless activity to no purpose"—which accurately characterizes his emotional state but obscures his ability to cope.

The participants are Ilbrahims in maturity—unsheltered by a family structure, untouched by affection, unprotected by society. Theirs is a world without the authority or the love of parents. There is no center. The mothers of the half-sisters are dead. Zenobia is abandoned first by Moodie and later by a guardian uncle who dies when she is six years old. She is involved in an anomalous but exploitative relationship with Westervelt, who uses for his own ends her abilities as a pamphleteer, her overwhelming beauty, and, above all, her desperate emotional needs. Her "womanliness incarnated" overawes Coverdale, who, like a character out of Henry James, closes his eyes in order to protect himself from such potency; but she surrenders meekly to Hollingsworth despite his disdain of the emancipated woman, attracted perhaps by his physical and patriarchal authority. Her posturings as an actress and exponent of women's rights hide the inner emptiness and dependency. Priscilla loses her mother at an early age and as a seamstress supports an alcoholic father who fails to protect her from Westervelt. If she idealizes Zenobia, it is because she searches for a replacement for her mother, and she falls in love with Hollingsworth to fill the void in her life created by an ineffectual father.

In a rare moment of confession Hollingsworth admits to having had a mother whom he "loved," speaks of her as "the most admirable handiwork of God," but adds immediately according to his Old Testament code, "in her true place and character." For she is to be "the Sympathizer ... lest man should utterly lose faith in himself."

> All the separate action of woman is, and ever has been, and always shall be, false, foolish, vain, destructive of her own best and holiest qualities, void of every good effect, and productive of intolerable mischiefs! Man is a wretch without woman; but woman is a monster—and, thank Heaven, an almost impossible and hitherto imaginary monster—without man, as her acknowledged principal!

For the "petticoated monstrosities" who have abandoned their ordained place, "I would call upon my own sex to use its physical force, that unmistakeable evidence of sovereignty, to scourge them back within their proper bounds! But it will not be needful. The heart of true womanhood knows where its own sphere is, and never seeks to stray beyond it!" Yet Hollingsworth during Coverdale's illness becomes an attentive nurse, and his climactic scene with the poet reveals that his dogma cloaks his dependency as well as his vulnerability. He is intellectually musclebound, emotionally in desperate need.

Coverdale is voluble on all subjects except his autobiography. Like Hawthorne himself he could have said, "So far as I am a man of really individual attitudes, I veil my face." At the same time the seemingly self-contained bachelor is in deep conflict. Supposedly a skeptic, he seeks out Blithedale and its dream, but on his arrival he uses illness to reestablish his privacy in "cosey" quarters where he gains the attention of Zenobia and Hollingsworth by establishing a child–parent relationship. From the sickbed he aggressively indulges in suggestive banter with Zenobia.

Because Hollingsworth is a monomaniac of the Ahab order, he underestimates Coverdale's character and resources and does not anticipate that after the poet repudiates his Old Testament views of women, he will also have the guts to reject the plea to be his "brother." After the fashion of Hester Prynne, Coverdale speaks with unusual intensity:

... Heaven grant that the ministry of souls may be left in charge
of women! ... God meant it for her. He has endowed her with the
religious sentiment in its utmost depth and purity, refined from
that gross, intellectual alloy.... I have always envied the Catholics
their faith in that sweet, sacred Virgin Mother, who stands
between them and the Deity, intercepting somewhat of His awful
splendor, but permitting His love to stream upon the worshipper,
more intelligibly to human comprehension, through the medium
of a woman's tenderness.

Perhaps the two women suspect his verbalizations since both are drawn to
Hollingsworth: despite his muscular and patriarchal rhetoric he is capable of
more affection than Coverdale and, at the same time, as disclosed in the
chapter entitled "A Crisis," is more dependent than the poet.

Nobody changes at Blithedale. Each plays minor variations upon
ingrained traits. As though imitating her biblical counterpart, Zenobia sets
out to be queen of the simple farm, but exotic flowers, perhaps from a
transcendental greenhouse, advertise her narcissism and her need for
attention. Priscilla continues to embroider purses which provide her father
with money for his "boozy kind of pleasure" and at the farm voluntarily
subordinates herself to Zenobia and Hollingsworth instead of to Westervelt
and Moodie. Hollingsworth, who has "immolated" himself on his quixotic
philanthropic scheme, finds another platform in Eliot's Pulpit at the base of
a granite rock formation twenty or thirty feet in height which like those in
"Roger Malvin's Burial" and "Young Goodman Brown" evokes ambiguous
associations of evil and death. Childlike and self-indulgent, always in search
of cover, as his name and his regression to the sickbed suggest, Coverdale
creates a "hermitage," a kind of womblike shelter in a tree. There he smokes
his cigars, spies on the activities of the members of the community, and, most
important, protects his privacy and celibacy. "At my height above the earth,"
he writes, "the whole matter looks ridiculous!"—but not ridiculous enough
to send him on his way.

Through physical and intellectual forces, Hollingsworth assumes the role
of the authoritarian parent and seeks to rule by fiat. Early in their relationship
Hollingsworth pronounces judgment, "Miles Coverdale is not in earnest, either
as poet or a laborer." Stung by this attack, Coverdale justifies himself feebly and
soon retaliates by prying into and magnifying Hollingsworth's "peculiarities,"
which he realizes is "a great wrong." But he rationalizes: "I could not help it.
Had I loved him less, I might have used him better." When the reformer
commands the support of his "brother," the seemingly ineffectual poet's "No!"
leads to his departure and later to the collapse of the commune.

Coverdale returns to Blithedale just as a second, even more devastating crisis is unfolding. In front of Eliot's Pulpit Zenobia has been tried and convicted by her accuser-judge-jury, Hollingsworth, in the presence of Priscilla. At last Zenobia has learned of her relationship to Priscilla, has suddenly been deprived of her inheritance, and has discovered that Hollingsworth's seeming love is tied to her wealth. In a rage of love and rejection Zenobia targets with keen insight Hollingsworth's greatest vulnerability, the intellectual defenses with which he has surrounded himself to create an illusion of authority and strength.

Zenobia shatters the illusion and his manhood. "Are you a man? No, but a monster! A cold, heartless, self-beginning and self-ending piece of mechanism!" "Aghast," Hollingsworth challenges, "show me one selfish end in all I ever aimed at, and you may cut it out of my bosom with a knife!" In her reply Zenobia wields the knife, an actress in the role of Salome or Judith.

> "It is all self!" answered Zenobia, with still intenser bitterness. "Nothing else; nothing but self, self, self! ... First, you aimed a death-blow, and a treacherous one, at this scheme of a purer and higher life, which so many noble spirits had wrought out. Then, because Coverdale could not quite be your slave, you threw him ruthlessly away. And you took me, too, into your plan, as long as there was hope of my being available, and now fling me aside again, a broken tool! But foremost, and blackest of your sins, you stifled down your inmost consciousness!—you did a deadly wrong to your own heart!—you were ready to sacrifice this girl [Priscilla], whom, if God ever visibly showed a purpose, He put into your charge, and through whom He was striving to redeem you!"

His faith in himself "shaken," his forceful voice suddenly "tremulous" like Arthur Dimmesdale's, Hollingsworth leaves the battle scene holding the arm of Priscilla, the overman now a child with a "mother." Zenobia has had, even perhaps enjoyed, her great dramatic moment—and illusion—for her victory, as she shortly realizes, is defeat, one more in an endless list of rejections. She has shattered the man she loves.

A few hours later, in guilt and despair, Zenobia turns her rage against herself and walks into one of the "blackest and most placid pools" of "the dark, sluggish river, ... with the barkless stump of a tree aslant-wise over the water." When Coverdale discovers her handkerchief near the edge of the pool, he awakens Hollingsworth and Silas Foster, the practical Yankee among the impractical Blithedalers. They set out in an "old leaky punt."

Hollingsworth sits "motionless, with the hooked-pole elevated in the air. But, by-and-by, with a nervous and jerky movement, he began to plunge it into the blackness that upbore us, setting his teeth, and making precisely such thrusts, methought, as if he were stabbing at a deadly enemy." Three times they row upstream and glide back. Suddenly Hollingsworth's pole strikes an object at the bottom of the river, and, "putting a fury of strength into the effort," he heaves up Zenobia's body.

When the men examine the body, they discover that Hollingsworth's pole "wounded the poor thing's breast.... Close by her heart, too." They have witnessed, as only Coverdale recognizes, the pursuit of a "deadly enemy" by the blacksmith-reformer, like Ahab in his love–hate relationship with the erotic white monster of the deep. Hollingsworth consummates the bond to Zenobia in what is a frightening parody of the primal scene and another of Hawthorne's extraordinary displacements.

In his fall from "topmost greatness" Ahab achieves a tragic apotheosis, Melville transforming the terrifying destructiveness of self and others into a heroic act of defiance. Hollingsworth is denied such release: now truly emasculated, he is to be the dependent of Priscilla, who will substitute for the mother whom he has termed "the most admirable handiwork of God."

A few years after Zenobia's death, Coverdale, still haunted by his experiences at Blithedale, journeys to see Priscilla and Hollingsworth, whose face has "a depressed and melancholy look." Worse, "the powerfully built man showed a self-distrustful weakness, and a childlike, or childish, tendency to press close, and closer still, to the side of the slender woman whose arm was within his." Priscilla is "protective and watchful ... as if she felt herself the guardian of her companion" and receives from Hollingsworth "a deep, submissive, unquestioning reverence." There is "a veiled happiness in her fair and quiet countenance."

Despite Priscilla's warning gestures, Coverdale makes himself known and then, "with a bitter and revengeful emotion, as if flinging a poisoned arrow at Hollingsworth's heart," which replicates the blacksmith's assault upon Zenobia, gloatingly asks how many criminals he has reformed.

> "Not one," said Hollingsworth, with his eyes still fixed on the ground. "Ever since we parted, I have been busy with a single murderer."
>
> Then the tears gushed into my eyes, and I forgave him.... I knew what murderer he meant, and whose vindictive shadow dogged the side where Priscilla was not.

Before the forgiveness, the intensity of Coverdale's feelings is not attributable to love of Zenobia but rests on Hawthorne's identification of Hollingsworth with Judge John Hathorne. "I saw in Hollingsworth," he writes, "all that an artist could desire for the grim portrait of a Puritan magistrate, holding inquest of life and death in a case of witchcraft." The body of the judge in the Charter Street Burying Point lies not far from the graves of William Hollingworth, age thirty-three (about Hollingsworth's age), and his mother Elianor.[5]

The last chapter is titled "Miles Coverdale's Confession." Now a middle-aged "bachelor, with no very decided purpose of ever being otherwise," no longer a poet or a believer in "human progress," Coverdale is not sure that "in this whole chaos of human struggle" there is anything worth dying for. He may "exaggerate" his defects, or he may be seeking sympathy. One thing is certain: nothing much has changed in his life. Yet he has "one secret" which, he avers, "will throw a gleam of light over my behavior throughout the foregoing incidents, and is, indeed, essential to the full understanding of my story." Like an adolescent he blushes and turns away his face as he declares with stumbling hesitations: "I—I myself—was in love—with—*Priscilla!*"

Miles Coverdale may be in love with Priscilla because she is the wife of Hollingsworth, that "great, stern, yet tender soul" to whom he is ambivalently attracted. Or he may be in love with her because she has transcended sexuality and its anxiety for the role of the mother or nurturer whom he seeks. Or Coverdale may be heeding the direction of Zenobia "to fall in love with Priscilla." Or he may be in love with an artifact of his own creation. With the cold remoteness of the artist, Coverdale suggests early in his tale that he does not care "for her realities—poor little seamstress, as Zenobia rightly called her!—but for the fancy-work with which I have idly decked her out!" Is the statement, then, simply another instance of self-love, or is it possible that what he says he means, that he transcends self-love? Coverdale keeps his "secret"; he is never uncovered.

To the consternation of later commentators, Hawthorne insisted on a number of occasions, perhaps with a great deal of delight, that *The House of the Seven Gables* was more characteristic of his genius than the hell-firedness of *The Scarlet Letter*. The obvious fact is that both romances are characteristic of divisions in his being and constitute a diptych. *The Blithedale Romance* creates a triptych, for it too unfolds other facets of its conflicted, evasive creator. *The Blithedale Romance* qualifies the exuberant excesses of the edenic motif and conclusion of *The House of the Seven Gables*, and no one assumes the hcroic stature of Hester, the refulgence of Phoebe, or the charm of Clifford and Hepzibah. Suicidal thoughts are translated into suicide. Depression and despair suffuse the atmosphere, and social schemes cannot lift despair. Survivors survive as best they can, but their freedoms are contracted by Hawthorne's seeming loss of faith or confidence.

One of the most perceptive contemporary comments on *The Blithedale Romance* appeared in a letter from Hawthorne's friend William Pike. "You probe deeply," Pike wrote; "you go down among the moody silences of the heart, and open those depths whence come motives that give complexion to actions, and make in men what are called states of mind." Other writers "go through only some of the strata; but you are the only one who breaks through the hard-pan."[6]

After he finished *The Blithedale Romance* early in May 1852, Hawthorne had his familiar doubts in the inevitable letdown that followed the birthing process. "Now that the book is off my mind," he explained to Edwin Whipple, "I feel as if it were out of the body; but (like a great many other translated spirits, I fear) the sense of it does not exactly increase my happiness." Not willing to trust Sophia's "too unreserved" judgment, he sought the counsel of Whipple, including advice as to the title which was at the time "Hollingsworth." On the basis of Whipple's opinion he stood ready, he emphasized, to "burn it or print it, just as he may decide." It was "a gesture on the order of Coverdale.[7]

NOTES

1. C.16: 462 (referring to *The House of the Seven Gables* and *A Wonder-Book*), 465.

2. C.3:2; A. Fields, 72.

3. R. W Emerson, *Complete Works*, 10: 363–364.

4. C.8: 261–267; Moncure Conway, Introduction to *The Blithedale Romance* (1901), xxvi–viii. Apparently this was not Martha Hunt's first attempt at suicide in the Concord River; see Mellow, 251–253.

5. Robert S. Rantoul was told by Edwin Whipple that Hollingworth was "the name of an ancestor and land-holder from whom the Hathorne Farm on Salem Neck descended"; see *EIHC* 41(1905): 4.

6. 1852-7-18, W. B. Pike to NH, in J. Hawthorne (1884), 1: 444.

7. C.16: 537, 539.

SAMUEL COALE

The Romance of Mesmerism:
Hawthorne's Medium of Romance

No one writing literary criticism today can deny the effects and influences of historical and cultural contexts on the text of a literary work. There is obviously a symbiotic relationship between the two, one as a kind of reflection of and interacting with the other. Hawthorne's psychology of idolatry did not appear out of nowhere. Several critics have, however subtly simplified this relationship by reducing it to bold assertions of power and ideology, with their accompanying tendency to empty out the actual content of things and see them merely as functions of one another. Thus the American "dilemma" between the individual self and society at large has been reduced to a kind of self-referential polarization, each polarity viewed as merely a function of the other, as part of a larger consensus-building ideology. Such a perspective often ignores the personal content and actual historical experience of such a dilemma, self-imposed, culturally induced, or, more than likely, some combination of the two. Such an approach tends to blur distinctions between all ideologies and muddy different degrees and kinds of social control. "To explain the novel's aesthetic design in terms of cultural strategies of control," as Sacvan Bercovitch explains it in his recent study, *The Office of the Scarlet Letter*, is a fascinating pursuit, but it may often empty out the visceral experience of art for the functional study of formal relationships.[1]

From *Studies in the American Renaissance* (1994), pp. 271–288. © 1994 by Joel Myerson.

Bercovitch attempts to equate the novel's aesthetic design with the strategies of control that a culture employs to indoctrinate and integrate its members. The attempt is a masterful one, reducing or explaining Hawthorne's apparent contradictions and polarities to functions of one another, thus ultimately upholding a hopeful and optimistic vision of a future consensus. What may at first, therefore, appear to be an irresolvable contradiction, such as individual freedom versus social oppression, may in fact be complementary polarities of an on-going debate or ideological argument whose resolution will occur at some future time. This belief is buoyed up by the American faith in and postponement of an ultimate consensus. This Bercovitch describes as "the code of liberal heroics," and his case is a strong one.[2]

Essentially, so Bercovitch's argument goes, a person or character interprets an event based on his or her own personal experience. These interpretations, which because of their very sources must be both personal and partial, tend in the minds of Hawthorne's characters "to polarize into symbolic oppositions, such as rumor and event, metaphor and fact, natural and supernatural, good and evil, head and heart, concealment and revelation, fusion and fragmentation." These polarities, as Bercovitch explains, are symbolic and thus "are never an inherent source of conflict, but instead they are always entwined in symbiotic antagonism and therefore mutually sustaining." And thus they ultimately suggest the hope of some future consensus or ultimate reconciliation based on faith "both in the value of experience ... and in some ultimate hermeneutical complementarity, as in an ideal prospect that impels us toward an ever-larger truth."[3] That idea of a future consensus underwrites an ultimate sense of progress and positive direction in American liberal politics. What seems, therefore, contradictory and ambiguous in the present circumstances of *The Scarlet Letter* turns out to predict a liberal consensus, an ultimate and consensual reconciliation in the distant but always possible future.

It seems to me, however, that if some kind of reconciliation presently framed in ambiguities will eventually take place on some higher, functional, and aesthetic-cultural plane, the present experience of it, as undergone by Hester Prynne and the other major characters in *The Scarlet Letter*, remains dark and ultimately tragic for those directly involved. Bercovitch's promising future seems all too easily to pass over the doom of individual passion and fulfillment, accepting it as the "dark necessity" for an ultimate consensus. He, in effect, confuses the abiding darkness of Hawthorne's vision with "overcompensation": "It is as though Hawthorne had to overcompensate for the enormous power of dissent potential in his characters and symbols."[4]

Emptying out the visceral power of Hawthorne's dark romance does not seem justified. Playing down certain dark "values" in order to emphasize their relational functions seems to miss the very nature of Hawthorne's vision, almost as if Bercovitch were substituting Emerson's "bipolarity of unity" for Hawthorne's more contradictory and paradoxical dualisms. That vision of individual isolation and resignation, of personal pain and enervation, prompted by a dark psychological dynamic of domination and submission, is built more upon the idea of irreconcilability than on some emerging and gratifying consensus. Hester's compulsion to resume wearing the scarlet letter may be her bowing to a future democratic consensus, as Bercovitch suggests, but her experience is in no way hopeful nor explicitly revealing of "a metaphysics of choosing."[5] It is grimmer than that, as is Hawthorne's vision, and however his contradictions may be viewed as polarized into symbolic oppositions, readied to become mutually sustaining and ultimately reciprocal in some future reconciliation, they still sustain an ultimate and impenetrable darkness and sorrow that will not disappear. The visceral vision of *The Scarlet Letter* leaves us only with "two sleepers [who] had no right to mingle," despite the fact that "one tombstone served for both"—ultimate reconciliation in the symbolic look of a democratic death?—and "an engraved escutcheon ... so sombre is it, and relieved only by one ever glowing point of light gloomier than the shadow: 'ON A FIELD, SABLE, THE LETTER A, GULES.'"

The general darkness and mystery of Hawthorne's romance was a product not only of his own apprehension of the world but also, in part, of the influence of mesmerism upon his vision and his fictional techniques. Mesmerism today is regarded as a discredited scientific theory that, nevertheless, left its mark on the developing psychology of the period, literature, and the culture. As Vincent Buranelli explains, "Mesmerism with animal magnetism is an interesting fallacy in the history of science. Mesmerism without animal magnetism is hypnosis."[6] Robert Fuller suggests that "the phenomenon of mesmerism, the nation's first popular psychology, now looms as a much larger determinant of the nineteenth-century's legacy to modern self-understanding than we had formerly observed."[7] Robert Darnton would add that "Mesmer might be considered the first German romantic to cross the Rhine."[8] I would like to examine this phenomenon in regard to Hawthorne's theory of the American romance, not so much in terms of mesmerism as a theme—that has been examined at some length, although it will be referred to here—but in terms of mesmerism as one of the most influential cultural phenomena to affect Hawthorne's chosen medium and the form of his fiction.

Mesmerism as a cultural influence affected Hawthorne and his art in several ways. For one, Hawthorne often described the artist as both a mesmerist, in the power he had over creating his characters, exploring and observing their intimate selves in his often cold-eyed, perceptive manner, and the spellbinding power he attempted to maintain over his readers, and as a medium, in which "the authentic artist subordinates his own will to an invisible current of sympathy vibrating through the universe. As the vessel of this higher force, he becomes a spiritual medium invested with the power to communicate life to his creations."[9] Hawthorne often used that "current of sympathy" to describe the psychological dynamics between his characters. His characters also gaze at one another in such a concentrated manner that it seems as if they are trying to mesmerize each other in an effort to strip individual souls of their social facades. And Hawthorne's law of human psychology that operates in many of his fictions summarily reflects that dynamic between mesmerist and medium, between domination and submission, master and slave, as if it were ineradicably at the root of the human condition.

Mesmerism clearly influenced the description of and approach to Hawthorne's romance. The process of entrancing the medium, or in this case the reader, as we shall see, was often reproduced in Hawthorne's fiction by his use of elongated, clause-ridden sentences and the repetition of certain names and details, calculated to create an hypnotic, spell-like effect. He intended to draw readers away from their ordinary daylight social world and lure them into the darker more remote recesses of his domain of romance, his "neutral territory." Descriptions of the mesmeric trance itself suggest Hawthorne's descriptions of his "neutral territory" in their sense of remoteness, suggestiveness, and mysteriousness, as, for example, in the case of the Pyncheon house, the "private theatre" at Blithedale, and the deadly shadows and yawning abysses of Rome.

Finally, the medium, having submitted to the trance, supposedly discovered new insights, wisdom, and revelations he or she may have been consciously unable to discover, just as the reader, once within the darker domain of a Hawthorne romance, was expected to discover more universal and often mysterious human sympathies and complicities, a glimpse into the human condition itself as Hawthorne suggested it. These discoveries, Hawthorne implied, would not be readily available to those confined only within the ordinary and social complexities of their own lives or of the social form of the novel as Hawthorne described it. These reverberations and revelations came to Hawthorne from the art or "science" of mesmerism, and we should turn to the beginnings of this phenomenon in the United States to see how and where he fits into the mesmeric tradition.

Charles Poyen St. Sauveur, "a self-proclaimed Professor of Animal Magnetism," who likened himself to Galileo, Columbus, and Christ,[10] and arrived in Boston in March 1836 to give a series of lectures, provides the link between European mesmerism and the American fascination with it. According to Slater Brown in *The Heyday of Spiritualism*, Poyen's lectures were preceded by the three lectures of a Dr. Joseph du Common, a former pupil of Puysegur and an instructor at West Point, at the Hall of Science in the summer of 1829, but these and the pamphlet that resulted from them were not widely publicized.[11] Poyen, who discovered mesmerism during his medical studies in Paris, had traveled to Martinique and Guadeloupe for a year in an effort to cure himself of a nervous ailment. On his family-owned plantations there, he discovered that the French planters were employing magnetism and "using their slaves as subjects." He moved on to Portland, Maine, thinking that the New England climate would be better for his health, and eventually found his way to Lowell, Massachusetts, where he taught French and drawing lessons to the daughters of *nouveau-riche* mill owners. He was encouraged by the mayor of Lowell, Dr. Elisha Bartlett, to pursue his interest in magnetism. An evangelical abolitionist, he originally wanted to write a book about slavery, but his publisher suggested that he choose another subject, and Poyen chose mesmerism: "The publisher agreed to print it, but only on one condition—that Dr. Poyen stir up as much excitement over animal magnetism as Dr. Spurzheim had created over phrenology."[12] Therefore he lectured in Boston and in 1836 published his *Report on the Magnetical Experiments*. This would be followed by his *Progress of Animal Magnetism in New England* in 1837.

In July 1836, B. F. Bugard, a teacher of French and pupil of Poyen, published a report in the *Boston Medical and Surgical Journal* that he had removed a decayed tooth from a twelve-year-old girl while she was in a trance. The trance functioned as an anesthetic, and during the operation, the girl felt no pain whatsoever. The curative effects of mesmerism were thus established early before it became more of a commercially successful stunt on the lecture circuit.

Poyen himself was welcomed more in Providence than in Boston, and while there he not only magnetized Cynthia Gleason, a poor weaver in a textile mill in Pawtucket, but cured her and discovered her clairvoyant powers as well. Thus began his long tour of New England that would take him to Taunton, Nantucket, and Salem. On that tour he magnetized Phineas Parkhurst Quimby who was more or less instrumental in curing Mary Baker Eddy through magnetism and, thus, laying part of the groundwork for her religious philosophy of Christian Science. According to Taylor Stoehr in *Hawthorne's Mad Scientists*, Dr. Joseph Emerson Fiske, a young dental assistant to Dr. Nathaniel Peabody, the father of Hawthorne's future wife Sophia, heard Poyen speak, was convinced that he too possessed magnetic powers, and offered to help cure Sophia of her headaches.[13] This would lead to Hawthorne's famous letter, warning Sophia about magnetic powers and control, which we will look at in more detail below. The link to Hawthorne from Mesmer to Poyen to Fiske to Sophia is thus complete.

Poyen performed his mesmeric experiments for a Salem audience, according to the *Salem Gazette* of 12 and 15 September 1837, and Hawthorne's future sister-in-law, the cause-oriented evangelical Elizabeth Peabody, heard him. Mesmerism and the fascination with it became so extensive that serious writers began to rely on such phrases as "magnetic trance" and "electric fluid" to describe certain psychological experiences and feelings shortly after Poyen's appearance.[14]

Hawthorne confided in his notebook of 1842 his notion of "questions as to unsettled points of History, and Mysteries of Nature, to be asked of a mesmerized person."[15] He also recorded in his American notebooks on 24 July 1837 his visit to the home of his friend, Horatio Bridge, and his discussions with a French visitor there, a Mr. Schaeffer: "When we sit in the twilight, or after Bridge is abed, talking of Christianity and Deism, of ways of life, of marriage, of benevolence,—in short all deep matters of this world and the next.... He generally gets close to me, in these displays of musical and histrionic talent. Once he offered to magnetize me, in the manner of Monsieur Poyen."[16]

The fascination with mesmerism spread quickly to New York and Ohio by 1838. Poyen returned to France, but the interest he had created did not die down. Robert Collyer arrived in New York on 15 June 1836, and in his pamphlet which he published in Boston in 1838, *Lights and Shadows of American Life*, he described himself as a Professor of Mesmerism and Psychography and as "the first man who ever brought the subject of Mesmerism before the American public ... the first one who ever gave the philosophy, or the rationale of Mesmerism ... the first who ever performed satisfactorily experiments in clairvoyance ... the first also who ever discovered Phreno-Mesmerism."[17] Stoehr examined his incredible career and decided that perhaps Hawthorne had used him as a model for Westervelt in *The Blithedale Romance*.[18]

One of the best eyewitness accounts we have of the era appears in Robert Collyer's pamphlet, however determined he is to show how much America needed him the moment he arrived. He finds a New York City full of

> humbugs ... and so much quackery abounds, where any one who
> has the impudence may leave his foreplane, or lapstone, or

latherbrush, and become a Physician; where any unlettered biped who has sufficient cant and hypocrisy may become a Minister of the Gospel, where ignorant and lousy pettifoggers may claim to be Lawyers, and are permitted in the Courts ... where even some of the most sacred Institutions of the Government bear upon their face the indelible blot of bribery and corruption, robbery, embezzlement, and every kind of moral guilt ... where in fact a cloud of moral depravity has arisen so dense and high as to eclipse from human sight the poor remains of virtue that still exist there. (p. 4)

Collyer is appalled by the "tall, red-faced man" who attended his lectures on Phrenology and then went on to imitate them, setting up his own travelling charts and skulls and lectures, "rising out of the dense obscurity that had always enshrouded him, and claiming to be the greatest, the most learned Phrenologist of the day" (p. 17). He marvels at the fact that most of English literature has been pirated and hawked inexpensively with no copyright laws to impede its public progress. Collyer surely has his axes to grind, but his observations of a professionally loose and "open market" for everything on the American scene from ministers to prophets, novels to phrenologists, certainly captures the Jacksonian spirit of the era and the manner in which apprentice cobblers could rise to the status of publicly acclaimed prophets. "The demon of money-making" (p. 14) was everywhere apparent, but so was the wide open opportunity for con-artist and charismatic clairvoyant.

Hawthorne's use of mesmerism as a theme and his moral injunctions against its powers are an old story and seem to spring from Collyer's own indignation at what the American scene could spawn. The cold, intellectual, Faustian powers of men like Maule and Westervelt, Aylmer and Rappaccini, and to a lesser degree Holgrave and Hollingsworth, have long since been discovered and discussed, as has Hawthorne's use of the medium as female stereotype, such as Priscilla in *The Blithedale Romance*, the passive, receptive creature so clearly if misguidedly identified in mid-nineteenth-century America. As Ann Braude explains, "Spiritualists used the language of electricity, also current in mesmerism and phrenology, to describe the relative positions of men and women in spirit communication." The woman suggested negativity in her susceptibility to magnetic and spiritual powers, and quite easily "nineteenth-century stereotypes of femininity were used to bolster the case for female mediumship ... purity, piety, passivity, and domesticity,"[19] despite the fact that there were almost as many male mediums as there were female. From such gender-specific and psychological roles emerged Hawthorne's broader themes of domination, emotional bondage, the reciprocity of slavery, and the battles between Freudian law and desire on the battlefield of the ego.

But there are three distinct areas in which the components and techniques of mesmerism influenced the shape of Hawthorne's fiction. These are "Transition," "The Trance," and "Within the Trance." The first occurs when the mesmerist magnetizes his subject, in effect releasing him or her from the ordinary daylight world, where the five senses predominate, into the more mysterious realm of the trance itself. This process involves the submission of the subject, the magnetic gaze of the mesmerizer, and the powers the mesmerizer employs. The trance itself suggests that enchanted and mysterious realm which we will call the domain of romance. In Hawthorne's domain, darkness and psychological domination prevail. Finally once within the trance, the subject may offer prophecies, insights, and revelations he or she otherwise could not conjure up when normally awake. Here discoveries are made, and healing processes of all kinds, both medical and spiritual, are possible.

THE PROCESS OF TRANSITION

The process of transition is described in a remarkably similar manner by different mesmerizers. Deleuze in 1825 suggests that the subject must be seated comfortably, the magnetizer must sit facing and exhorting him, and the subject must be willing "to surrender himself entirely to the operation ... to think of nothing."[20] The mesmerizer's eyes must be fixed entirely upon the subject, allowing no break with the mood of tranquillity and repose. Puysegur in 1784 described the "manipulations" of the magnetizer, "while fixing the patient with a *concentrated gaze*" (emphasis added).[21] "The immediate response of the subject [must be] to the unexpressed will of the magnetist." Both mesmerist and subject must establish a rapport within which thought transference and/or telepathy will result, and that rapport produces "the 'community of sensation,' in which the subject shares the sensations experienced by the hypnotist."[22] In *Report on the Magnetic Experiments*, which Charles Poyen translated and had published in 1836, in this transition period, according to a Dr. Georget, there must take place the "suspension, more or less complete, of the external senses," followed by an increase in energy resulting from "a concentration of the thinking power *upon one object*" (emphasis added). The possibility also exists "in some cases, to find a substitute for the ordinary action of the senses."[23] As Chauncy Townsend described the process in his *Facts in Mesmerism* in 1844, the "normal waking state [remains] dependent on information from the five senses," a perfectly logical and Lockean statement of the times, and hypnosis in order to succeed must abstract thinking from the external world and fill the subject's mind with the "mesmerist's suggestions."[24]

Surely our increased knowledge of the act of reading and of reader response theory suggests the "falling into a dreamworld" description that novelist John Gardner used when describing the "pact" the reader makes with a text. But in Hawthorne's case the use of long clauses and a hypnotic litany of language, particularly in the opening paragraph of *The House of the Seven Gables*, establishes his own concentrated gaze upon his material and by creating his linguistic spell disconnects the reader from the every-day world of consciousness and experience:

> Halfway down a bystreet of one of our New England towns stands a rusty wooden house, with seven acutely peaked gables, facing towards various points of the compass, and a huge, clustered chimney in the midst. The street is Pyncheon Street; the house is the old Pyncheon House; and an elm tree, of wide circumference, rooted before the door, is familiar to every town-born child by the title of the Pyncheon Elm. On my occasional visits to the town aforesaid, I seldom failed to turn down Pyncheon Street, for the sake of passing through the shadow of these two antiquities—the great elm tree and the weather-beaten edifice.

Hawthorne suspends the workings of the every-day world of sunlight and ordinary incidents, "of the external senses," by drawing the reader into a more remote and shadowy domain, the "neutral territory" of his romances. This part-psychological, part-dreamlike, and part-social space, the interior of what Hawthorne suspected would occur within the mesmeric trance, is located "*halfway* down a *bystreet*" (emphasis added) of an old New England town, a curious "middle" area away from the main thoroughfare, reserved in Hawthorne's sense of it for the more visibly social realm of the novel as he defined it. It is a place where the author cannot resist "passing through the shadow of these two antiquities," a passage similar to his idea of passing beneath the sway of a mesmerist's powers. He is drawn to them almost against his will, as is the medium in some cases, for when he occasionally visits the town, "I seldom failed to turn down Pyncheon Street." That "seldom failed" suggests the lack of personal choice that the more positive and active phrase, "often succeeded," would not.

Hawthorne also repeats the name "Pyncheon" four times as if summoning up some strange place or object like a mesmerist's incantation in casting a spell: Pyncheon Street, the old Pyncheon House, the Pyncheon

Elm, and again Pyncheon Street. The sentences contain several clauses which extend and elongate them, adding to the developing atmosphere of the place in a hypnotic manner with its "rusty wooden house, with seven acutely peaked gables, facing towards various points of the compass, and a huge, clustered chimney in the midst." The narrator's sympathies with the setting are, therefore, made clearly and eerily apparent, as is his "concentration of the thinking power upon one object."

At the beginning of the second paragraph, Hawthorne acknowledges that "[t]he aspect of the venerable mansion has always affected me like a human countenance." We are about to enter into that domain of dark romance, the interior of a soul, the territory which the mesmerist also must discover and reveal. And finally Hawthorne finds "a substitute for the ordinary action of the senses" by connecting the reader to the evocation of and "connection with the long past" within the mysterious shadow of the old house and the old elm. Again, the long hypnotic clauses themselves disconnect the reader from "the ordinary action of the senses" and "hypnotize" her, luring her into darker mysteries within the "human countenance."

This short sequence also parallels Townsend's progress from a normal waking state into the space "occupied by the mesmerist's suggestions." In Hawthorne's first two paragraphs, we begin with a "rusty wooden house," the name "Pyncheon" provides an almost spellbinding "animating principle" for that house, we are lured into "passing through the shadow," and the house is transformed before our eyes into "a human countenance." The normal, every-day, sunlit world succumbs to a darker, more shadowy, trance-like realm in which the author will attempt to connect us to some long and mysterious past and "a more enduring growth, which may darkly overshadow [our] posterity."

THE TRANCE

Hawthorne's "concentrated gaze ... upon one object" not only induces a trance-like state in his characters and also in his own narrative voice, but it also seems to endow the scarlet letter, for instance, with extraordinary powers: "My eyes *fastened themselves upon* the old scarlet letter, and would not be turned aside" (emphasis added).[25] This is the sort of decoration that was devised by white men "in order to *take the eyes* of Indians" (emphasis added; pp. 31–32). Such a gaze half-generates Hawthorne's "absorbing contemplation" of the letter. As Hiram Mattison, writing about the spiritualist rappers in 1854, suggested, "The fixing of the eyes upon an object so long ... is so evidently allied with ... animal magnetism, that no arguments seem necessary to prove the intimacy of the connection.... This condition may be produced spontaneously. By fixing the eye upon an object, by concentrating the thought upon an idea, by isolating one's self in the completest manner from all surrounding and extraneous things, the state of semi-trance may be induced."[26]

"*The Scarlet Letter*," Evan Carton maintains, "produces an illumination that unsettles the objectivity of objects by revealing the act of perception that figures in their constitution."[27] One of the best descriptions of this gaze as Hawthorne "created" it can be found in John Dolis's 1984 article on "Hawthorne's Metonymic Gaze."[28] He suggests that objects become meaningful in the very act of perceiving them. In effect the gaze invests the object with meaning at some pre-personal, pre-reflective, unself-conscious level. That gaze operates like a cinematic close-up, focusing upon a detail of the object which then becomes in the gazer's response to it, the single most important feature of that object: "Hawthorne's gaze zooms to the single aspect, the lonely detail which not only counts as a figure but expresses the whole of his 'person' as well" (371). "The unity of the object is therefore never complete or 'finished' but endures, as such, only so long as it is taken up by the subject and invested with a 'living' significance" (373). Hawthorne's images, therefore, constitute "the visible 'reply' to those interrogations which the object inaugurates" (373). The image "is an icon of vision itself" (375). Thus no object or image can ever exist free and independent from the gaze which engulfs it, and what it ultimately expresses is inherent in that concentrated gaze. The mesmeric gaze, therefore, invests all objects or images with meaning, just as the act of perception itself first perceives the expressive detail which comes to symbolize the significance of the entire object. The act of perception unites both observer and observed, both subject and object, so that the object has revealed certain expressive and significant details—its shape, its color, its condition, its emblematic "essence"—and the observer has sensed meaning in those details, an expression of them inherent in the very act of his or her perceiving them.

In effect the concentrated, mesmeric gaze fetishizes the object. As David Freedberg suggests in his provocative *The Power of Images*, "By looking in this way we are placed in the object's thrall; it is always there for us to engage with, in whatever way we like. Through looking we make it into a fetish." In such a manner, "the image becomes like a fetish: it is lovingly cherished, rouses sweet affection or tears, and may be touched and handled as frequently and as fondly as one likes."[29] Or in other words, the mesmeric gaze has helped produce the very idolatrous psychology that compulsively motivates both Hawthorne and his characters to begin with, whether they are fascinated by a scarlet letter, veiled ladies, dark houses, or a marble faun.

The trance itself as explained by mesmerists and their colleagues suggests a kind of sleep in which the subject's will has been suspended, and the mesmerist is in control of his or her responses. It suggests what Sir Walter Scott had described, in his *Demonology and Witchcraft* (which Hawthorne borrowed from the Salem Athenaeum on 4 October 1837), as "phantasmata," a series of dreamlike states, "somnambulism and other nocturnal deceptions [which] are formed in this middle state, betwixt sleeping and waking."[30] Fuller maintains that the mesmerists were "the first Americans to directly study the psychodynamic nature of interpersonal relationships,"[31] a phrase which strikes at the heart of Hawthorne's description of the American romance.

The dark domain of Hawthorne's romance shares many of its attributes with the mesmeric trance. It is a dim, dark place, colored by Hawthorne's darker sense of things, filled with strange images and powerful icons, a realm of the haunted mind often visited by ghosts and shadowed by the doom of the past, some primeval curse or original sin, a territory Hawthorne describes as "neutral" only because it is a few steps removed from the ordinary daylight world, more remote in time and space from the social probabilities he associated with novels. It is, as the Goldfarbs describe the Custom House, "a haunted place, appropriate for a seance, for ghostly visits, and for physical manifestations,"[32] whether it be on the second floor of the Custom House in Salem, within the gloomy walls of the house of the seven gables, in the forest of Blithedale, or in the monumental ruins and dark catacombs of Rome.

In the prefaces to his romances, Hawthorne described this domain clearly, both in suggesting a working theory of and an apology for his ways of creating a romance. In *The House of the Seven Gables* he wishes to "manage his atmospherical medium [so] as to bring out or mellow the lights and deepen and enrich the shadows of the picture," all the while creating in this realm "a legend prolonging itself," filled with "its legendary mist," pointing toward "the truth, namely, that the wrongdoing of one generation lives into the successive ones [as] a pure and uncontrollable mischief." He does this for the sole purpose of avoiding the "very minute fidelity" of the novel, "the probable and ordinary course of man's experience," a description of "local manners," and "the characteristics of a community" in order to reveal the innermost and secretive "truth of the human heart." The mesmeric trance existed to do likewise, either to cure a diseased patient or, when it was "taken over" by spiritualism, to reveal ultimate truths about the human condition, personality, and immortality.

Likewise in the preface to *The Blithedale Romance*, Hawthorne hoped to create a "Faery Land, so like the real world, that, in a suitable remoteness, one cannot well tell the difference, but with an atmosphere of strange enchantment ... essentially a daydream, and yet a fact ... thus offering an available foothold between fiction and reality." In such an enchanted place, the author can allow "the creatures of his brain [to] play their phantasmagorical antics." "Phantasmata" is precisely the world Sir Walter Scott used to describe this somnambulistic state, halfway between the waking and the sleeping world. And Hawthorne knew his Scott.

In the preface to *The Marble Faun*, the description of the domain of romance has become much more conventional—there is an eight-year gap between his third and fourth romances—but the focus remains the same. Hawthorne has chosen Italy to be "a sort of poetic or fairy precinct, where actualities would not be so terribly insisted upon, as they are, and must needs be, in America." And in this precinct ruin must exist to make romance and poetry grow. The domain and Hawthorne's descriptions of it, therefore, reflect the central tenets and contours of the mesmeric trance and Hawthorne's own haunted mind, where the mind itself becomes passive and cannot control the strange images and icons that appear within and before it.

In all these prefaces, the domain is opposed to but reflective of the "ordinary" world in which we live. It is both natural and supernatural at once. Such a description also applied to the mesmeric trance. "Mesmeric control constituted for Hawthorne a mingling of psychic influence with magnetic powers," Tatar suggests, "and it thus represented for him a kind of natural supernaturalism." In effect "mesmeric control hovers somewhere between the natural and the supernatural. It is at once the psychosexual control of the magnetic personality and the witchcraft of the evil eye.... The romance, by Hawthorne's own definition, weds the real to the fantastic: it stimulates the reader's own imagination, yet remains within the bounds of the plausible."[33] As Taylor Stoehr concludes, "Hawthorne's art could be taken as a variety of mesmerism, a spell he wove over his readers.... He was like the 'writing mediums' that began to spring up in the 1840s, mesmerist and somnambulist in one, whose magnetic trances could be self-induced."[34]

WITHIN THE TRANCE

The third area of comparison between the mesmeric trance and the domain of Hawthorne's romance—after the transition period and the description of the trance/domain itself—occurs within the trance itself, within the area of the domain. According to Chauncy Townsend in 1844, once within the trance, the medium experiences the expansion of interior perceptions, strange vibrations and the suggestion of telepathy, and a "final stage of clairvoyant wisdom," a kind of spiritual omniscience. Here "individuals might learn to participate in some ultimate reality." And, according to Fuller, this higher spiritual state suggested "a distinct inward transformation [which] was thought to be logically and ontologically prior to authentic self-improvement."[35] Here, according to Poyen's 1836 translation of the 1831 report on mesmerism by the Commission of the Royal Academy of Medicine in Paris, "curative effects" became possible, and the medium achieved a kind of moral insight into her or his own illness or disease.[36] Other possibilities suggested the patient's total surrender to the mesmerist's powers, the darker possibilities that Hawthorne judged and described. But in every case the insights achieved within the trance suggest insights similar to those often ascribed to the romantic reverie, bristling with prophecy, visions, and revelation.

Whatever insights Hawthorne's characters achieve in the domain of his major romances, they usually lead to further isolation and/or collapse. Hester's wandering in the moral wilderness of her mind leads to her attempted flight with Dimmesdale, which leads to Dimmesdale's death and Chillingworth's eventual withering. Hester survives because of her fortitude and courage, but she survives to live on alone in the scene of her tragedy. Holgrave and Phoebe may find love, but the studied ends of Hepzibah's and Clifford's diminished redemption reveal more completely the lasting effects of the abandoned Pyncheon mansion. Coverdale may express a love for Priscilla, but it has been twelve years since his sojourn to Blithedale, and such love is too timid and too late (if it is real at all) to accomplish anything; Priscilla has married the broken Hollingsworth; and Zenobia has killed herself. Likewise Miriam and Donatello remain forever separated, and the shrill repressive exhortations of Hilda to Kenyon and his submission to her do not suggest moral growth so much as they suggest moral evasion. The interior perceptions and moral insights of these characters do not so much heal as hurt them.

Hawthorne's is a darker world than Mesmer's. It foregrounds the disconnections and disruptions between people and the world around them more than it includes them in some universal, health-inducing medium. And it does so because of Hawthorne's moral objections to the psychological powers of mesmerism, its master/slave potentials, and the ease with which the self can fall prey to its powers. But it is the reader who might be expected to experience Hawthorne's romances as a health-inducing medium because of what he or she sees in terms of the characters' failure to act sympathetically. And it is Hawthorne's notion of mesmerism's powers and descriptions that he has borrowed to explain the process his romance is supposed to undergo and achieve. He "accepted mesmeric clairvoyance as physiological fact," Howard Kerr concludes, "even though he distrusted utterly its ethical use."[37] In any case, however, his romance becomes the mesmerized medium within which the reader, suitably entranced, should realize the potential of that great invisible fluid of human sympathy that surrounds us all, if we but recognize and acknowledge it.

THE HIDDEN SELF AS ULTIMATE DOMAIN

At the center of Hawthorne's romances and itself described as a more interior dark domain of the same "neutral territory" lies the individual self. This self can be all too easily manipulated by mesmeric powers and conjured up by authorial speculations, but as fictional character, narrator, medium, or mesmerist, it remains essentially hidden, indeterminate, and dangerous to "know." Hawthorne cannot bring himself to stare directly at it, and even if he could, he felt it should be left, almost religiously, as an unfathomable mystery, a kind of compulsive but invisible force. In effect his description of this self is as much empty as it is full, an entity that remains an elusive shadow, seen to exist only by its visible actions and contemplations, a thing of smoke in the act of "lights and shadows flitting across" it, without the mind's having "the power of selecting or controlling" whatever may arise from it.

Hawthorne's hidden self may most be like his house of the seven gables which comes to represent the dark interior of the human psyche, a place where ultimate confrontations with the self must transpire. And those whose selves are found wanting are necessarily doomed. The descent into the dark interior of the house parallels the descent into one's own dark and nearly imageless psyche, and only those with an inner integrity and intuitive human sympathies will get out alive. Moments after the evil judge Jaffrey Pyncheon crosses the threshold of the old Pyncheon house, he dies. The other characters, however problematic their possible rebirth, escape.

Terry Eagleton, in his Marxist approach to literature and the ideology of aesthetics, has suggested that the kind of soul or self Hawthorne subscribes to—that hidden, deep well of mystery which can only know itself, that is as much absent as it is present, and whose presence can be felt only by its enigmatic absence—is really a bourgeois invention. It came about because "Power is shifting its location from centralized institutions to the silent, invisible depths of the subject itself." Eagleton continues: "That the individual subject should come to occupy central stage, reinterpreting the world with reference to itself, follows logically enough from bourgeois economic and political practice. But the more the world is thus subjectivized, the more the all-priviledged [sic] subject begins to undermine the very objective conditions of its own preeminence." This could, indeed, be one approach to the very subject of Hawthornian romance: "The wider the subject extends its imperial sway over reality, the more it relativizes that terrain to its own needs and desires, dissolving the world's substance into the stuff of its own senses."[38] However perceptive this assessment may be from a more social and political perspective, the matter remains that Hawthorne's essential dualism between mesmerist and medium, victor and victim, male and female, however jeopardized by the slipperiness and fragility of its own possible dissolution and interaction, remained virtually intact throughout his fiction, drawn as it was along gender stereotypes—the man as mesmerist, the woman as medium—and revealing as it did an ultimately parasitic relationship that seems essential to Hawthorne's understanding of the compulsions hidden in the human psyche.

Hawthorne suggested that the "soul" or hidden, inner self could only be known by the shadows cast by its outer shell, that "what was" could only be hinted at and described in veiled terms by "what it was not." In effect the conscious self could never really hope to understand or to fathom the more compulsive and ultimately hidden subconscious self. As Hawthorne wrote to Sophia: "Words may be a thick and darksome veil of mystery between the soul and the truth which it seeks.... Yet words are not without their use ... merely for explaining outward acts, and all sorts of external things, leaving the soul's life and action to explain itself in its own way."[39] Words, therefore, become the visible carapace of invisible, intangible forces and experiences, the outer garment of the mesmeric act, the litany used to enhance the inner self, forever elusive and forever present.

Language for Hawthorne suggests Terry Eagleton's description of Walter Benjamin's approach to language, having "its roots in the acting out of magical correspondences between humanity and Nature; it is thus originally a matter of sensuous images, and only subsequently of ideas."[40] For all of Hawthorne's allegorical and anti-allegorical musings—and one must recognize the inevitable collapse of all allegorical interpretations in his fiction, leaving the compulsive need to continue to interpret and allegorize the events of his characters and of his fiction intact—the scarlet letter and the gaze that both invests it with and takes from it the power of its mysterious and suggestive presence appear first before the allegory "sets in" to try and analyze these powers. As a sensuous and fiery object, perceived first by the senses as such, deep within an almost self-imposed self-hypnosis, that letter conjures up the very act of enchantment and trance which lie at the heart of Mesmer's misguided theories. Thus, suggests Robert Levine, does Hawthorne "like the spiritualist ... as romancer behind the romancer, entice a restless democratic readership [in *The Blithedale Romance*] with melodrama and mystery."[41]

The other half of the process is the incarnation of the image, the power that Hawthorne suggests, because of the mesmeric gaze, remains inherent in, for example, the scarlet letter, the house of the seven gables, the minister's black veil, and the marble faun. All too easily his characters transform these images into idols, into icons to worship and uphold, a mesmeric process itself a product of the interpenetration between self-hypnotic gaze and external object. Mesmer's magnetic fluid, his pervasive invisible agent, and his hypnotic powers became transformed in Hawthorne's art into the magnetic chain of human sympathies, the powers of the artist, and the medium of his art. Mesmerism itself is a dead and discredited theory, but in the context of its time and place, particularly in the America of the 1830s and 1840s, it corroborated much of Hawthorne's own theories of fiction.

Hawthorne's romance thus initiates and re-enacts a way of seeing and apprehending the mysteries of the human psyche and its elusive motives that borrows the description of its process from the tenets and tendencies of mesmerism. Whether in the conjurings up of the incarnation of the scarlet letter, entering within the moonlit places of the house of the seven gables, in which "common-place characteristics ... were now transformed by a charm of romance," musing upon the various veils, masks, and misplaced eye-patches in and around the environs of Blithedale, or succumbing to the stiffling ruin and ancient waste of Rome, the process in Hawthorne's major romances and much of his fiction reenacts that of the mesmeric trance. The reader finds himself or herself lured into the dark domain, armed with his or her own speculations and musings, attempting to interpret events in many of the same ways that the characters do. Yet the reader becomes aware of a wider "fluid" of sympathy that the characters evade or repress, in much the same way as he or she would be if hypnotized by a powerful mesmerist. And in this enchanted process, the work of Hawthornian romance is momentarily completed and ongoing.

Hawthorne distrusted the literalist and dogmatic language of the mesmerist and the spiritualist, reducing such mysteries to physical and material explanations and occurrences. He opted for a more open-ended and ambiguous series of speculations, part allegorical, part unexplained riddle in order to leave that mysteriously "empty" process of the growth of human sympathy and, perhaps, the human soul intact, to leave "the mysteries which it knows within itself, but never transmits to the earthly eye or ear."[42] The mesmeric process, if not the product, which he both condemned and described as an essential part of human psychology, allowed him the room, the "neutral territory" to do just that. It was a delicate balancing act always, and it was not always successful. He achieved it in his major romances only in *The Scarlet Letter* and then spent the rest of his energies trying to withdraw from that conjured up, gloomy domain that imprisoned him all too easily. He occupied the realm of mesmerism without believing in its possible curing abilities and made of it his vision of the American romance.

Sacvan Bercovitch is correct when he suggests "that text and context are reciprocal." It is the nature of that reciprocity, however, that remains open to question and investigation, that is finally more than "ideological analysis [as] a richly aesthetic form of criticism," and that goes beyond the description, however brilliant and subtle, of "the novel's aesthetic design in terms of cultural strategies of control."[43] Art does participate in ideology and can be described "as ideological mimesis," but the boundaries are far less certain and far less rigid than the way in which Bercovitch describes them. Mesmerism is one of those cultural "strategies of control" and more: it provided the dark context for and the visceral experience of Hawthorne's art, and the textures of his texts reveal again and again its pervasive and persuasive powers.

NOTES

1. Sacvan Bercovitch, *The Office of the Scarlet Letter* (Baltimore: Johns Hopkins University Press, 1991), p. xvii.

2. Bercovitch, *Scarlet Letter*, p. 17.

3. Bercovitch, *Scarlet Letter*, p. 23.

4. Bercovitch, *Scarlet Letter*, p. 156.

5. Bercovitch, *Scarlet Letter*, p. 88.

6. Vincent Buranelli, *The Wizard from Vienna: Franz Anton Mesmer* (New York: Coward, McCann and Geoghegan, 1975), p. 120.

7. Robert C. Fuller, *Mesmerism and the American Cure of Souls* (Philadelphia: University of Pennsylvania Press, 1982), p. x.

8. Robert Darnton, *Mesmerism and the End of the Enlightenment in France* (Cambridge: Harvard University Press, 1968), p. 149.

9. Maria M. Tatar, *Spellbound: Studies on Mesmerism and Literature* (Princeton: Princeton University Press, 1978), p. 229.

10. Darnton, *Mesmerism*, p. 17.

11. See Slater Brown, *The Heyday of Spiritualism* (New York: Hawthorn, 1970).

12. Grace Adams and Edward Hutter, *The Mad Forties* (New York: Harper and Row, 1942), p. 90.

13. See Taylor Stoehr, *Hawthorne's Mad Scientists* (Hamden, Conn: Shoe String Press, 1978).

14. Clare R. Goldfarb and Russell M. Goldfarb, *Spiritualism and Nineteenth-Century Letters* (Rutherford, N.J.: Fairleigh Dickinson University Press, 1978), p. 30.

15. *The Centenary Edition of the Works of Nathaniel Hawthorne*, ed. William Charvat et al., 20 vols. to date (Columbus: Ohio State University Press, 1962–), vol. 8, *The American Notebooks*, ed. by Claude M. Simpson (1972), p. 228.

16. *American Notebooks*, p. 58.

17. Robert H. Collyer, *Lights and Shadows of American Life* (Boston: Redding, 1838), p. 17.

18. Stoehr, *Hawthorne's Mad Scientists*, p. 35.

19. Ann Braude, *Radical Spirits: Spiritualism and Women's Rights in Nineteenth-Century America* (Boston: Beacon, 1989), pp. 23, 83, 82.

20. Brown, *Spiritualism*, p. 7.

21. Brown, *Spiritualism*, p. 2.

22. Brown, *Spiritualism*, p. 4.

23. Charles Poyen, *Report on the Magnetic Experiments Made By the Commission of the Royal Academy of Medicine, of Paris, Read in the Meetings of June 21 and 28, 1831* (Boston: D. K. Hitchcock, 1836), p. xxv.

24. Fuller, *Mesmerism*, p. 44.

25. *Works*, vol. 1, *The Scarlet Letter* (1962), p. 31.

26. Hiram Mattison, *The Rappers* (New York: H. Long & Brother, 1854), pp. 226–71.

27. Evan Carton, *The Rhetoric of American Romance* (Baltimore: Johns Hopkins University Press, 1985), p. 207.

28. John Dolis, "Hawthorne's Metonymic Gaze: Image and Object," *American Literature*, 56 (October 1984): 362–78.

29. David Freedberg, *The Power Of Images* (Chicago: University of Chicago Press, 1989), pp. 373, 178.

30. Sir Walter Scott, *Demonology and Witchcraft* (London: William Tegg, 1972 ([1831]), p. 8.

31. Fuller, *Mesmerism*, p. 8.

32. Goldfarb and Goldfarb, *Spiritualism*, p. 142.

33. Tatar, *Spellbound*, pp. 227, 212.

34. Stoehr, *Hawthorne's Mad Scientists*, p. 61.

35. Fuller, *Mesmerism*, pp. 45, 46, xii, 52.

36. Poyen, *Report*, p. xlv.

37. Howard Kerr, *Mediums, and Spirit-Rappers, and Roaring Radicals: Spiritualism in American Literature, 1850–1900* (Urbana: University of Illinois Press, 1972), p. 56.

38. Terry Eagleton, *The Ideology of the Aesthetic* (Oxford: Basil Blackwell, 1990), pp. 27–28, 70.

39. *Works*, vol. 15, *The Letters, 1813–1843*, ed. by Thomas Woodson et al. (1984), p. 462.

40. Eagleton, *Ideology of the Aesthetic*, p. 335.

41. Robert S. Levine, *Conspiracy and Romance: Studies in Brockden Brown, Cooper Hawthorne, and Melville* (Cambridge, England: Cambridge University Press, 1989), p. 147.

42. Stoehr, *Hawthorne's Mad Scientists*, p. 43.

43. Bercovitch, *Scarlet Letter*, pp. 155, xvii.

MICHAEL DUNNE

Narrative Transformations of Romanticism

My argument in the previous chapter was that Hawthorne deliberately appropriated and transformed the elements of history—in which he had considerable interest and personal involvement—to create problematic fictional narratives available to repeated reevaluation and interpretation. In creating other fictional works, Hawthorne freely exploited more contemporary materials including the semiotics, ideology, and literary structures central to his own mid-nineteenth-century culture—once again despite whatever attraction these romantic properties exercised on Hawthorne the man. In this respect, larger thematic narrative elements including historical events and romantic ideology can be seen to function analogously with the smaller narratological elements of verb tenses and personal pronouns as forces useful for destabilizing reader responses. When confronting these larger elements of Hawthorne's narratives, our natural tendency as readers is to interpret organically, to select the more "correct" alternative. As George Haggerty wisely concludes, "It is the nature of Hawthorne's affective form ... to create an indeterminacy that encourages closure in private and personal terms" (109). Even while recognizing this tendency, it is still possible simply to recognize the presence of two or more contending choices. Insofar as I am able, therefore, I will attempt to defer interpretive closure in favor of tracking some instances in which Hawthorne

From *Hawthorne's Narrative Strategies*, pp. 129–154. © 1995 by the University Press of Mississippi.

both solicits conventional romantic responses from his readers and problematizes them.

It is unsurprising that Hawthorne incorporated contemporary as well as historical materials into his narratives, since the first admonition given to apprentice writers of fiction is that they should write about what they know. However, Hawthorne rejected absolute realism, the most obvious strategy for fulfilling this literary program, as he explains in the preface to his most patently contemporary longer work of fiction, *The Blithedale Romance*. Having conceded that "many readers will probably suspect a faint and not very faithful shadowing of BROOK FARM" in Hawthorne's depiction of the Blithedale commune, the preface continues:

> The Author does not wish to deny, that he had this Community in his mind, and that (having had the good fortune, for a time, to be personally connected with it) he has occasionally availed himself of his actual reminiscences, in the hope of giving a more lifelike tint to the fancy-sketch in the following pages. He begs it to be understood, however, that he has considered the Institution itself as not less fairly the subject of fictitious handling, than the imaginary personages whom he has introduced there. (3:1)

That is to say, Hawthorne will write directly and realistically about contemporary culture when this approach seems most useful, and he will transform these materials imaginatively when that strategy seems more immediately appropriate.

In a similarly mixed formula, Hawthorne explains in the preface to *The House of the Seven Gables* that, although "The Reader may perhaps choose to assign an actual locality to the imaginary events of this narrative," the author would prefer that "the book ... be read strictly as a Romance, having a great deal more to do with the clouds overhead, than with any portion of the actual soil of the County of Essex" (2:3). Both prefaces insist that, despite any reader's desire for unmixed realistic depiction, realism will constitute only one element of Hawthorne's narratives. These narratological discussions in Hawthorne's prefaces furnish the materials upon which the generic critics cited in my first chapter develop their theories about Hawthorne's theory of romance. From my perspective, these discussions are also interesting in what they reveal about how Hawthorne approaches his readers' attitudes toward contemporary materials.

As was true of history, moreover, no matter how much or how little autobiographical significance some element of contemporary culture might represent, Hawthorne accords it authority in his fiction primarily as his immediate narrative strategy requires. Hawthorne was, in this sense, simultaneously a highly aware participant in the romantic culture of his time and an exploiter of its dearest beliefs in the service of narrative effect. In some fictional works, Hawthorne both dramatizes and undermines contemporary attitudes toward natural symbols. In other works, he exploits and challenges his contemporaries' confidence in the inevitability of progress. Elsewhere, he imitates through parody the popular narrative structure of the romantic quest. As was true of the more narrowly technical experiments considered in earlier chapters, Hawthorne's adoption of this complex approach creates thematic ambiguity. D. H. Lawrence speaks for many when he writes: "That blue-eyed darling Nathaniel knew disagreeable things in his inner soul. He was careful to send them out in disguise" (83). At the same time, these strategies also allowed Hawthorne to continue writing originally about subjects that might appear to have been exhausted by other writers.

A fundamental doctrine of many mid-nineteenth-century American writers was a belief in the symbolic authority of nature. In 1836 Ralph Waldo Emerson enunciated a theory of symbol in his first book, *Nature*, that retained its validity through much of the century: "Particular natural facts are symbols of particular spiritual facts" (31). In consequence, as he later explains, "To the wise ... a fact is true poetry, and the most beautiful of fables" (55). In illustration of this doctrine, Emerson's poetry and prose during the 1830s and 1840s—the decades in which Hawthorne was writing his tales and sketches—are filled with particular natural facts directing attention onward and upward to the inspiring spiritual facts of truth, beauty, and unity. Gertrude Reif Hughes observes about this transcendental practice: "The relationship between affirmation and confirmation is subtle.... Temporally of course, affirmation comes first. Without affirmation there can exist no confirmation, for where nothing has been projected nothing can be verified" (xi). In the work of Hawthorne's contemporaries, optimistic assumptions so often authorized symbolic literary confirmations that readers might easily assume an inescapable causal relationship. Even today, we can hardly ignore the rhetorical force of this symbolic equation when reading these works.

In 1849 Emerson appended to *Nature* a verse epigraph that captures both the semiotics and the teleological metaphysic of contemporary romanticism. The poem concludes: "[S]triving to be man, the worm / Mounts through all the spires of form" (21). To the optimistic romantic imagination, this representation of the worm's successful efforts to evolve can stand as an emblem of the soul's quest for spiritual transcendence. Emerson's verse narrative of a worm's ascent therefore articulates an act of great romantic faith, even if symbolically displaced to what some might consider a trivial level of experience. Emerson reveals little discomfort with this possible discrepancy, however, as is clear in another passage from *Nature*: "In their primary sense these are trivial facts, but we repeat them for the value of their analogical import" (35); and what the worm analogically represents is spiritual progress.

Such literary appropriations of the natural world do not indicate merely a private inclination of Emerson's. Throughout *Walden*, Henry David Thoreau shows his agreement with this program by using imagery drawn from nature to validate romantic optimism. Thus in the chapter "The Bean-Field," Thoreau identifies his literary purpose in undertaking this physical exercise: "[S]ome must work in fields if only for the sake of tropes and expression" (142). Such natural tropes abound in *Walden*. In a brilliantly metaphorical explanation of metaphor, Thoreau writes about animals that "they are all beasts of burden, in a sense, made to carry some portion of our thoughts" (189). One such animal, reminiscent of Emerson's striving worm, is the grub, which functions successfully in two metaphorical capacities. First the grub serves as an illustration during Thoreau's lecture on etymological evolution: "Thus, also, you pass from the lumpish grub in the earth to the airy and fluttering butterfly. The very globe continually transcends and translates itself, and becomes winged in its orbit" (247). Physical transcendence is suggested as the tenor. Second and more significantly, the grub functions as the first stage in a process intended to symbolize the evolution of consciousness that Thoreau sees as the ultimate goal of all naturalistic study: "The perch swallows the grub-worm, the pickerel swallows the perch, and the fisherman swallows the pickerel; and so all the chinks in the scale of being are filled" (231). In one sense, the most striking facet of this literary exercise is Thoreau's refusal to develop the process logically into a completed circle. Shakespeare or Marvell could not resist concluding the anecdote with the fisherman's death and subsequent return to the earth and the grub-worm. The symbolic strategy of American romanticism is unlikely to turn in this ironic direction, however, as readers are well aware.

Hawthorne's narrators frequently problematize the rhetorical assumptions implicit in this symbolic system. In *The Scarlet Letter*, for example, the narrator ironically explains that "nothing was more common" among the American Puritans "than to interpret all meteoric appearances, and other natural phenomena, that occurred with less regularity than the rise and set of sun and moon, as so many revelations from a supernatural source" (1:154). Comments of this sort are, of course, valuable to critics investigating Hawthorne's attitudes toward Puritanism or toward the exceptionality of American democracy. At the same time, the narrator's reservations may also be aptly applied to the interpretive dispositions of Hawthorne's romantic contemporaries. At this point in *The Scarlet Letter*, the narrator raises the issue of Puritanical interpretation primarily to contextualize Arthur Dimmesdale's conviction that a meteor has just signified across the sky his concealed adultery. The narrator continues:

> We impute it, therefore, solely to the disease in his own eye and heart, that the minister, looking upward to the zenith, beheld there the appearance of an immense letter,—the letter A,— marked out in lines of dull red light. Not but the meteor may have shown itself at that point, burning duskily through a veil of cloud; but with no such shape as his guilty imagination gave it; or, at least, with so little definiteness, that another's guilt might have seen another symbol in it. (1:155)

This narrator insists that when fictional characters engage in interpretation, the results are highly subjective. The sexton therefore explains to Dimmesdale at the end of this chapter how the members of his congregation have otherwise deciphered the same natural fact: "[W]e interpret [the meteor] to stand for Angel. For, as our good Governor Winthrop was made an angel this past night, it was doubtless held fit that there should be some notice thereof" (1:158). These contradictory interpretations surely problematize Dimmesdale's private interpretation within Hawthorne's narrative. At the same time, the interpretive conflicts may suggest why later critics have discovered so many metaphorical tenors for the scarlet letter.

Hawthorne also exploits his contemporaries' fondness for symbolic interpretation in his seldom-discussed tale "The Great Stone Face." At first glance, this material seems particularly suited to a transcendental treatment since its plot as well as its title is derived from a sublime freak of nature whose spiritual significance depends entirely on human perception. According to the narrator, the Great Stone Face seemed, "when viewed at a proper distance, precisely to resemble the features of the human countenance" (11:27), thus affording an opportunity for the kind of symbolic interpretation practiced by Hawthorne's Concord neighbors. Hawthorne complicates the process, however, when the narrator adds: "True it is, that if the spectator approached too near, he lost the outline of the gigantic visage, and could discern only a heap of ponderous and gigantic rocks, piled in chaotic ruin one upon another." According to the narrator, any resemblance between a human being and these rocks is probably more coincidental than profoundly spiritual, since the formation is merely "a work of Nature in her mood of majestic playfulness" (11:27). As this explanation implies, the natural facts in this tale have been carefully preselected by the author to make the whole issue of interpretation problematic. If the rocks do represent a face, "it seemed as if an enormous giant, or a Titan, had sculptured his own likeness on the precipice." In other words, the natural sign would have been produced by another product of human imagination rather than by the tutelary genius of unmediated nature. Furthermore, the Great Stone Face may be seen to affect nature, rather than vice versa: "According to the belief of many people, the valley owed much of its fertility to this benign aspect that was continually beaming over it, illuminating the clouds, and infusing its tenderness into the sunshine" (11:27). Throughout the introductory paragraphs, Hawthorne's narrator insists on the effects of human consciousness. The implication is that the villagers see in natural facts what they expect to see, that their ideas precede their experiences of nature. As Larzer Ziff says in *Literary Democracy: The Declaration of Cultural Independence in America*, Hawthorne "treats the sky, forest, and river as impersonal carriers of messages projected by the beholder, not those sent down from a higher reality" (145).

The narrator's description of the tale's setting also stresses human intervention rather than primal nature:

> Embosomed amongst a family of lofty mountains, there was a valley so spacious that it contained many thousand inhabitants. Some of these good people dwelt in log huts, with the black forest all around them, on the steep and difficult hill-sides. Others had their homes in comfortable farmhouses, and cultivated the rich soil on the gentle slopes or level surfaces of the valley. Others, again, were congregated into populous villages, where some wild, highland rivulet, tumbling down from its birth-place in the upper mountain region, had been caught and tamed by human cunning, and compelled to turn the machinery of cotton factories. (11:26)

These people do not live in an unspoiled natural environment charged with spiritual truth. Even apart from the agriculture and manufacturing, the narrator's description emphasizes human agency and creativity. These villagers probably do not live even in New England, but in a story book. The narrator's vocabulary—"good people," "gentle slopes," "highland rivulet"— clearly signals a chronotope of pastoralism rather than of realism.

Another element in the tale shows Hawthorne's transformation of another contemporary belief. The central character, aptly named Ernest, is one of nature's noblemen, somewhat like William Wordsworth's shepherd, Michael. Ernest spends his whole life in this pastoral valley, working conscientiously at simple agricultural tasks and meditating constantly on the primary natural fact in the story. Although "Ernest had had no teacher, save only that the Great Stone Face became one to him" (11:29), he nevertheless becomes wise and good. Eventually wise men flock to Ernest because "the report had gone abroad that this simple husbandman had ideas unlike those of other men, not gained from books, but of a higher tone—a tranquil and familiar majesty, as if he had been talking with the angels as his daily friends" (11:42). In this light, the tale seems compatible with contemporary romantic thinking about nature and natural imagery. Since Hawthorne is not Wordsworth—or Emerson or Thoreau—the experiences of his natural man often run contrary to expectations. At one point, after his great spiritual development has taken place, Ernest gazes at the source of his wisdom and "could hardly believe but that a smile beamed over the whole visage, with a radiance still brightening, although without motion of the lips." Since the object of Ernest's perception is a rock formation, the narrator is surely correct in noting that there is no movement of the lips, but even this qualification is insufficient. The narrator goes on to insist that, in any case, Ernest's perception should be understood as uncanny rather than marvelous: "It was probably the effect of the western sunshine, melting through the thinly diffused vapors that had swept between him and the object that he gazed at" (11:37). Thus, even while creating a character perfectly suited to interpret natural facts according to the prevailing romantic mode, Hawthorne cannot help problematizing the issue.

Since the tale is about interpreting natural facts, its very few incidents all hinge on the villagers' acceptance of the Great Stone Face as a sign that some great man will eventually come to their valley. The narrator questions this interpretation first of all by presenting the view of those who "had seen more of the world, had watched and waited till they were weary, and had beheld no man with such a face, nor any man that proved to be much greater or nobler than his neighbors." These people have come to the conclusion that the prophecy is "nothing but an idle tale" (11:28). Despite all their worldly experience, these folk may be mistaken, and yet the plot's unfolding tends to support rather than contradict their view. As the tale develops, the narrator satirizes the gullibility and foolish optimism of the less-traveled characters as they perceive the fulfillment of the prophecy in the successive arrivals of Mr. Gathergold, a rich merchant; General Blood-and-Thunder, a military hero; Old Stony Phiz, an eminent statesman; and a great poet. They are mistaken in each case, but unschooled by their errors, they continue to await the desired event as if practicing some form of Emersonian optimism.

The only hope that this tale might achieve romantic closure lies in Ernest's moral superiority to the other characters. In a negative sense,

Ernest's great simplicity of heart enables him eventually to understand that none of the four claimants can be accepted as the long-awaited great man. In a positive sense, Ernest's mode of life eventually establishes an Emersonian connection among his deeds and words. As the narrator says, Ernest's "words had power, because they accorded with his thoughts, and his thoughts had reality and depth, because they harmonized with the life which he had always lived" (11:47). In the writings of most citizens of Concord, this passage would probably inspire a narrative in which Ernest correctly interprets for his neighbors the spiritual facts underlying the facts of their natural environment. Hawthorne rejects this plot development, however. Ernest believes in the prophecy of a great man's coming as devotedly as do his gullible neighbors: "Though more than once disappointed, as we have seen, he had such a hopeful and confiding nature, that he was always ready to believe in whatever seemed beautiful and good" (11:39). Although he is never fooled for long, Ernest initially accepts the candidacy of each claimant and is bitterly disappointed each time. His spiritual growth has done little to replace his illusions or to guarantee the validity of his interpretations of natural facts.

Ironically enough, by the end of the tale, Ernest's virtues have transformed him into the great man. He has come to resemble the Great Stone Face himself. The narrator observes that, even if Ernest has become the Great Stone Face, Ernest cannot perceive the resemblance. The tale's last paragraph insists on this irony rather than on the Emersonian perfection of Ernest's preaching:

> Then all the people looked, and saw that what the deep-sighted poet said was true. The prophecy was fulfilled. But Ernest, having finished what he had to say, took the poet's arm, and walked slowly homeward, still hoping that some wiser and better man than himself would by-and-by appear, bearing a resemblance to the GREAT STONE FACE. (11:48)

The beauties of nature are emphasized in this tale, as they might be in conventional romantic writing. One of nature's noblemen is celebrated. The possibility of natural–supernatural correspondences is raised. In the end, though, it is uncertain whether the natural facts in this tale actually signify spiritual facts; if they do so signify, these spiritual facts are not very sunny.

As "The Great Stone Face" suggests, Hawthorne was willing to transform his contemporaries' fondest images and ideas into fictional materials. One idea usually unquestioned by these contemporaries was the inevitability of material or spiritual progress. In recognition of this belief,

Hawthorne's fiction often represents romantic aspiration in terns compatible with the writing of Emerson and Thoreau. Hester Prynne maintains a "firm belief, that, at some brighter period, when the world should have grown ripe for it ... a new truth would be revealed, in order to establish the whole relation between man and woman on a surer ground of mutual happiness" (1:263). Despite all his Prufrockian quibbles, Miles Coverdale can still affirm some sort of optimism: "Yet, after all, let us acknowledge it wiser, if not more sagacious, to follow out one's day-dream to its natural consummation ..." (3:10). Perhaps most impressively, in *The House of the Seven Gables*, the narrator applauds Holgrave's conviction that "we are not doomed to creep on forever in the old, bad way, but that, this very now, there are harbingers abroad of a golden era, to be accomplished in his own lifetime" (2:179). When Hawthorne's narrators provide romantic affirmations of this sort, however, they nearly always qualify them by offering the reader a statement of conservative skepticism. Hester realizes that she will not live to see the hoped-for day on which sexual inequality disappears. Similarly, Coverdale reflects: "... although, if the vision have been worth the having, it is certain never to be consummated otherwise than by a failure" (3:10–11). Holgrave moves to the country to found a rural dynasty. Through the tension between these two forces, Hawthorne consistently destabilizes the belief in inevitable progress central to contemporary romanticism, leaving the issue open to further literary investigation—and also to later critical argument.

Hawthorne's complex strategy may be seen in a series of passages that carefully balance affirmations and qualifications. In the first chapter of *The Scarlet Letter*, the narrator explains: "The founders of a new colony, whatever Utopia of human virtue and happiness they might originally project, have invariably recognized it among their earliest practical necessities to allot a portion of the virgin soil as a cemetery, and another portion as the site of a prison" (1:47). The sentence epitomizes Hawthorne's practice of juxtaposing the idealistic and the pragmatic: "Utopia" and "practical necessities." An equally illuminating example is the passage in which Coverdale explains the unlikelihood of establishing "Paradise" in "our bleak little world of New England": "Nor, with such materials as were at hand, could the most skilful architect have constructed any better imitation of Eve's bower, than might be seen in the snow-hut of an Esquimaux" (3:9–10).

"The New Adam and Eve," first published in 1843 and then included in *Mosses from an Old Manse*, provides an extended treatment of this ideological tension. This tale provides two characters a chance to act out the fantasies of romantic reformers: to begin all over, this time in keeping with man's "true" nature rather than under the influence of "the old, bad way"— those social institutions that reformers held responsible for the defects of modern life. In this tale there are no jaded world travelers, no cynics, no merchants, politicians, or generals to spoil the experiment by reminding the pair of age-old practices or historic unhappiness. In the opening paragraphs, human potential seems so great that Adam and Eve expect apotheosis. Hawthorne's narrator is less optimistic:

> In the energy of new life, it appears no such impracticable feat to climb into the sky! But they have already received a woful lesson, which may finally go far towards reducing them to the level of the departed race, when they acknowledge the necessity of keeping the beaten track of earth. (10:250)

Many critics—from Chester E. Eisinger in 1954 to Milton R. Stern in 1991—have argued that the beaten track is Hawthorne's recommended path through life. This thematic approach to Hawthorne has always seemed sensible to me, striking a middle course between idealism and conservatism. As I have been arguing previously, however, I believe that it is also useful to watch how Hawthorne lays down this track, especially how he qualifies contemporary romantic thinking in the process.

Like many modern Utopian and dystopian fantasies, Hawthorne's speculative tale is set just following the near-extinction of the world. The sketch has as its premise not a war or a natural disaster, but the prophecy of Father William Miller that the world would end in 1843. Here is a wonderful chance to convert both the Millerites, who professed an imminent end to time, and contemporary optimists, who professed an endlessly expanding future, into narrative materials. The first sentence establishes the tale's thesis: "We, who are born into the world's artificial system, can never adequately know how little in our present state and circumstances is natural, and how much is merely the interpolation of the perverted mind and heart of man" (10:247). "We," in company with Hawthorne's narrator, are therefore free to investigate the romantic distinction between what ought to be and what exists merely as a result of social expediency. Adam and Eve quickly discover for us that social pressures cannot be easily ignored, even in Utopia. Their first step down the beaten track requires them to recognize and accept the external world. At the beginning, they are "content with an inner sphere which they inhabit together." Soon, though, "they feel the invincible necessity of this earthly life, and begin to make acquaintance with the objects and circumstances that surround them" (10:248–49). If even Adam and Eve, alone in the universe, cannot exist within their own sphere, it is highly problematic whether a citizen of Concord might hope to fulfill Emerson's injunction in the stirring conclusion to *Nature*:

Build therefore your own world. As fast as you conform your life to the pure idea in your mind, that will unfold its great proportions. A correspondent revolution in things will attend the influx of the spirit. So fast will disagreeable appearances, swine, spiders, snakes, pests, mad-houses, prisons, enemies, vanish; they are temporary and shall be no more seen. (56)

By taking seriously Emerson's question "Why should not we also enjoy an original relation to the universe?" (21), "The New Adam and Eve" both dramatizes and undermines such romantic optimism.

One impediment confronting Hawthorne's fictional pair is the powerful force of gender roles. In an uninhabited mansion, the only woman in the world soon experiences very conventional feelings:

Eve ransacks a work-basket, and instinctively thrusts the rosy tip of her finger into a thimble. She takes up a piece of embroidery; glowing with mimic flowers, in one of which a fair damsel of the departed race has left her needle.... Eve feels almost conscious of the skill to finish it.... Passing through a dark entry, they find a broom behind a door; and Eve, who comprises the whole nature of womanhood, has a dim idea that it is an instrument proper for her hand. (10:257–58)

Later Adam intuits his true "maleness" in the abandoned library at Harvard. Just as Eve is instinctively attracted to her broom, so Adam's masculine intellectual curiosity is naturally roused by a book: "He stands poring over the regular columns of mystic characters, seemingly in studious mood; for the unintelligible thought upon the page has a mysterious relation to his mind, and makes itself felt, as if it were a burthen flung upon him" (10:264). Eve does not begin to sew and sweep, and she manages to drag Adam out of the library before he learns to read. The tale suggests, however, that contemporary social practices are not the only forces postponing the arrival of Utopia.

It is crucial at this point to distinguish the narrative strategies of tale writing from the imperatives of social responsibility. In *The Art of Authorial Presence*, G. R. Thompson warns against "the purely formal naivete of certain critical assertions about the univocal narrators of Hawthorne's fictions and the congruence or identity of Hawthorne's early narrators with Hawthorne" (37). The warning might also be appropriately raised here. "The New Adam and Eve" forces its characters into familiar gender roles. It does not necessarily follow, however, that the author of

"The New Adam and Eve" believed only these roles appropriate to all men and women. Hawthorne's characters Hester Prynne, Miriam Schaefer, and Zenobia do not hold such restricted views of gender roles. Hawthorne's wife, Sophia, and her sister Elizabeth thought of gender in broader terms, as did their friend Margaret Fuller. We might assume that there was sufficient stimulus in Hawthorne's environment for him to write tales showing women happily fulfilling other roles—if not to illustrate his deepest convictions, at least to accommodate an important element of contemporary ideology. On the other hand, there was probably also sufficient stimulus for him to resist the influence of advanced thinkers and to side with the conservatives—again, if not to illustrate his deepest convictions, at least to write against the current grain. In any event, the issue under consideration is not what Hawthorne believed but how he manipulated the narrative materials available to him.

One form of manipulation involves the equation of narrative inevitability with social determinism. Hawthorne's strategy, is clear when the narrator considers what might have happened if Eve had not been able to lure Adam away from his study:

> Happy influence of woman! Had he lingered there long enough to obtain a clue to its treasures,—as was not impossible, his intellect being of human structure, indeed, but with an untransmitted vigor and acuteness,—had he then and there become a student, the annalist of our poor world would soon have recorded the downfall of a second Adam. (10:265)

The implication is that Adam would have systematically gone about reestablishing the institutions of contemporary society simply because his studies would inevitably lead him to projective reasoning and social organization. Adam does not get a chance to re-create these social evils in the tale. Even so, this nonevent seriously challenges the romantic optimism of Hawthorne's contemporaries—whether or not Hawthorne actually believed in progress. In such cases, whether the subject is a Utopian project or an individual quest for fulfillment, Hawthorne's fiction often challenges contemporary orthodoxy by presenting a disjunction between desire and experience, as in "The New Adam and Eve," rather than a romantic unity of the two. His narrators draw their wit from an affectation of surprise that after so many centuries of human history, people still attempt to ignore this discrepancy.

"The Lily's Quest," a simple tale first published in 1839 and then added to the second edition of *Twice-told Tales*, provides a direct illustration.

The plot sends an allegorically named young couple, Adam Forrester and Lily Fay, in search of the perfect piece of land on which to build their dream house. Natural facts signal their initial anticipations of success: "[T]here all pure delights were to cluster like roses among the pillars of the edifice, and blossom ever new and spontaneously" (9:442). Throughout the tale, however, the narrator views this youthful optimism with an amused tolerance that forces readers to suspect a dichotomy between desire and possibility. After the young lovers have been forced to abandon three promising sites because each has been emotionally polluted by earlier human sufferings, the narrator observes: "They set forth again, young Pilgrims on that quest which millions—which every child of Earth—has tried in turn." Establishing the pattern that will be thoroughly examined by R. W. B. Lewis in *The American Adam* a century later, the narrator then questions whether this lovely and loving couple can transcend the limits of earlier generations: "And were the Lily and her lover to be more fortunate than all those millions?" (9:446). Are they—in Lewis's words—"to be acknowledged in [their] complete emancipation from the history of mankind" (41)? Unhappily, they are not. The spot they finally select conceals, unbeknownst to them, an ancient cemetery. Lily dies there as so many have before, and her dream house becomes her tomb. To soften this bitter conclusion, Hawthorne's narrator brings the grieving Adam to accept mortality and to express a faith in immortality. Adam's final speech affirms that transcendence will be achieved: "On a Grave be the site of our Temple; and now our happiness is for Eternity!" (9:450). Contrary to most readers' desires, however, this triumph will take place only in another world, after death. Hawthorne's narrator affirms that Adam and Lily pursue the highest goals with the highest hearts for the highest motives, but he frustrates them even so. As is often the case in Hawthorne's fiction, furthermore, natural facts serve as both signs and agents of the gap between optimistic projection and achievement.

Dualistic tales of this sort contributed greatly to Herman Melville's judgment of Hawthorne, expressed in a letter written in 1851:

> There is the grand truth about Nathaniel Hawthorne. He says NO! in thunder; but the Devil himself cannot make him say *yes*. For all men who say *yes*, lie; and all men who say *no*,—why, they are in the happy condition of judicious, unencumbered travellers in Europe; they cross the frontiers into Eternity with nothing but a carpet-bag,—that is to say, the Ego. Whereas those *yes*-gentry, they travel with heaps of baggage, and, damn them! they will never get through the Custom House. (125)

'Today, most critics of nineteenth-century American literature would probably endorse Melville's view, because anyone alternately reading the works of Hawthorne and Emerson—for example—cannot help but recognize two very different literary sensibilities at work on two very different thematic projects. I wish to reassert that the differences are not only thematic: they can be traced through Hawthorne's narrative strategies as well as through the patterns of thought created by these strategies.

Hawthorne's plot structures often make this clear. As the plot of "The Lily's Quest" suggests, Hawthorne sometimes uses simple quest narratives to reinflect contemporary romantic thinking. M. H. Abrams's *Natural Supernaturalism* supplies a helpful context for Hawthorne's experiments by exhaustively analyzing quests for spiritual significance in the works of many European romantic writers. According to Abrams, the basic narrative pattern adopted by both literary and philosophical writers of the time may be represented as follows:

> [T]he most apt and available vehicle was the traditional one of the history of mankind as a circuitous journey back home. So represented, the protagonist is the collective mind or consciousness of men, and the story is that of its painful pilgrimage through difficulties, sufferings, and recurrent disasters in quest of a goal which, unwittingly, is the place it had left behind when it first set out and which, when reachieved, turns out to be even better than it had been at the beginning. (191)

Abrams easily supplies illustrations of this psychomachia from the writings of G. W. F. Hegel, F. W. J. von Schelling, S. T. Coleridge, and Thomas Carlyle. Since, according to Abrams, "The chief antecedent of this narrative form is the Christian allegory of the journey of life" (193), we might also assume Hawthorne's candidacy for the list, in light of his pronounced fondness for the works of Edmund Spenser and John Bunyan. In fact, Hawthorne's fiction shows both his involvement in this world-historical imaginative project and his transformations of its elements to suit his own narrative purposes.

Typical of Hawthorne's approach is the narrator's ironic description, in "Passages from a Relinquished Work," of how he initiated his own quest: "Never was Childe Harold's sentiment adopted in a spirit more unlike his own." Another typically parodic note is struck when this narrator continues: "Naturally enough, I thought of Don Quixote" (10:410). Usually, Hawthorne's romantic questers attain much less distance from their own enterprises than this highly fictionalized narrator exhibits, and so it falls to the undifferentiated narrator to ridicule the quest and its hero for unreasonable assumptions about the malleability of existence. The plot that appeals most strongly to Hawthorne is not, then, the romantic quest that terminates in the hero's psychic unity, but the ironic quest that terminates in making the hero, as Northrop Frye says in "The Archetypes of Literature," "a prey to [the] frustration and weakness" that blight everyday existence (18). I suspect that the principal appeal of this structure for Hawthorne probably lay in the tonal and emotional variety that it provided narratives such as "The Threefold Destiny," "Wakefield," and "Ethan Brand."

In "The Threefold Destiny," Hawthorne presents an ironic quest schematically, without the displacement required in his more realistic tales. According to the narrator—perhaps the Ashley Allen Royce identified as the author when the tale first appeared in *American Monthly Magazine* in 1838— the tale is actually "a Faery Legend":

> Rather than a story of events claiming to be real, it may be considered as an allegory, such as the writers of the last century would have expressed in the shape of an eastern tale, but to which I have endeavored to give a more life-like warmth than could be infused into those fanciful productions. (9:472).

As Luther Luedtke explains (128–32), Hawthorne's mention of the eastern tale serves to justify the introduction of all sorts of romantic exoticism: Hindostan, Spain, Arabia, Turkey, the Arctic. The reader suspects that "The Threefold Destiny" is intended primarily as a literary exercise. Therefore, as Frye proposes in "Myth, Fiction, and Displacement" (27–29), structure may take prominence—here, the forthright structure of a circle.

The hero of this quest, Ralph Cranfield, left his native New England village many years ago to search throughout the world for a treasure, a position of "extensive influence and sway over his fellow-creatures" (9:474), and a beautiful woman. As the tale opens, he returns to the village frustrated, soon to discover the treasure to be his boyhood home, the position of influence to be master of the village school, and the beautiful woman to be his childhood sweetheart, Faith Egerton. In a sense, this tale has a happy ending because Cranfield does find his destiny in life, and—more significantly in light of the issues discussed in Chapter 7—he has hope of domestic salvation. Even so, the ironies of the tale are striking. Since everything Cranfield sought was available to him in the same form before his departure, his "long and remote travel" (9:472) has been a futile quest. This moral is stated explicitly in the narrator's concluding remarks:

Would all, who cherish such wild wishes, but look around them, they would oftenest find their sphere of duty, of prosperity, and happiness, within those precincts and in that station where Providence itself has cast their lot. Happy they who read the riddle without a weary world-search, or a lifetime spent in vain! (9:482)

Cranfield is spared the more devastating consequences of his "wild wishes" in that his whole "lifetime" has not been "spent in vain," merely the years of his young manhood in which he pursued his "weary world-search." Throughout the tale, though, Hawthorne uses devices that might be redirected to scathing ridicule by the slightest change of emphasis.

The narrator presents the inspiration for Cranfield's quest in terms that subtly discount its wisdom in advance. He says first that "Ralph Cranfield, from his youth upward, had felt himself marked out for a high destiny." Readers may accept this information univocally if they choose, because the stress on "felt himself" is so slight. The next sentence forecloses a univocal reading, however, and invites readers to share the narrator's amused scorn of Cranfield's design:

He had imbibed the idea—we say not whether it were revealed to him by witchcraft, or in a dream of prophecy, or that his brooding fancy had palmed its own dictates upon him as the oracles of a Sybil—but he had imbibed the idea, and held it firmest among his articles of faith, that three marvellous events of his life were to be confirmed to him by three signs. (9:473)

The discrepancy here between the "high destiny" of the previous sentence and the judgmental terms "imbibed" and "palmed ... upon him" creates an ironic context that shadows the narrator's subsequent treatment of Cranfield's "destiny." Because of this context, the narrator is able to dispense with the quest itself in three sentences of deflation:

With this proud fate before him, in the flush of his imaginative youth, Ralph Cranfield had set forth to seek the maid, the treasure, and the venerable sage, with his gift of extended empire. And had he found them? Alas! it was not with the aspect of a triumphant man, who had achieved a nobler destiny than all his fellows, but rather with the gloom of one struggling against peculiar and continual adversity, that he now passed homeward to his mothers cottage. (9:475)

The commonplace terminus of this quest—"his mother's cottage"—epitomizes the disproportion of Cranfield's world-wide search for significance. A few sentences later the narrator underscores this point by stressing the inconsequence of these efforts: "There had been few changes in the village ..." (9:475). That is to say, Cranfield's effect on the world, great and small, has been nil, and his adventure has been circular rather than an evolutionary movement toward a "higher good."

About midpoint in the tale, Cranfield begins to think about his life in more down-to-earth terms. As he is preparing to enter his mother's cottage after so many years' absence, he sees on a tree in the front yard something resembling the sign that was to have marked the treasure he has sought. He reflects, "Now a credulous man ... might suppose that the treasure which I have sought round the world, lies buried, after all, at the very door of my mother's dwelling. That would be a jest indeed!" (9:476). That would be, in fact, the jest that Hawthorne intends here, a joke he often used to undermine the pretensions of the romantic quest. In this case, the severity of the joke is benignly muted. Although Cranfield is exposed as an egotistical fool, he is not humiliated by the narrator as many of Hawthorne's protagonists are.

Cranfield's conversion to domesticity is appropriately depicted in terms of his interpretive activities. When the squire and two selectmen of the village come to offer Cranfield the position of schoolmaster, he begins by "enveloping their homely figures in the misty romance that pervaded his mental world" (9:478). This misinterpretation is soon corrected, however, when "At every effort of his memory he recognized some trait of the dreamy Messenger of Destiny, in this pompous, bustling, self-important, little great man of the village" (9:480). Once Cranfield can see the squire without the distortion produced by "misty romance," he is on the road to domestic happiness. He may thus be spared the narrator's more severe judgments. This changed position is evident when the squire takes on the role of pompous victim and absorbs the sort of ridicule that the narrator earlier directed toward Cranfield. Cranfield's salvation is confirmed when he is overwhelmed by sudden affection for the village children. As soon as "a flow of natural feeling gushed like a well-spring in his heart" (9:480), Cranfield is free of his delusion and safe from the more severe exactions of Hawthorne's narrator. Elsewhere, Hawthorne rearranges the constituents of Cranfield's quest to produce a bitter and biting condemnation.

In "Wakefield" Hawthorne uses the same plot to organize a more vigorous critique. As we have seen in Chapter 2, the protagonist of this tale leaves home in order to discover "how the little sphere of creatures and circumstances, in which he was a central object, will be affected by his removal" (9:134). Like Cranfield's, Wakefield's quest is ironically fulfilled.

Returning home after twenty years, he discovers his absence to have been of little consequence to anyone. The principal difference between Cranfield's fate and Wakefield's lies in the fact that the former is destined for domestic salvation and the latter is destined, by the newspaper account from which the tale originates, to enact "as remarkable a freak as may be found in the whole list of human oddities" (9:130). Because Wakefield is intended to fulfill this absurd role, the narrator feels free to abuse him throughout the narrative.

After summarizing the newspaper account of Wakefield's quest, the narrator affects a pose of objectivity: "The fact, thus abstractly stated, is not very uncommon, nor—without a proper distinction of circumstances—to be condemned either as naughty or nonsensical" (9:130). Immediately, the narrator shows that he will not be treating the matter "abstractly." Having raised the question "What sort of a man was Wakefield?", the narrator explains that "We are free to shape out our own idea, and call it by his name." "We" may—if the narrator wishes—create a Wakefield capable of experiencing Cranfield's deep rush of love or Adam Forrester's supernatural reassurance. The narrator says instead that Wakefield "was intellectual, but not actively so; his mind occupied itself in long and lazy musings, that tended to no purpose...." More ominous is the judgment that Wakefield had "a cold, but not depraved nor wandering heart" (9:131). Most damaging is the opinion of Wakefield's wife. She was "partly aware of a quiet selfishness, that had rusted into his inactive mind—of a peculiar sort of vanity, the most uneasy attribute about him—of a disposition to craft, which had seldom produced more positive effects than the keeping of petty secrets, hardly worth revealing ..." (9:132). Having attributed intellectual abstraction, emotional coldness, egotism, and pointless craftiness to Wakefield, the narrator goes on to criticize these qualities throughout the tale, finally reaching the condemnation that he originally affects to withhold.

One sign of the narrator's attitude is his use of the mock-heroic when discussing Wakefield's quest. As Wakefield prepares to depart, he is described in terms that effectively discount the quest through ironic echoes of chivalric trappings: "His equipment is a drab great-coat, a hat covered with an oil-cloth, top-boots, an umbrella in one hand and a small portmanteau in the other" (9:132). Here the distance between these pedestrian details and their romantic antecedents is insistent: an umbrella in place of a sword, for example. Elsewhere the effect is even more obvious, as when the narrator describes Wakefield's recovery after almost entering his home inadvertently: "Will not the whole household ... raise a hue-and-cry, through London Streets, in pursuit of their fugitive lord and master? Wonderful escape!" (9:135). The disproportionate chivalric term "lord and master" so impugns Wakefield's imagined importance that the concluding exclamation—

"Wonderful escape!"—can function with ironic appropriateness. The most damaging of these mock-heroic deflations goes right to the heart of the quest itself. After Wakefield leaves home to discover his importance in the world, he settles down for twenty years in the next street. The narrator dispatches this physical quest in one sentence: "He is in the next street to his own, and at his journey's end" (9:133). Describing Wakefield's activity with the elevated term "journey" mocks his enterprise even in relation to Ralph Cranfield's foolish quest.

As a result of such ridicule, the narrator can easily descend from satire to lampoon, as when he calls Wakefield a "crafty nincompoop" and his quest a "long whim-wham" (9:135). This low abuse prevents any positive movement comparable to Cranfield's developing self-knowledge. A higher unity is out of the question for Wakefield because the narrator insists throughout the tale that—contrary to the prevailing ideology—Wakefield's consciousness does not evolve. The natural symbol for this fixity of character is Wakefield's smile, the outer sign of his "craftiness." After he has taken leave of his wife, Wakefield opens the door for a last look, and his wife sees a strange smile on his face. As his absence lengthens, she often thinks of this smile:

> In her many musings, she surrounds the original smile with a multitude of fantasies, which make it strange and awful; as, for instance, if she imagines him in a coffin, that parting look is frozen on his pale features; or, if she dreams of him in Heaven, still his blessed spirit wears a quiet and crafty smile. (9:132–33)

When Wakefield enters the same house again after twenty years, the narrator observes: "As he passes in, we have a parting glimpse of his visage, and recognize the crafty smile, which was the precursor of the little joke, that he has ever since been playing off at his wife's expense" (9:139–40). The Wakefield invented by this narrator is more like a "humour" character from an English stage comedy than like a romantic protagonist.

Wakefield's story thus sheds a very unflattering light on the romantic quests for spiritual knowledge popular with Hawthorne's contemporaries. Like Ralph Cranfield, Wakefield completes a circular quest and returns home, but, because there has been no growth in his perception of his place in the world, Wakefield's quest has resulted in ironic frustration. He has "los[t] his place forever." The narrator is thus appropriately severe: "Stay, Wakefield! Would you go to the sole home that is left you? Then step into your grave!" (9:139). "Wakefield" suggests a picture of Hawthorne sitting at his writing desk with the grid of a romantic quest for higher knowledge laid out before him and a conversion chart by which every positive element can be represented negatively, every negative element, positively.

Hawthorne problematizes the romantic quest most profoundly in "Ethan Brand." In this highly esteemed tale, the title character devotes eighteen years to a quest far nobler than Wakefield's or Cranfield's, but eventually he also comes full circle—back to the lime kiln from which he set forth. Then, as if following the advice offered by the narrator to Wakefield, Brand jumps to his fiery death. The narrator diminishes Brand's quest by insisting that his absence, like Cranfield's and Wakefield's, has had very little effect on the world he left behind. In this tale, the unbroken continuity of ordinary life is represented by the experience of "three or four individuals who had drunk flip beside the bar-room fire, through all the winters, and smoked their pipes beneath the stoop, through all the summers, since Ethan Brand's departure" (11:90). While Brand has roamed the world pursuing spiritual truth, the world has gone on just fine without him. Additional evidence appears when these townsfolk are joined by "A number of the youth of the village, young men and girls, [who] had hurried up the hill-side, impelled by curiosity to see Ethan Brand, the hero of so many a legend familiar to their childhood." They are quickly disappointed: "Finding nothing, however, very remarkable in his aspect—nothing but a sun-burnt wayfarer, in plain garb and dusty shoes ... these young people speedily grew tired of observing him" (11:94). By opposing the chivalric vocabulary of "hero" and "legend" to details like Brand's "dusty shoes," the narrator undercuts the character, his quest, and his motives.

The narrator's attitude is surprising since, unlike Cranfield and Wakefield, Ethan Brand is motivated by an admirable, even noble, intention. Eighteen years ago, Brand was "a simple and loving man" whose concern for his fellow creatures led him to meditate on the doctrine of the Unpardonable Sin, the cause of much human fear and anguish. Looking back from the present of the tale, Brand "remembered with what tenderness, with what love and sympathy for mankind, and what pity for human guilt and wo, he had first begun to contemplate those ideas which afterwards became the inspiration of his life ..." (11:98). If he were to discover this sin, Brand could show others that they were innocent of it and that they could therefore anticipate divine forgiveness. What nobler motive could one have?

The tale's moral complexity has led generations of critics to devote their energies to mapping the theological implications of Brand's search and the moral implications of his methods. In 1955, James E. Miller, Jr., writes that Brand "takes upon himself the heavy knowledge which man was not meant to have, the unbearable knowledge of the supreme evil which only God can determine" (103). In 1965, Ely Stock quotes Martin Buber to explain that the tale "tells how human knowledge of good and evil works out in post-Paridisial time—'not as "original sin," but as the specific sin, only possible in relation to God, which alone makes possible general sin against the fellow-man and hence, of course, once more against God as his guardian"' (133). In 1985, Agnes McNeill Donohue argues that Brand "blasphemes against the Holy Spirit by violating the soul of another human being and studying it out of cold curiosity. This violation is blasphemous because the investigator has coolly and defiantly assumed the role of the deity" (214–15). These readings embody great wisdom but, when all is said and done, the structure of Brand's quest is narratologically just as circular as Cranfield's or Wakefield's.

Brand discovers that while seeking the Unforgivable Sin, he has committed it himself. Like Cranfield, Brand suspects that he has been the victim of a joke: "And then, without mirth in his countenance, but as if moved by an involuntary recognition of the infinite absurdity of seeking throughout the world for what was the closest of all things to himself, and looking into every heart, save his own, for what was hidden in no other breast, [Brand] broke into a laugh of scorn" (11:87). As in Hawthorne's other quest narratives, laughs, smiles, and some form of mental disequilibrium appear together. The narrator goes on to explain helpfully:

> Laughter, when out of place, mistimed, or bursting forth from a disordered state of feeling, may be the most terrible modulation of the human voice. The laughter of one asleep, even if it be a little child—the madman's laugh—the wild, screaming laugh of a born idiot, are sounds that we sometimes tremble to hear, and would always willingly forget. Poets have imagined no utterance of fiends or hobgoblins so fearfully appropriate as a laugh. (11:87)

We should assume that writers of fiction—of tales like "Ethan Brand," for example—have made the same discovery about uncanny laughter. The cause of Brand's madness, or whatever his maniacal laughs signifies, is not far to seek: "The whole question on which he had exhausted life, and more than life, looked like a delusion" (11:93).

This discovery is practically an affront to Hawthorne's transcendental contemporaries—and to most readers today. Surely, none of us would have developed the story this way, none of us would have had Brand throw himself into the lime kiln, none of us would have written that "The whole question on which he had exhausted life, and more than life, looked like a delusion." But none of us is Hawthorne. Even Hawthorne's narrator seems somewhat unsatisfied when Brand makes this discovery—not because the conclusion

Brand draws is too bleak, however, but because it is expressed baldly, in a direct statement. Even a spiritual fact unwelcome to the transcendental mind should be presented through an appropriate natural fact. Thus, the narrator soon represents Brand's circular quest through one of Hawthorne's finest symbols, an old dog chasing his own tail. The passage is lengthy but worth quoting in its entirety:

> But, now, all of a sudden, this grave and venerable quadruped, of his own mere notion, and without the slightest suggestion from anybody else, began to run round after his tail, which, to heighten the absurdity of the proceeding, was a great deal shorter than it should have been. Never was seen such headlong eagerness in pursuit of an object that could not possibly be attained; never was heard such a tremendous outbreak of growling, snarling, barking, and snapping—as if one end of the ridiculous brute's body were at deadly and most unforgivable enmity with the other. Faster and faster, roundabout went the cur; and faster and still faster fled the unapproachable brevity of his tail; and louder and fiercer grew his yells of rage and animosity; until, utterly exhausted, and as far from the goal as ever, the foolish old dog ceased his performance as suddenly as he had begun it. (11:96)

As Cyril A. Reilly has shown, Hawthorne's reworking of a journal entry into this richly symbolic passage clearly evidences the seriousness of his intentions. Thematically, as many critics have demonstrated, the tale is very complex. Structurally, it is very simple. Like this old dog, Brand has returned to his point of origin. Brand's circle is completed, and it is definitely a circle, not an Emersonian spiral.

In "Ethan Brand," Hawthorne uses the literary elements of plot and imagery created by his contemporaries to produce narrative effects that none of them—with the possible exception of Melville—would endorse. To the romantic imagination, the circle, a sign potentially signifying the static and finite, easily converts into a spiral, a "natural fact" signifying the inevitability of material and spiritual progress. Emerson, for example, writes in his essay "Circles": "The life of man is a self-evolving circle, which, from a ring imperceptibly small, rushes on all sides outwards to new and larger circles, and that without end" (2:304). Abrams says about Hegel:

> The self-moving circle ... rotates along a third, a vertical dimension, to close where it had begun, but on a higher plane of value. It thus fuses the idea of the circular return with the idea of

linear progress, to describe a distinctive figure of Romantic
thought and imagination—the ascending circle, or spiral. (184)

In contrast, Brian Way accurately describes Ethan Brand's quest as follows:
"He had thought he was engaged in a vast cosmic journey through time and
space, whereas in fact he was travelling along the circumference of a circle—
a movement which gives the illusion of constant progress, although it is in
reality constricted, always returning upon itself" (21). Even as the plot of
such tales opens the way to an organically appropriate happy ending,
Hawthorne's handling of the plot complicates the tale's progress,
problematizes the hero's actions, and frustrates the reader's more optimistic
inclinations.

Hawthorne was as familiar with romantic modes of symbolic
interpretation as his readers were. Therefore his character Ethan Brand can
easily construe the significance of a dog's chasing his own tail: "Meanwhile,
Ethan Brand had resumed his seat upon the log; and moved, it might be, by
a perception of some remote analogy between his own case and that of the
self-pursuing cur, he broke into the awful laugh, which, more than any other
token, expressed the condition of his inward being" (11:97). Hawthorne was
also familiar with the dominant contemporary theories of progress, and yet
Ralph Cranfield comes to realize that if "the treasure which I have sought
round the world, lies buried, after all, at the very door of my mother's
dwelling ... [t]hat would be a jest indeed!" (9:476). Hawthorne was surrounded
by romantic ideology. In "Chiefly About War Matters" he consequently wrote
the following about a figure highly esteemed by most romantic thinkers, the
abolitionist John Brown: "Any common-sensible man, looking at the matter
unsentimentally, must have felt a certain intellectual satisfaction in seeing him
hanged, if it were only in requital of his preposterous miscalculation of
possibilities" (328). Whether Hawthorne set out to project some "Utopia of
human virtue and happiness" or—more usually—to "acknowledge the
necessity of keeping the beaten track of earth," he constructed his narratives
out of the materials available to him in his own contemporary culture,
ingeniously transforming these narrative materials by writing against the
grain of his readers' expectations. Hawthorne freely appropriated elements of
contemporary romanticism, as he appropriated elements from the history of
New England, not only to fulfill his own narrative strategies, but to keep
readers reading attentively, to prevent their easy acquiescence in what goes
without saying, to problematize even the simplest of matters, to make
subsequent readings possible and productive. These are the usual effects
today upon readers who long ago repudiated—eagerly or with reluctance—
the romantic values of Hawthorne's contemporaries.

Works Cited

Abcarian, Richard, and Marvin Klotz, eds. *Literature: The Human Experience*. 3rd ed. New York: St. Martin's, 1982.

Abrams, M. H. *Natural Supernaturalism: Tradition and Revolution in Romantic Literature*. New York: Norton, 1971.

Adkins, Nelson F. "The Early Projected Works of Nathaniel Hawthorne." *Papers of the Bibliographical Society of America* 39 (1945): 39–57.

Allen, Margaret V. "Imagination and History in Hawthorne's 'Legends of the Province House.'" *American Literature* 43 (1971): 432–37.

Aristotle. *Poetics*. In Bate, 19–39.

Auerbach, Jonathan. "Executing the Model: Painting, Sculpture, and Romance-Writing in Hawthorne's The *Marble Faun*." *ELH* 47 (1980): 103–20.

Bakhtin, M. M. *The Dialogic Imagination: Four Essays*. Ed. Michael Holquist. Trans. Caryl Emerson and Michael Holquist. Austin: University of Texas Press, 1981.

Barth, John. "Lost in the Funhouse." 1967. Reprinted in *Lost in the Funhouse: Fiction for Print, Tape, Live Voice*, 72–97. Garden City, New York: Doubleday, 1968.

Barthes, Roland. "Introduction to the Structural Analysis of Narratives." In *Image-Music-Text*, 79–124. Trans. Stephen Heath. New York: Hill and Wang, 1977.

Bate, Walter Jackson, ed. *Criticism: The Major Texts*. Enlarged ed. New York: Harcourt, 1970.

Baym, Nina. *Novels, Readers, and Reviewers: Responses to Fiction in Antebellum America*. Ithaca: Cornell University Press, 1984.

———. *The Shape of Hawthorne's Career*. Ithaca: Cornell University Press, 1976.

———. *Woman's Fiction: A Guide to Novels by and about Women in America, 1820–1870*. Ithaca: Cornell University Press, 1978.

Bell, Michael Davitt. *The Development of American Romance: The Sacrifice of Relation*. 1980. Reprint, Chicago: University of Chicago Press, 1983.

———. *Hawthorne and the Historical Romance of New England*. Princeton: Princeton University Press, 1971.

Bensick, Carol Marie. *La Nouvelle Beatrice: Renaissance and Romance in "Rappaccini's Daughter"*. New Brunswick: Rutgers University Press, 1985.

Benveniste, Emile. *Problems in General Linguistics*. Trans. Mary Elizabeth Mack. Coral Gables, FL: University of Miami Press, 1971.

Bercovitch, Sacvan. *The Office of The Scarlet Letter*. Baltimore: The Johns Hopkins University Press, 1991.

Berlant, Lauren. *The Anatomy of National Fantasy: Hawthorne, Utopia, and Everyday Life*. Chicago: University of Chicago Press, 1991.

Booth, Wayne C. "Rhetorical Critics Old and New: the Case of Gerard Genette." In *Reconstructing Literature*, 123–41. Ed. Laurence Lerner. Totowa, NJ: Barnes & Noble, 1983.

———. *The Rhetoric of Fiction*. 2nd ed. Chicago: University of Chicago Press, 1983.

Brodhead, Richard H. *The School of Hawthorne*. New York: Oxford, 1986.

Brooks, Cleanth, Jr., and Robert Penn Warren, eds. *Understanding Fiction*. 2nd ed. New York: Appleton, 1959.

Brown, Gillian. "Getting in the Kitchen with Dinah: Domestic Politics in *Uncle Tom's Cabin*." *American Quarterly* 36 (1984): 503–23.

Budick, E. Miller. *Fiction and Historical Consciousness: The American Romance Tradition*. New Haven: Yale University Press, 1989.

———. "Sacvan Bercovitch, Stanley Cavell, and the Romance Theory of American Fiction." *PMLA* 107 (1992): 78–91.

Byers, John R., Jr., and James J. Owen. *A Concordance to the Five Novels of Nathaniel Hawthorne*. 2 vols. New York: Garland, 1979.

Cameron, Kenneth Walter. *Genesis of Hawthorne's "The Ambitious Guest"*. Hartford, CT: Transcendental Books, 1955.

Carpenter, Frederick I. "Puritans Preferred Blondes: The Heroines of Melville and Hawthorne." *NEQ* 9 (1936): 253–72.

Carton, Evan. "Hawthorne and the Province of Romance." *ELH* 47 (1980): 331–54.

———. *The Marble Faun: Hawthorne's Transformations*. New York: Twayne, 1992.

———. *The Rhetoric of American Romance: Dialectic and Identity in Emerson, Dickinson, Poe, and Hawthorne*. Baltimore: The Johns Hopkins University Press, 1985.

Chase, Richard. *The American Novel and Its Tradition*. 1957. Reprint, Baltimore: The Johns Hopkins University Press, 1980.

Coffey, Dennis G. "Hawthorne's 'Alice Doane's Appeal': The Artist Absolved." *ESQ* 21 (1975): 230–40.

Cohen, B. Bernard. "The Sources of Hawthorne's 'The Ambitious Guest.'" *Boston Public Library Quarterly* 4 (1952): 221–24.

Colacurcio, Michael J. "Idealism and Independence." In Elliott, 207–26.

———. Introduction to *Nathaniel Hawthorne: Selected Tales and Sketches*. New York: Penguin, 1987. vii–xxxv.

———. *The Province of Piety: Moral History in Hawthorne's Early Tales*. Cambridge: Harvard University Press, 1984.

Coover, Robert. "The Babysitter." In *Pricksongs & Descants: Fictions*, 206–39. New York: Dutton, 1969.

Crane, R.S. "Questions and Answers in the Teaching of Literary Texts." 1953. Reprinted in *The Idea of the Humanities and Other Essays Critical and Historical*, 2: 176–93. 2 vols. Chicago: University of Chicago Press, 1967.

Crews, Frederick C. *The Sins of the Fathers: Hawthorne's Psychological Themes*. New York: Oxford University Press, 1966.

Crowley, J. Donald. "The Unity of Hawthorne's *Twice-Told Tales*." *Studies in American Fiction* 1 (1973): 35–61.

———, ed. *Hawthorne: The Critical Heritage*. New York: Barnes & Noble, 1970.

———, ed. *Mosses from an Old Manse*. Vol. 10 of *The Centenary Edition of the Works of Nathaniel Hawthorne*.

———, ed. *Twice-told Tales*. Vol. 9 of *The Centenary Edition of the Works of Nathaniel Hawthorne*.

Dekker, George. "Once More: Hawthorne and the Genealogy of American Romanticism." *ESQ* 35 (1989): 69–83.

Donohue, Agnes McNeill. *Hawthorne: Calvin's Ironic Stepchild*. Kent, OH: Kent State University Press, 1985.

Doubleday, Neal Frank. *Hawthorne's Early Tales: A Critical Study*. Durham: Duke University Press, 1972.

Dryden, Edgar A. *The Form of American Romance*. Baltimore: The Johns Hopkins University Press, 1988.

Duyckynck, Evert Augustus. Review of *The House of the Seven Gables*, by Nathaniel Hawthorne. *The Literary World* (26 April 1851): 334–35. Reprinted in Crowley, *The Critical Heritage*, 192–94.

Eberwein, Jane Donahue. "Temporal Perspective in 'The Legends of the Province House.'" *American Transcendental Quarterly* 14 (1972):41–45.

Eisinger, Chester E. "Hawthorne as Champion of the Middle Way." *NEQ* 28 (1954): 27–52.

Eliot, T. S. *The Complete Poems and Plays, 1909–1950*. New York: Harcourt, 1952.

Elliott, Emory, et al., eds. *Columbia Literary History of the United States*. New York: Columbia University Press, 1988.

Emerson, Ralph Waldo. *Selections from Ralph Waldo Emerson*. Ed. Stephen E. Whicher. Boston: Houghton Mifflin, 1960.

Erlich, Gloria C. *Family Themes and Hawthorne's Fiction: The Tenaceous Web*. New Brunswick, NJ: Rutgers University Press, 1984.

Faust, Bertha. *Hawthorne's Contemporaneous Reputation: A Study of Literary Opinion in America and England 1828–1864*. 1939. Reprint, New York: Octagon, 1968.

Federman, Raymond. "Self-Reflexive Fiction." In Elliott, 1142–57.

Feidelson, Charles, Jr. *Symbolism and American Literature*. Chicago: University of Chicago Press, 1953.

Felperin, Howard. *Beyond Deconstruction: The Uses and Abuses of Literary Theory*. 1985. Oxford: Clarendon Press, 1987.

Foerster, Norman, ed. *American Poetry and Prose*. 4th ed. Boston: Houghton Mifflin, 1957.

Fogle, Richard Harter. *Hawthorne's Fiction: The Light and the Dark*. Norman: University of Oklahoma Press, 1964.

———, ed. *The Romantic Movement in American Writing*. New York: Odyssey, 1966.

Fossum, Robert H. "Time and the Artist in 'Legends of the Province House.'" *NCF* 21 (1967): 337–48.

Frye, Northrop. *Fables of Identity: Studies in Poetic Mythology*. New York: Harcourt, 1963.

Gallagher, Susan Van Zanten. "A Domestic Reading of *The House of the Seven Gables*." *Studies in the Novel* 21 (1989): 1–13.

Genette, Gerard. *Figures of Literary Discourse*. Trans. Alan Sheridan. Oxford: Basil Blackwell, 1982.

———. *Narrative Discourse: An Essay in Method*. Trans. Jane E. Lewin. Ithaca: Cornell University Press, 1980.

———. *Narrative Discourse Revisited*. Trans. Jane E. Lewin. Ithaca: Cornell University Press, 1988.

Gollin, Rita K. *Nathaniel Hawthorne and the Truth of Dreams*. Baton Rouge: Louisiana State University Press, 1979.

Griffith, Clark. "Substance and Shadow: Language and Meaning in *The House of the Seven Gables*." *MP* 51 (1954): 187–95.

Haggerty, George. *Gothic Fiction/Gothic Form*. University Park: Pennsylvania State University Press, 1989.

Harris, Kenneth Marc. *Hypocrisy and Self-Deception in Hawthorne's Fiction*. Charlottesville: University Press of Virginia, 1988.

Hawthorne, Nathaniel. *The Centenary Edition of the Works of Nathaniel Hawthorne*. 20 vols. Ed. William Charvat, et al. Columbus: Ohio State University Press, 1962–

———. "Chiefly About War Matters." In *Tales, Sketches, and Other Papers*. Vol. 12 of *The Complete Works of Nathaniel Hawthorne*, 299–345. Ed. George Parsons Lathrop. Cambridge, MA: Riverside Press, 1885.

———. *The English Notebooks*. Ed. Randall Stewart. 1941. Reprint, New York: Russell & Russell, 1991.

Hoeltje, Hubert H. *Inward Sky: The Mind and Heart of Nathaniel Hawthorne*. Durham, NC: Duke University Press, 1962.

Howe, Daniel Walker. "Victorian Culture in America." In *Victorian America*, 3–28. Ed. Howe. Philadelphia: University of Pennsylvania Press, 1976.

Hughes, Gertrude Reif. *Emerson's Demanding Optimism*. Baton Rouge: Louisiana State University Press, 1984.

Iser, Wolfgang. *The Implied Reader: Patterns of Communication in Prose Fiction from Bunyan to Beckett*. Baltimore: The Johns Hopkins University Press, 1974.

———. "Representation: A Performative Act." In *Prospecting: From Reader Response to Literary Anthropology*, 236–48. Baltimore: The Johns Hopkins University Press, 1989.

James, Henry. "The Art of Fiction." 1884. Reprinted in *The House of Fiction*, 23–45. Ed. Leon Edel. 1957. Westport, CT: Greenwood, 1973.

———. *Hawthorne*. 1887. New York: AMS, 1968.

Johnson, Samuel. "Preface to Shakespeare." In Bate, 207–17.

Kent, Thomas. *Interpretation and Genre: The Role of Generic Perception in the Study of Narrative Texts*. Lewisburg, PA: Bucknell University Press, 1986.

Kirby, John T. "Toward a Rhetoric of Poetics: Rhetor as Author and Narrator." *The Journal of Narrative Technique* 21.1 (1992): 1–22.

Kraditor, Aileen S. Introduction to *Up From the Pedestal: Selected Writings in the History of American Feminism*. Chicago: Quadrangle, 1968. 3–24.

Lawrence, D. H. *Studies in Classic American Literature*. 1923. Reprint, New York: Viking, 1964.

Leavis, Q. D. "Hawthorne as Poet." 1951. In *Collected Essays*, 2: 30–76. 2 vols. Ed. G. Singh. Cambridge: Cambridge University Press, 1985.

Levin, David. *In Defense of Historical Literature*. New York: Hill and Wang, 1967.

Lewis, R. W. B. *The American Adam: Innocence, Tragedy, and Tradition in the Nineteenth Century*. Chicago: University of Chicago Press, 1955.

Longfellow, Henry Wadsworth. *The Poetical Works of Henry Wadsworth Longfellow in Six Volumes*. Vol. 3. New York: AMS, 1966.

Longinus. *On the Sublime*. In Bate, 62–75.

Lowell, James Russell. "To Nathaniel Hawthorne." 24 April 1851. In *Nathaniel Hawthorne and his Wife: A Biography*, by Julian Hawthorne, 1: 390–92. 2 vols. 1884. Reprint, [Hamden, CT]: Archon Books, 1968.

Luedtke, Luther S. *Nathaniel Hawthorne and the Romance of the Orient*. Bloomington: Indiana University Press, 1989.

Lundblad, Jane. *Nathaniel Hawthorne and the European Literary Tradition*. New York: Russell & Russell, 1965.

Male, Roy R. *Hawthorne's Tragic Vision*. Austin: University of Texas Press, 1957.

Marks, Alfred H. "German Romantic Irony in Hawthorne's Tales." *Symposium* 7 (1953): 274–305.

Martin, Terence. *Nathaniel Hawthorne*. New York: Twayne, 1965.

Martin, Wallace. *Recent Theories of Narrative*. Ithaca: Cornell University Press, 1986.

Matthiessen, F. O. *American Renaissance: Art and Expression in the Age of Emerson and Whitman*. 1941. Reprint, New York: Oxford University Press, 1968.

McWilliams, John P., Jr. "'Thorough-going Democrat' and 'Modern Tory': Hawthorne and the Puritan Revolution of 1776." *Studies in Romanticism* 15 (1976): 549–71.

Melville, Herman. "To Nathaniel Hawthorne." 16? April? 1851. In *The Letters of Herman Melville*, 123–25. Ed. Merrell R. Davis and William H. Gilman. New York: Yale University Press, 1960.

Michael, John. "History and Romance, Sympathy and Uncertainty: The Moral of the Stones in Hawthorne's *Marble Faun*." *PMLA* 103 (1988): 150–61.

Miller, Edwin Haviland. *Salem Is My Dwelling Place: A Life of Nathaniel Hawthorne*. Iowa City: University of Iowa Press, 1991.

Miller, James E., Jr. "Hawthorne and Melville: The Unpardonable Sin." *PMLA* 70.1 (1955): 91–114.

Millington, Richard H. *Practicing Romance: Narrative Form and Cultural Engagement in Hawthorne's Fiction*. Princeton: Princeton University Press, 1992.

Mizruchi, Susan L. *The Power of Historical Knowledge: Narrating the Past in Hawthorne, James, and Dreiser*. Princeton: Princeton University Press, 1988.

Newberry, Frederick. *Hawthorne's Divided Loyalties: England and America in His Works*. Rutherford, NJ: Associated University Presses, 1987.

Newman, Lea Bertani Vozar. *A Reader's Guide to the Short Stories of Nathaniel Hawthorne*. Boston: G. K. Hall, 1979.

Ong, Walter J., S. J. "The Writer's Audience is Always a Fiction." *PMLA* 90 (1975): 9–21.

Orians, G. Harrison. "The Angel of Hadley in Fiction: A Study of the Sources of Hawthorne's 'The Grey Champion.'" *AL* 4 (1932): 257–69.

Pauly, Thomas H. "The Literary Sketch in Nineteenth-Century America." *Texas Studies in Literature and Language* 17 (1975): 489–503.

Pearce, Roy Harvey. "Romance and the Study of History." In Pearce, 221–44.

———, ed. *Hawthorne Centenary Essays*. Columbus: Ohio State University Press, 1964.

Poe, Edgar Allan. "The Balloon-Hoax." In *Tales*. Ed. James A. Harrison. Vol. 4 of *The Complete Works of Edgar Allan Poe*, 224–40. 17 vols. 1902. Reprint, New York: AMS, 1965.

Ponder, Melinda M. *Hawthorne's Early Narrative Art*. Lewiston, NY: Edwin Mellen, 1990.

Prince, Gerald. *A Dictionary of Narratology*. Lincoln: University of Nebraska Press, 1987.

———. "Introduction to the Study of the Narratee." Trans. Francis Mariner. In *Reader-Response Criticism: From Formalism to Post-Structuralism*, 7–25. Ed. Jane P. Tompkins. Baltimore: The Johns Hopkins University Press, 1980.

Rahv, Philip. "The Dark Lady of Salem." *Partisan Review* 8 (1941): 362–81.

Reed, P. L. "The Telling Frame of Hawthorne's 'Legends of the Province-House.'" *Studies in American Fiction* 4 (1976): 105–11.

Reilly, Cyril A. "On the Dog's Chasing His Own Tail in 'Ethan Brand.'" *PMLA* 68 (1953): 975–81.

Reynolds, David S. *Beneath the American Renaissance: The Subversive Imagination in the Age of Emerson and Melville*. New York: Knopf, 1988.

Richards, Jeffrey H. "Hawthorne's Posturing Observer: The Case of 'Sights from a Steeple.'" *ATQ* 59 (March 1986): 35–41.

Ricoeur, Paul. "The Model of the Text: Meaningful Action Considered as a Text." *New Literary History* 5 (1973): 91–117.

Scholes, Robert, and Robert Kellogg. *The Nature of Narrative*. New York: Oxford, 1966.

Schorer, Mark. "Technique as Discovery." *The Hudson Review* 1 (1948): 67–87.

Simpson, Claude M., ed. *The Marble Faun*. Vol. 4 of *The Centenary Edition of the Works of Nathaniel Hawthorne*.

Smith, Julian. "Hawthorne's 'Legends of the Province-House.'" *NCF* 24 (1969): 31–44.

Spengemann, William C. *The Adventurous Muse: The Poetics of American Fiction, 1789–1900*. New Haven: Yale University Press, 1977.

St. Armand, Barton L. "The Love Song of Miles Coverdale: Intimations of Eliot's 'Prufrock' in Hawthorne's *Blithedale Romance*." *ATQ* 2.2 (1988): 97–100.

Stern, Milton. *Contexts for Hawthorne: The Marble Faun and the Politics of Openness and Closure in American Literature*. Urbana: University of Illinois Press, 1991.

Stock, Ely. "The Biblical Context of 'Ethan Brand.'" *AL* 37 (1965): 115–34.

Stowe, Harriet Beecher. *Uncle Tom's Cabin*. 1852. Reprint, New York: Bantam, 1981.

Stubbs, John Caldwell. *The Pursuit of Form: A Study of Hawthorne and the Romance*. Urbana: University of Illinois Press, 1970.

Swann, C. S. B. "The Practice and Theory of Storytelling: Nathaniel Hawthorne and Walter Benjamin." *Journal of American Studies* 12 (1978): 185–202.

Thompson, G. R. *The Art of Authorial Presence: Hawthorne's Provincial Tales*. Durham: Duke University Press, 1993.

Thoreau, Henry David. *The Variorum Walden*. Ed. Walter Harding. New York: Twayne, 1962.

Thorpe, T. B. "The Big Bear of Arkansas." In *The Hive of "The Bee–Hunter": A Repository of Sketches*, 72–93. New York: D. Appleton, 1854.

Todorov, Tzvetan. *The Fantastic: A Structural Approach to a Literary Genre*. Trans. Richard Howard. Cleveland: Case Western Reserve University Press, 1973.

———. "The Limits of Edgar Allan Poe." In *Genres in Discourse*, 93–102. 1978. Trans. Catherine Porter. Reprint, Cambridge: Cambridge University Press, 1990.

———. *The Poetics of Prose*. Trans. Richard Howard. Ithaca: Cornell University Press, 1977.

Tompkins, Jane. Afterword to *The Wide, Wide World*, by Susan Warner, 584–608. New York: Feminist Press, 1987.

———. *Sensational Designs: The Cultural Work of American Fiction, 1790–1860*. New York: Oxford University Press, 1985.

Tuckerman, Frederick Goddard. *The Complete Poems of Frederick Goddard Tuckerman*. Ed. N. Scott Momaday. New York: Oxford University Press, 1965.

Turner, Arlin. *Nathaniel Hawthorne: An Introduction and Interpretation*. New York: Barnes & Noble, 1961.

Updike, John. "Man of Secrets." Review of *Salem Is My Dwelling Place: A Life of Nathaniel Hawthorne*, by Edwin Haviland Miller. *The New Yorker* 28 September 1992, 114–19.

Van Tassel, Mary M. "Hawthorne, His Narrator, and His Readers in 'Little Annie's Ramble.'" *ESQ* 33 (1987): 168–79.

Wagenknecht, Edward. *Nathaniel Hawthorne: The Man, His Tales and Romances*. New York: Ungar, 1989.

Waggoner, Hyatt H. "Art and Belief." In Pearce, 167–95.

———. *Hawthorne: A Critical Study*. 1955. Cambridge: Harvard University Press, 1963.

Walsh, Thomas F., Jr. "'Wakefield' and Hawthorne's Illustrated Ideas: A Study in Form." *Emerson Society Quarterly* 25 (1961): 29–35.

Warhol, Robyn R. "Toward a Theory of the Engaging Narrator: Earnest Interventions in Gaskell, Stowe, and Eliot." *PMLA* 101 (1986): 811–18.

Warner, Susan. *The Wide, Wide World*. 1850. Reprint, New York: Feminist Press, 1987.

Way, Brian. "Art and the Spirit of Anarchy: A Reading of Hawthorne's Short Stories." In *Nathaniel Hawthorne: New Critical Essays*, 11–30. Ed. A. Robert Lee. Totowa, NJ: Barnes & Noble, 1982.

Webster, Grant. *The Republic of Letters: A History of Postwar American Literary Opinion*. Baltimore: The Johns Hopkins University Press, 1979.

Whipple, E. P. Review of *The House of the Seven Gables*, by Nathaniel Hawthorne. *Graham's Magazine*, May 1851, 467–68. Reprinted in Crowley, *The Critical Heritage*, 197–201.

White, Hayden. "The Value of Narrativity in the Representation of Reality." *Critical Inquiry* 7 (Autumn 1980): 5–28. Reprinted in *The Content of the Form: Narrative Discourse and Historical Representation*, 1–25. Baltimore: The Johns Hopkins University Press, 1987.

Winters, Yvor. "Maule's Curse, or Hawthorne and the Problem of Allegory." 1938. In *In Defense of Reason*, 157–75. 3rd ed. Reprint, Chicago: Swallow, 1947.

Ziff, Larzer. *Literary Democracy: The Declaration of Cultural Independence in America*. New York: Viking, 1981.

JOSEPH FLIBBERT

"That Look Beneath":
Hawthorne's Portrait of Benevolence in
The House of the Seven Gables

The most common activity in *The House of the Seven Gables* is looking at faces. This should not be surprising. Among the most vivid impressions Nathaniel Hawthorne creates in the work are those associated with facial features. Like Dickens, Hawthorne displays a talent for using fixed physical features to reveal attributes of character. Thus, the dark, stern, and massive countenance of Colonel Pyncheon's portrait accurately reflects the "iron-hearted" character of "the grasping and strong-willed man."[1] But fixed features do not always mirror the inner attributes of the characters in the story. Hepzibah's near-sighted but fierce scowl creates the distorted impression that the "naturally tender, sensitive" woman is ill-tempered and as stern as her ancestor (p. 34). Facial features are also not always frozen—the liquid elusiveness of Judge Pyncheon's mien being the most striking example.

There is, however, an element of consistency in even the fluid aspect of Judge Pyncheon's face, which alternates between a natural expression of sternness that exhibits his true character—"sly, subtle, hard, imperious, and, withal, cold as ice"—and the grinning public posture "indicative of benevolence" (p. 92). Hawthorne reserves the term "benevolence" in order to fix in the reader's mind a definite impression of the smile as feigned and hollow. The devastatingly satirical effect of the benevolent smile has

From *Critical Essays on Hawthorne's "The House of the Seven Gables,"* ed. Bernard Rosenthal, pp. 114–128. © 1995 by Bernard Rosenthal.

accurately been associated with Hawthorne's intention in this work to satirize the duplicity of a Charles Upham or the well-intentioned but heavy-handed paternal intrusions of the surrogate father, Robert Manning.[2] His antagonism, however, seems to be directed at least as venomously against the notion of benevolence itself.

I

The word "benevolence" may be used to signify a particular attitude displayed by one individual toward another in a specific situation or to denote an inherent disposition of character that tends to govern action. In the first kind—what I will call personal benevolence—the benevolent individual acts in a kindly and thoughtful manner, for example, toward a street beggar looking for a handout. In the latter the benevolent person is one who displays a cheerful good will (as the etymology of the word implies) toward that collective tag termed "humanity."

Judging from comments in *Our Old Home*, Hawthorne appears to have had a grudging affinity for the former—specific acts of benevolence. Unlike his English hosts who resisted "street-charity," they affirmed, because it "promotes idleness and vice," Hawthorne was an easy mark for English and Italian beggars while abroad in the 1850s. Although he occasionally resisted characters like the "sickly-looking wretch" of Assisi and the "phenomenon abridged of his lower half" of Liverpool, more often he bought a clear conscience and "the little luxury of beneficence at a cheap rate." Like Emerson, he succumbed and gave the wicked dollar. As consul, he was assaulted by "another class of beggarly, depradators—ministers, tradesmen, ladies, and authors—humbugs all, but successful suppliants for a cut of his valued emoluments.[3]

While instances of such instinctive acts of kindliness and generosity are relatively rare in Hawthorne's fiction, with its emphasis upon figures driven by self-centered goals, they do occur and are treated with favorable regard by their creator. The most conspicuous example is the role Hester assumes as a "Sister of Charity" in Boston. The depth, the spontaneity, and the sincerity of her impulse to help the poor, the sick, and the afflicted in the community is charitable in the truest sense, for she asks for nothing in return, not even acknowledgment. It is not "Christian" charity; Hester's thoughts have taken her well beyond the rigid confines of religious orthodoxy. Moreover, she is not motivated by some vague impulse of love for humanity. She merely responds to a community need in an area for which she seems uniquely and wholly suited.

Hawthorne's attitude toward humanitarian benevolence is quite different from that which he displayed toward personal acts of benevolence.

Those who assume an attitude of love for humanity in Hawthorne's works are almost always posturing egotists who cultivate the sentiment as a form of self-aggrandizement. The individual whose benevolence extends to everyone usually steps on those closest to him. Rappaccini destroys his daughter to heal the world. Ethan Brand annihilates Esther in an experiment that originated in hillside musings prompted by love of mankind. Ironically, Rappaccini's benevolence is paternal; in an attempt to find a cure for all illness, he assumes the role of the benevolent Father of all, with providential power to alter the nature of things. Brand's benevolence is rooted in a conviction of brotherhood; but the lime-kiln tender who can feel no connection to former friends and even less to a fellow of his trade is "no longer a brother-man" to anyone. In Brand's case, and, we might reasonably assume, in Rappaccini's as well, the sentiment of benevolence—as a conviction of universal kinship—promotes a perception attuned to larger patterns but blind to proximate and tangible realities. In effect, they see the whole forest, but not the trees. While they delude themselves in believing that they embrace all of mankind, they separate themselves from all individuals. This isolation leads to obsessive fixation on some grand scheme, reflecting an inordinate sense of self-importance. Ultimately, the sentiment corrodes and distorts intellectual pursuits, for these individuals always fail grandly at the schemes they devise.

An alternative to intellectual pursuits for the man of humanitarian benevolence is philanthropic activity (*philos* + *anthropos* = loving mankind). The prototype of such activity is Hollingsworth in *The Blithedale Romance*. Consumed by a passion for criminal reform, Hollingsworth manipulates personal relationships in an effort to achieve his "overruling purpose," unaware of the debilitating effect his goals have on his "sympathies, and affections, and celestial spirit," unable to recognize the process "by which godlike benevolence has been debased into all-devouring egotism."[4] Ironically, Hollingsworth's recognition of the devastating effect of his posture begins with his confrontation of another man of humanitarian benevolence, Westervelt. This huckster of "mystic sensuality," envisions "one great, mutually conscious brotherhood" based upon a "universally pervasive fluid" that dissolves the limitations of time and space.[5]

Before exploring Judge Pyncheon's kinship with these putatively well-intentioned lovers of humanity, I want to comment on the source of Hawthorne's attack on humanitarian benevolence. An acute observer of human nature—as certainly Hawthorne was—will note in his personal relationships an occasional disparity between the outward display of humanitarian goodwill and an inner penury of actual benignity, and will conclude that such displays are fraudulent. Experiences like these undoubtedly influenced Hawthorne's attitudes, but if we stop there at least one problem arises. Underlying the sentiment of humanitarian benevolence is the assumption that all humans are linked—an assumption Hawthorne strongly advocated throughout his career. In attacking humanitarian benevolence, Hawthorne is not striking out at the notion of universal bonds; no one reminds us more often than he does of the great chain of humanity to which we all belong. Rather, he suggests that the truest experience of connectedness does not proceed from some vague affirmation of love for humanity but from sensitive and observant response to the needs of those closest to us. In the works of Hawthorne, that response is almost always one of sympathy.

II

Hawthorne immersed himself in reading on the ethics of sympathy during a six-month period in 1827, beginning in March when he borrowed Adam Smith's *Theory of Moral Sentiments* (1759) from the Salem Athenaeum and ending in August with the withdrawal of Francis Hutcheson's *An Inquiry Into the Original of Our Ideas of Beauty and Virtue* (1725).[6] Best known today as a pioneer political economist, Smith, a professor of moral philosophy at the University of Glasgow in the 1750s, established an early reputation in the area of moral theory. Along with David Hume, Smith was the most influential proponent in his time of a theory of moral behavior that derives from feeling or emotion. A former student of Francis Hutcheson, Smith's ideas both derive from and respond to Hutcheson's theories, which are based on the notion that apprehension of virtue results from a faculty he calls the "moral sense."[7] When functioning properly, the moral sense guides one to approve of actions that appear to be benevolent, that is, "flowing from Good-will to others," because they appear morally good.[8] Benevolence is "the internal Spring of Virtue," the highest form being "a calm, extensive Affection, or Good-will toward all beings," the "humanitarian" benevolence I noted earlier. In Hutcheson's view, there is a "universal Determination to Benevolence in Mankind."[9]

Smith accepts the view of a nonrational moral faculty but rejects the vagaries of a "moral sense" by which we approve or censure the conduct of others. He advocates a specific and easily identifiable human sentiment he calls sympathy. In doing so, Smith separates himself from Hutcheson's view that virtue consists in benevolence, for the sentiment of sympathy is not directed toward all humans but is a response of fellow-feeling with the affections of a particular individual. Thus, although it is probably true, as one critic has suggested, that Hawthorne discarded most of Smith's theories, he appears to have been influenced by Smith's distinction between benevolence and sympathy.[10] As we shall see, Hawthorne consistently relies upon this distinction to differentiate the behavior of Judge Pyncheon from that of the other principal characters in *The House of the Seven Gables*. Smith also emphasizes the perceptual aspect of the relationship between the sympathizer and the subject of sympathy by describing the relationship as one between spectator and spectacle, suggesting that the mechanism of sympathy is activated initially by the sense of sight. In this respect, Smith, like most of his contemporaries, reflects the influence of Locke's theory that knowledge has its origin in perceptions which arrive in the mind either through reflection or sensation. Sympathy becomes a "moral sentiment" when we develop an analogous feeling to the one we imagine the observed person to be experiencing and respond to the propriety and merit of that feeling. Sensitive observation is also the key to sympathy as a moral faculty in *The House of the Seven Gables*.

Between his reading of Smith and Hutcheson, Hawthorne perused the works of two moral philosophers affiliated with the Scottish school of "common sense," Thomas Brown (*Lecturer on the Philosophy of the Human Mind*, 1820) and Dugald Stewart (*Philosophical Essays*, 1811). Hawthorne had already become acquainted with Stewart in his last year at Bowdoin College, where two terms were devoted to the study of *Philosophy of the Human Mind* (1808).[11] Stewart was a disciple of Thomas Reid who succeeded Adam Smith as professor of moral philosophy at the University of Glasgow. Brown was a student of Stewart and was later to hold jointly the chair in moral philosophy with him at the University of Edinburgh. Like Smith, Stewart and Brown produce their own modulations on moral sentiment. The intuitional feature of "common sense" is reminiscent of Hutcheson's "moral sense" but is now part of a "Science of Mind"; that is, it has moved from the domain of philosophical speculation to the verges of empirical inquiry. Brown is especially forceful in his objections to Smith's doctrine of universal sympathy, arguing that to trace the moral sentiments to "occasional sympathies" is like deriving "the water of an ever-flowing stream from the sunshine or shade which may occasionally gleam over it."[12] While he acknowledges that "benevolent affections" are among the objects of "moral science," he distinguishes between benevolence as a desire for "the good of all" and as a "principle of moral feeling" that actually prompts us to promote the happiness of others.[13] Brown endorses this latter notion of benevolence as "the moral link which connects man with man" through "benefactions" that include "consolations, counsels, cares, friendships, protection."[14]

But for Brown, sympathy (as only one of the affections that involve moral feeling) has its basis in physiological mechanisms that have a direct bearing on human behavior. These mechanisms are activated by an "external sign" which, through the agency of suggestion, produces that state of mind by which we identify with the feelings of others. Brown's theory of suggestion was derived from the influence of David Hartley's doctrine of associationism. Hartley's chief work, *Observations on Man, His Frame, His Duty, and His Expectations* (1749), was withdrawn from the Salem Athenaeum about a month after Brown's *Lectures*.

In the first volume of his treatise—concerned with man's "frame" or physical constitution—Hartley, a physician, lays the groundwork for his notions in a theory of vibrations and association which posits a neurological basis for our sensations and thoughts. Sympathy is treated as the fourth of six classes of intellectual pleasures and pains but is distinguished from the moral sense—the sixth and the most elevated of the emanations from the mind. Here benevolence, in the sense of humanitarian goodwill, seems to have a modest place as one of four tendencies that arise from the first class of sympathetic affections by which we rejoice at the pleasure of others. But in the second volume of the treatise—concerned with human duty and expectations—the terms sympathy and benevolence are used interchangeably to identify a pivotal faculty that regulates the lower pleasures of sensation, imagination, ambition, and self-interest while it feeds into the higher pleasures of theopathy and the moral sense. In analyzing the dynamics of this faculty, Hartley emphasizes the personal outcomes and sources of satisfaction of the benevolent impulse (happiness, reciprocation, a feeling of unity, development of the moral sense, etc.) and thus affirms as "the grand design and purport of life" not some vague sentiment of good will toward humanity but a particular "benevolent act by A to B" based in part on self interest and resulting in the cultivation of the moral sentiment.[15]

Even a cursory glance at the moral concepts of these theorists reveals that Hawthorne did not accept their moral system but rather tested his own more sober contentions against theirs, harvesting some of their more lofty pronouncements, as we shall see, for ironic purposes. The element of high-minded meliorism in the works of all five of these authors is incompatible with the darker view of human potential presented in Hawthorne's fiction. These moral philosophers stand unanimously against the dark stain of innate depravity that blights the world of Hawthorne's characters and perverts even their nobler ambitions. The philosophers have, in effect, lifted the curse. For while there are occasional obligatory acknowledgments of the "consequences and marks of our fallen and degenerate nature" (Hartley's attempt to account for the difficulty in subordinating lower pleasures to higher ones) they are, to a man, committed to "the doctrine of the tendency of all beings to unlimited happiness through benevolence," a view Hartley uses to support the contention that malevolence is unnatural.[16]

Hawthorne may have been reading these authors (who acknowledge indebtedness to one another) one after the other to obtain as broad a view as possible of the nature and origin of moral knowledge and moral behavior at a time when he was also absorbing Puritan history and doctrine. While he may not have adopted their view of human nature, his works display a similarly strong commitment to the notion that feeling plays a crucial role in moral experience, that our apprehension of good and evil is triggered by a moral "sentiment." The consistent distinction in his works between a natural sentiment that bonds us to fellow humans and a parallel tendency that prompts us to exploit even those closest to us appears to have been influenced by the debate in these works concerning the nature of this sentiment. In *The House of the Seven Gables*, he portrays in the most vivid manner the differences between the sham of humanitarian benevolence and the sincerity of the human sentiment of sympathy.

III

Our first view of Judge Pyncheon at the beginning of chapter 4, "A Day Behind the Counter," is suggestive and revealing. He arrives on Pyncheon Street, pauses across from the House of the Seven Gables, and "scrutinizes" the shopwindow. Hawthorne repeatedly presents Pyncheon as an observer of the scene before him ("His eye rested on the shop-window"; "he minutely surveyed Hepzibah's little arrangements"; "the elderly gentleman stood looking at the Pyncheon-house"; "The gentleman had paused in the street ... still with his eyes fixed on the shop-window") (56–58). The face of this observer has a "capacity for varied expression" (57). While Pyncheon stares at the house, we are invited to observe him for he is "as well worth looking at as the house" (56). What we see is an elderly man with an outward appearance of respectability. We learn that this distinctive appearance— which sets him off in dignity, influence, and wealth from those around him— has been carefully cultivated. Every look, gesture, movement of the body, his clothing and his cane, his bearing—all are calculated to uphold the impression of a kindly gentleman of superior social position.

But we also see other things. His eyes are "too cold"; one of his most frequent expressions is a frown; his facial features are pinched and crabbed; his physical frame is obese; and his smile has an "acrid and disagreeable" quality to it (57). These externals seem to more accurately reflect the inner man when he manufactures a smile of "the sunniest complaisance and benevolence" in response to Hepzibah's presence in the shop window (57).

As he departs, she retreats to the parlor where she observes the portrait of Colonel Pyncheon. Like Jaffrey's, "the unlovely truth" of the Puritan's character surfaces with age. Despite her hesitancy to judge her ancestor, compelled by a "perception of the truth," Hepzibah reads the same decadent look on both faces (59).

In this scene, the posture of benevolence comes face to face with the sentiment of sympathy. Judge Pyncheon parades his smile and his vestments past the house in a deliberate display of concocted kindness. But the studied mannerisms, the self-absorbed smugness, the self-indulgent corpulence of the man hardly suggest genuine benevolence. Pyncheon rivets most of his attention on the shop window, barely gazing long enough at Hepzibah to modify his sagging smile, intent upon the implications for his own devices of the opening of a cent shop. Hawthorne strongly implies that his demeanor of benevolence is a front for greed and treachery—an ironic inversion of Hutcheson's conviction that displays of benevolence are, by their nature, displays of virtue.[17] Hepzibah, on the other hand, looks long and hard at the judge and then gazes as intensely at the portrait of Colonel Pyncheon. The look on Judge Pyncheon's face causes "a very bitter emotion" to arise in her; she tries to "drive it back into her heart" (57). She trembles under the stern look of Colonel Pyncheon but perseveres because it enables her to "read more accurately, and to a greater depth, the face which she had just seen in the street" (p. 59). Because she reads "with feeling" (*sym pathos*), she penetrates the deception, revealing the real man: "Let Jaffrey Pyncheon smile as he will, there is that look beneath!" (59). In later years, Hawthorne would observe, "There is a decorum which restrains you ... from breaking through a crust of plausible respectability, even when you are certain that there is a knave beneath it."[18] Hepzibah maintains that decorum out of respect for the family patriarch until the face of her cousin prompts a moral judgment from her.

The sketch of Judge Pyncheon in chapter 4 is developed into a full-blown portrait in his next appearance in chapter 8. The most prominent features are those introduced in the first sketch—the judge's excessive attention to his physical appearance, his obesity, his artificial smile, and the general air of benevolence he exudes. Expansion of each of these features of the portrait is carefully calculated to reveal some facet of the judge's depravity. The shine on his boots seems too "conscientious," like his glowing smile. The "massive accumulation of animal substance" below his chin belies the "spiritual" posture he affects (116–17). A prominent aspect of his portliness is humorously associated with his posterior, described as "favored with a remarkable degree of fundamental developement, well adapting him for the judicial bench" (121). The smile, described merely as sunny in the earlier sketch, blazes forth with heated intensity, inspiring the extravagant hyperbole that it required "an extra passage of the water-carts ... to lay the dust occasioned by so much extra sunshine!" (130). His look of "paternal benevolence" alternates with an appearance of "all-comprehensive benignity" (each term appears six times in the chapter) by which he gathers not only Hepzibah, Phoebe, and Clifford but "the whole world besides, into his immense heart" (130–31).

The observer of this bowing and smiling spectacle is Phoebe. Her observations quicken when she becomes the unwilling recipient of a kiss from the "unctuously-benevolent Judge" (118). The same instincts that prompt her to dodge the caress provoke a sudden recognition of a likeness between the dark-visaged face her embarrassed eyes now see and the stern face in the miniature that Holgrave had shown her earlier in the garden. Holgrave had captured the judge's true character when for a moment he dropped the "exceedingly pleasant countenance, indicative of benevolence" that he wears "to the world's eye" (92). Such a moment recurs now, one of two flash revelations of the judge's true character in the chapter. In this instance, Phoebe instinctively sees a resemblance between Judge Pyncheon and Colonel Pyncheon, just as Hepzibah had done earlier.

Hawthorne reveals differences between the public posture the judge assumes and the private life he has lived. His consummate performance of the role of benevolence has enhanced his reputation with the public as a pillar of the community. He has "etherealized" the "rude benevolence" of his ancestor into a "broad benignity" displayed in each of his public persona— Christian, philanthropist, judge, and politician (122). His unblemished reputation in these public roles is a measure of the success of the spectacle. Hutcheson, Smith and their followers worked hard to offset the darker implications of the Hobbesian view that human behavior is motivated by grasping self-interest; in their scheme of things, virtuous behavior promotes private interest. For Judge Pyncheon, the appearance of virtuous behavior will do. But "private diurnal gossip" discloses a more intimate and less flattering view of his destructiveness in personal relationships. His exploitation of his wife, who died a few years after they married, is said to have given her a "death-blow in the honey-moon" from which she never recovered (122–23).

Phoebe's spontaneous repulsion at the prospect of being kissed by this man of animal substance arises from a suspicion of lecherous intent behind the "sultry, dog-day heat ... of benevolence" (119). But her "sensible" nature prevents her from following her instincts. Moments later, she is inclined to grant him the withheld kiss, seduced by the sentiments of good will and kindliness he expresses toward Clifford and diffuses throughout the atmosphere of the room. The judge's display of compassion is, quite literally, a "spectacle"—not, as Adam Smith suggests, an observed scene of real and spontaneous feeling, but a staged performance put on for the spectator. Ironically, false feelings elicit true sentiments. Phoebe accepts what she sees at face value. At this point, she has retreated to the snug and superficial view that the judge's display of benevolence reflects his true character. Her "trim, orderly, limit-loving" mind refuses to acknowledge the darker truth under the veil of radiant deceit (131).

Not so with Hepzibah, whose resistance prompts the second and most startling glimpse of the real Jaffrey Pyncheon. Braced by "the moral force of a deeply grounded antipathy," she provokes a fierce and dark look on his face, expressive of "a certain hot fellness of purpose, which annihilated everything but itself" (127, 129). The profound disparity between this image of self-absorbed malevolence and the pretense of benevolent concern suggests the depth of Pyncheon's hypocrisy and the iron inflexibility of his purpose.[19] At the end of the chapter, Hawthorne implies that Pyncheon is the embodiment of a type, the public individual—"judges, clergymen, and other characters of that eminent stamp and respectability." While Phoebe remains perplexed by what has ensued, the observer capable of "a wider scope of view" and "deeper insight" would recognize that displays of humanitarian benevolence by public figures, cloaked in feigned sentiments of sympathetic identification with human misery, conveniently conceal the true motives of greed and ambition (131). In another ironic inversion—this time of an observation by Hartley—Jaffrey's "benevolence" regulates the higher pleasures of the moral sense while feeding the lower ones of ambition and self-interest.[20]

Judge Pyncheon succeeds in masking his intentions from Phoebe at this stage of the work. Her lack of astuteness is not surprising. Phoebe is not a Hester, a Zenobia, or a Miriam, women whose intellectual development and profound penetration into evil reflect their earlier experiences with the powers of darkness. Phoebe is Phoebe. She is the "ocher" woman—like the pursemaker Priscilla or the dovekeeper Hilda—a figure of virginal innocence. Judge Pyncheon's sunshine blazes forth with the blinding intensity of noon on the hottest summer day. Holgrave's is the angled ray that sharpens and clarifies the shadows of dusk on a clear autumn day. Phoebe's sunshine is the warming glow of an April morning. Her obtuseness is self-willed. She will go just so far. When Clifford exclaims, as he peers into Maule's Well, "the dark face gazes at me!" Phoebe "could see nothing of all this" because her "sphere lay so much in the Actual" (154). When Holgrave asks her if Clifford's disturbed state of mind is the result of dark thoughts, she replies, "I cannot see his thoughts!" and adds: "When he is cheerful—when the sun shines into his mind—then I venture to peep in, just as far as the light reaches, but no farther. It is holy ground where the shadow falls!" (178).

Phoebe misjudges Jaffrey's intentions because her perception is deflected by a moral sentiment that remains, at that moment, untested and undeveloped. Hutcheson notes that the moral sense prompts one to approve of actions that appear to be benevolent, regardless of their effect or utility.[21] Hawthorne implies that the spectator of such a display may not realize that she is witness to a performance. The difference in perspective is profound. Hutcheson assumes that such a display is an outward sign of virtue; Hawthorne presents it as a diversion from sinister goals. Phoebe will eventually do better, but the refinement of her sense of discernment will never be the result of intellectual growth. By nature, she is cautious and "limit-loving," just as she is naturally compassionate and generous. Her affection for and kindliness toward Clifford is grounded on "the simple appeal of a heart so forlorn as his, to one so full of genuine sympathy" (143).

Initially, she makes the same mistake with Holgrave. Even before she sees him, she has uneasy presentiments of his wild and lawless nature. When they first meet, she is "perplexed" by him. She does not "altogether like him" but is attracted by a "certain magnetic element" in him (94). Sympathy seeks affinities. The woman capable of sympathizing with the gaiety of the robins, and, "to such a depth as she could," with Hepzibah's "dark anxiety" and Clifford's "vague moan" will soon overcome her reticence about Holgrave (137). Hawthorne affirms a "spiritual force" in that kind of disposition which is rarely acknowledged (137). The "girlish" observer of feigned benevolence and apparent lawlessness overcomes her deficiencies of perception as the moral power of sympathetic association transforms her eyes into "larger, and darker, and deeper" recipients of her experience.

The same is true of Holgrave, but not because of any self-imposed limits. Whereas Phoebe will settle for the surface sunshine in Clifford's nature, Holgrave is intent on "fathoming Clifford to the full depth of his plummet-line" (178). At twenty-two, Holgrave is already a man of the world, a risk taker, one who ventures to ask and to answer the fundamental questions. Somewhat impetuous, rebellious, vaguely resentful of the oppression he senses, and given to strong preconceptions, like Phoebe he is not always accurate in his estimate of people. When he meets Phoebe, he is surprised by her simple, natural warmth and cheerfulness, having been predisposed to believe that all Pyncheons labor under the curse of his ancestors.

Also like Phoebe, Holgrave is sometimes bewildered by the "odd and incomprehensible world" he sees. Despite his readiness to probe the depths of humans, he reflects skeptically on the ability to "guess what they have been, from what he sees them to be, now." If Phoebe accepts limitations of intellectual curiosity, Holgrave acknowledges the constriction of perception that comes from being a "mere observer" (178–79).

Hawthorne's uneasiness with dispassionate observation is well known and best exemplified by his self-characterization in a letter to Longfellow as an owl peering out of the darkness at his prey, removed from "the main current of life."[22] Hawthorne projects this perspective into a host of characters: the narrator of "Sights From a Steeple" who "so coldly" describes the scene below him and who can but "guess" about "the interior of brick walls, or the mystery of human bosoms"; Wakefield, who aloofly observes the center of his social and emotional life for twenty years from the next street; the Rev. Mr. Hooper, who looks at his congregation through alienating shades of a dark veil; Heidegger and Aylmer, whose chilling detachment blind them to their deadly purposes; Ethan Brand, described as a "cold observer, looking on mankind as the subject of his experiment"; Chillingworth, peering into the soul of Dimmesdale; Coverdale, staring into Zenobia's and Priscilla's chamber with "that cold tendency ... which made me pry with a speculative interest into people's passions and impulses." Recall the image of Jaffrey Pyncheon staring into the shop window. In a notebook entry, Hawthorne once commented that "men of cold passions have quick eyes." The consequences of such a way of seeing are devastating—for the observer (alienation, bitter recognition of failure, insanity, suicide, cynicism) and for the observed (guilt, loneliness, a sense of entrapment, heartache, and premature death).

Holgrave, on the verge of such an error, has set his mind on prying out Pyncheon secrets. Phoebe says he is "too calm and cool an observer." She "felt his eye, often; his heart, seldom or never." In his relationship with Hepzibah and Clifford, "he studied them attentively" (177). It is no accident that his current occupation is that of daguerreotypist. He is attempting to be an artist of the ugly. The brush and easel won't do; the painter invariably represents his own renditions of the scene before him, coloring them with the hues of his own subjective sentiments. With a camera, he can record merely what is visible to a mechanical eye. To be sure, some of his portraits penetrate character, notably the daguerreotype of Judge Pyncheon, which reveals the man in his true aspect. But the mechanical eye does not disclose the judge's nature. It is "the wonderful insight in heaven's broad and simple sunshine"—the warm "eye" of nature—whose beams penetrate the core of Judge Pyncheon's darkness (91). When Holgrave looks through the lens, his perception is as controlled by physical phenomena as is the eye of the camera and its chemical solutions. When he observes the Pyncheon world with studied detachment, he submits to the same mechanistic devices. But when he begins to look with sympathy, his observations become as acute as the rays of the sun.

By the time Holgrave and Phoebe discuss the regions of Clifford's mind, he has already begun to glimpse this truth. He observes that solving the "complex riddle" of human nature "requires intuitive sympathy" (179). What he does not appreciate is the extent to which he has already moved in that direction. Consciously, he is the embodiment of the probing mind. Unconsciously, he is the model of the quick heart. As early as chapter 3, as Hepzibah prepares to open her shop, she senses "genuine sympathy" in his voice and aspect when he offers to help, and she reveals her fears to him. When she comments that the genteel family tradition will tumble with the vulgar business of penny profits, Holgrave offers this advice: "Let it go! You are the better without it" (44). Holgrave needs to do the same thing, to let go of the past. The corrosive influence of vindictiveness and detached observation have not consumed him yet, as they do Chillingworth, perhaps because, unlike Chillingworth, his impulses to mesmeric inquiry have not yet become a life pattern.

Holgrave's moment of surrender and of triumph over the past comes as he finishes telling the story of Alice Pyncheon. As Phoebe hovers on the brink of a mesmeric trance, the "speculative" side of Holgrave's disposition tempts him to "acquire power over her human spirit." This is one of the rare instances in Hawthorne's fiction of a man with occult powers resisting the impulse to control the destiny of a woman, largely through the influence of another spellbinder on the scene, nature. The converging rays of a setting sun and a rising moon create an atmosphere of enchantment powerful enough to make Holgrave feel "sympathy with the eternal youth of nature" (213). In a moment of near animistic identification with nature, the other side of Holgrave's disposition—his inclination toward sympathetic association—prompts him to show "reverence for another's individuality" (212).

This scene, often disparaged by critics as maudlin mush, is the inescapable result of a subcurrent of forces as compelling as the "curse" of the story. It is not the "heart" alone, as we often vaguely assert, that prevails here. The specific disposition of sympathy, with its powerful moral promptings, pushes Holgrave past the temptations of manipulation and domination to see the need to respect each individual. Having released himself from the emotionally insulating influences of suspicion, acrimony, and resentment, and impassioned by an awakening of love, Holgrave the man rhapsodizes the beauty, goodness, and youthfulness of the world. Having sensitized his powers of observation by surrendering detachment for affective association, Holgrave the artist transforms the House of the Seven

Gables into a "bower of Eden," achieving what Hawthorne refers to as "poetic insight": "the gift of discerning, in this sphere of strangely mingled elements, the beauty and the majesty which are compelled to assume a garb so sordid" (41).

Thus sympathy is not presented as a corollary to or a type of benevolence, as it is in the theorists Hawthorne read, but as a distinct sentiment operating in personal relationships, activating both the moral and emotional sensibilities of the individual, quickening the power of perception, and serving as a counteragent to specious benevolence. It diffuses its influence through the house principally through the agency of Hepzibah, Phoebe, and Holgrave, but also through the ruined Clifford—both as the object of the sentiment and as one who experiences it the most elementally in his identification with children, birds, and flowers. "The sympathy of this little circle of not unkindly souls" breaks the curse (157). Their eventual retreat to the countryside is not the "bathetic turn" it has been made out to be.[23] They go not to the bower of Eden but from it, aware of the limitation that "man's best-directed effort accomplishes a kind of dream, while God is the sole worker of realities" (180).

But to return to our judge. His third and final visit to the House is his deepest and most threatening penetration of it. He is there to wrest the secret of the lost estate from Clifford. At first, he raises the facade of "a visage of composed benignity" enhanced by "the genial benevolence of his smile" (226). When he claims compassion for Clifford, cloaking these sentiments in professions of duty, conscience, and law, Hepzibah assaults "this loathsome pretense of affection," denying him the right "to stand in the ring of human sympathies" (228). The progress of the scene is arrested for a moment as Hawthorne deliberates upon the judge's public reputation as a man of respectability, acknowledged by church and state, "denied by nobody." In the next paragraph, Hawthorne expands his earlier portrait of the public man, detailing the methods and motives of "Judge Pyncheon's brotherhood." They are "men to whom forms are of paramount importance, ... grasping, and arranging, and appropriating ... landed estate ... and public honors." Their good deeds are "done in the public eye" and out of this they build a glittering "palace." Only the "sadly gifted eye," such a one as Hepzibah's, can perceive the "secret abomination" within. Hawthorne then parades his public roles past the reader again—judge, public servant, political party faithful, Bible society officer, philanthropist—culminating in a sardonic reference to his "smile of broad benevolence" (229–31).

The most devastating portrait of the sham of public benevolence is saved for the last. As "Governor Pyncheon" sits quite dead in the ancestral chair in chapter 18, his watch ticking in his hand, the narrator reveals his schedule of activities for the morning, juxtaposing with trenchant irony the commitments of his private life with his public engagements. His assault on Clifford is to be followed by a visit to a broker to invest "a few loose thousands." Next, he will try to purchase former Pyncheon land before he attends the meeting of a charitable society, whose name he has forgotten, "in the multiplicity of his benevolence." The acquisition of fruit trees for his country estate is adjoined to the purchase of a tombstone to replace the broken one at his wife's grave site, which he will do "if he have time." The contribution of hundreds of dollars to a committee of his political party is measured against the "small bank-note" he might give to the destitute widow of a friend who he "partly intends" to call on (270–72). The Judge Pyncheon who is insensitive to the dignity of Clifford, his wife, and the widow of a friend is incapable of affective response to individuals. His lifelong pursuit of power and wealth has deadened him to truly sympathetic personal relationships. The final image of him is vaguely reminiscent of the opening scene where we find him staring intently at the house. Well before the fly that has "smelt out" the judge begins to crawl across his face to his "wide-open eyes," we sense that the man who has lost "that dog-day smile of elaborate benevolence" sees nothing and feels nothing (282–83).

NOTES

1. *The House of the Seven Gables*, Ohio State Centenary Edition, vol. 2, ed. William Charvat et al. (Columbus, OH: Ohio State University Press, 1965), 15. All citations are from this edition and will be identified by page number within parentheses in the text.

2. Gloria C. Erlich, *Family Themes and Hawthorne's Fiction: The Tenacious Web* (New Brunswick, NJ: Rutgers University Press, 1984), 138–40; James R. Mellow, *Nathaniel Hawthorne in His Times* (Boston: Houghton Mifflin Co., 1980), 360–61.

3. *Our Old Home*, ed. Roy Harvey Pearce et al. (Columbus: Ohio State University Press, 1970), 289–92.

4. *The Blithedale Romance*, Ohio State Centenary Edition, vol. 3, ed. William Charvat et al. (Columbus, OH: Ohio State University Press, 1965), 70–71.

5. Hawthorne, *Blithedale*, 198–200.

6. Marion L. Kesselring, *Hawthorne's Reading, 1828–1850* (New York: New York Public Library, 1949), 53, 61. Although Hawthorne did not have borrower's privileges at the Salem Athenaeum at this time, it is likely that his aunt, Mary Manning purchased a share in October, 1826 to make the library's collection available to him and that most of the books borrowed while she owned the share were for Hawthorne. Kesselring presents evidence to support this view, especially pages 6–7. Mary's share was transferred to Nathaniel in May 1828.

7. Hutcheson derived his notion of the moral sense from the third earl of Shaftesbury's arguments for a moral faculty that balances the tendency toward self-interest and moves the individual toward virtuous behavior.

8. Francis Hutcheson, *An Inquiry Into the Original of Our Ideas of Beauty and Virtue*, 4th ed. (London: D. Midwinter, 1738), 166. I have used the edition of the Salem

Athenaeum which, according to Kesselring, Hawthorne borrowed, for this and all other works Hawthorne used during this period.

9. Hutcheson, 177, 218.

10. Lester H. Hunt's reading of *The Scarlet Letter* in the light of Smith's theories eventually concludes that Hawthorne's notion of sympathy in *The Scarlet Letter* discredits Smith's views. See especially page 86 in "*The Scarlet Letter*: Hawthorne's Theory of Moral Sentiments," *Philosophy and Literature* 8 (April 1984), 75–88. In an unpublished dissertation, Marie L. Foley argues that Hawthorne absorbed the influences of Smith's theories principally through his reading of Shelley, "'The Key of Holy Sympathy': Hawthorne's Social Ideal" (Ph.D. diss., Tulane University, 1969). Roy R. Male had earlier argued that Hawthorne's concept of sympathy derived from organicism in "'From the Innermost Germ': The Organic Principle in Hawthorne's Fiction," *English Literary History* 20 (1953), 218–36; "Hawthorne and the Concept of Sympathy," *PMLA* 68 (1953), 138–49; and "Sympathy—A Key Word in American Romanticism," *Emerson Society Quarterly* 35 (1964), 19–23.

11. Randall Stewart, *Nathaniel Hawthorne: A Biography* (New Haven: Yale University Press, 1948), 17.

12. Thomas Brown, *Lecturer on the Philosophy of the Human Mind*, 3 vols. (Andover: Mark Newman, 1822), 3:246.

13. Brown, 1:150.

14. Brown, 3:340–42.

15. David Hartley, *Observations on Man, His Frame, His Duty, and His Expectations*, 4th ed., 2 vols. (London: W. Eyres, 1801), 2:285–88.

16. Hartley, 2:289–90.

17. Hutcheson, 166.

18. *Our Old Home*, 292.

19. Kenneth Harris argues that Hawthorne derived his notions of hypocrisy from Puritan theories in "'Judge Pyncheon's Brotherhood': Puritan Theories of Hypocrisy in *The House of the Seven Gables*," *Nineteenth-Century Fiction* 39 (September 1984), 144–62. Harris's book, *Hypocrisy and Self-Deception in Hawthorne's Fiction* (Charlottesville: University of Virginia Press, 1988) treats the subject in other works by Hawthorne.

20. Hartley, 2:183.

21. Hutcheson, 166–67.

22. *The Letters, 1813–1843*, ed. Thomas Woodson et al. (Columbus, OH: Ohio State University Press: 1984), 251.

23. Leslie Fiedler, *Love and Death in the American Novel*, rev. ed. (New York: Dell, 1966), 444.

DAN McCALL

The Tongue of Flame

Sigmund Freud was not (so far as I know) thinking about *The Scarlet Letter* when he wrote *Civilization and Its Discontents*. But a brief paragraph from Freud's book can be applied with accuracy and force to the history of Hester Prynne in Puritan Boston:

> Human life in communities only becomes possible when a number of men unite together in strength superior to any single individual and remain united against all single individuals. The strength of this united body is then opposed as "Right" against the strength of any individual, which is condemned as "brute force." This substitution of the power of a united number for the power of a single man is the decisive step towards civilization. The essence of it lies in the circumstance that the members of the community have restricted their possibilities of gratification whereas the individual recognized no such restrictions. The first requisite of culture, therefore, is justice—that is, the assurance that a law once made will not be broken in favor of any individual.

Hawthorne wrote *The Scarlet Letter* with great speed, often working over nine hours a day. Henry James said, "the subject had probably lain a

From *Citizens of Somewhere Else: Nathaniel Hawthorne and Henry James*, pp. 45-70. © 1999 by Cornell University Press.

long time in his mind." Indeed it had: for over a decade Hawthorne had pondered a slowly ripening image, a scarlet letter, A, on a woman's bodice. In "Endicott and the Red Cross" (1837) he had asked us to see

> a young woman, with no mean share of beauty, whose doom it was to wear the letter A on the breast of her gown, in the eyes of all the world and her own children. And even her own children knew what the initial signified. Sporting with her infamy, the lost and desperate creature had embroidered the fatal token in scarlet cloth, with golden thread and the nicest art of needlework, so that the capital A might have been thought to mean Admirable, or anything rather than Adulteress.

When he was forced out of his job at the Salem Custom-House, Hawthorne picked up that letter again; now he was ready to invest the symbol with its full power.

We should remember that from early on he had had in mind both the starkness of the brand and the luxuriance of the embroidery. In almost Miltonic stately cadences—"Sporting with her infamy the lost / And desperate creature"—the golden thread says adultery is beautiful, says Right you are, and richer than you know!

Hawthorne mentions the letter, on average, more than once every two pages. The modulations he plays on the A are not always successful, and when he talks of its lurid gleam and magical properties he stumbles. The superhuman badge that protects Hester from Indian arrows, the flaming A in the night sky—these are examples of Hawthorne's burdening a meaningful symbol with distracting and overwrought effects. These errors are open enough and sufficiently commented upon, but something may still be said about the way the A focuses our attention on the central issues Hawthorne confronts in Puritan Boston.

First of all, we must take it literally. Critics have been overly ingenious, telling us that the A stands not only for Adultery and Able but also for Art, America, and Arthur. No. As John Thompson has written, "the title truly is *The Scarlet Letter*, and it is truly about sex: about what happens to our sex in the condition of American culture." Hawthorne, skittish at first (skittish as always), worried about the lurid quality of *Scarlet*, and suggested that perhaps *The Judgment Letter* might be a better title. But then, persuaded by the other side of his temperament, he suggested that the title be printed in flaming red on the cover of the book. The scarlet A is the ideal mythic type of the portion of the American past that he was exploring, the least far-fetched symbol he could have used to tell this story of Massachusetts. Historically grounded, pictorially vivid, the letter calls into play the central impulses of the colony. Yvor Winters has written that "in the setting which Hawthorne chose, allegory was realism, the idea was life itself." Hawthorne's "inveterate love of allegory," his desire constantly to work with symbolic signs rather than experiential particulars, here is turned into a chief merit of his writing style and not a temperamental defect. The A is the focal point not just for our eyes; it embodies where the Puritans were and who they were and why they lived as they did. The A becomes, in Kenneth Burke's phrase, "the informing anecdote," the one resonant symbol which carries with it all that the story will reveal. In chapter 15, "Hester and Pearl," we read that "as the last touch to her mermaid's garb, Pearl took some eel-grass, and imitated, as best she could, on her own bosom, the decoration with which she was so familiar on her mother's. A letter,—the letter A,—but freshly green, instead of scarlet!" Three times Pearl asks, "What does the letter mean, mother?" And finally Hester answers, "Silly Pearl, what questions are these? There are many things in this world that a child must not ask about," and she resonantly concludes, "as for the scarlet letter, I wear it for the sake of its gold thread!" Exactly. And, as I said, the "gold thread" is not something else, or something that happens later. The gold thread is there from the very beginning, an essential, virtually instinctual part of the larger plan. Punitive scarlet and celebratory gold. Those two. That one.

In choosing the image Hawthorne made the greatest choice of his writing life; never again would he find that single dramatic and coherent symbol around which to build a fiction. The furry ears of Donatello in *The Marble Faun*, for example, are in no way "the informing anecdote" of that book and are curiously inadequate as a vehicle for the questions the book raises. But the scarlet letter raises a very great question: by what signs shall ye know them? The business of the book is to elaborate the A, to put it in different terms. The letter stands as a brutally clear meaning, but since it is only a letter, the heroine may change by her actions the word in which the letter belongs. She has already done so when we meet her; she has made "a pride of what they, worthy gentlemen, meant for a punishment."

In the first scene Hester stands there, an emblem of sin. The Puritan community has designed the letter to erase the sinner, to obliterate her individuality. She is supposed to be the general symbol of "woman's sinful passion." But Hawthorne keeps taking us into Hester's "inward sphere" behind the letter to show us the discrepancy between what the community can see and who Hester is. Thus, the reality that society has defined provides the fighting terms of the book: either the meaning assigned by the community will retain its repressive function or it will yield through the efforts of the central character to a new meaning. Hester's embroidery has already begun to answer the question; it is the visible sign that she has taken her place and will endure it with a vengeance.

Hawthorne had already jotted down in his notebook, in capital letters, "A Secret Thing In Public." It is a perfect description of the scarlet letter. That is who Hester is, when we first see her trapped, helpless and lonely on the pillory undergoing the censure of the assembled townspeople. All they do is look at her in silent punishment. Or, as D. H. Lawrence flamboyantly claimed, the citizens of Boston are really worshipping Hester as the incarnation of their forbidden desires.

Whatever way you look at it, there is a dark feeling of despair and loss, something extremely strange in the air of mid-nineteenth-century New England. Hawthorne's great neighbors, Emerson and Thoreau, were busy proclaiming "the infinitude of the private man." Walt Whitman was very soon to proclaim the United States itself "the greatest poem." But Hawthorne's tragic heroine is constantly confined by American society, entrapped and tortured by the massive *fact* of it. Her story bleakly contradicts the prevailing optimism of the day, as do her essential life and most telling gestures.

She is radically unlike the stereotypic heroines in the popular literature of 1850. Oliver Wendell Holmes found her a profound relief from the "languid, lifeless, sexless creations" he usually encountered in American novels. Hester Prynne is an absolutely astonishing figure in nineteenth-century New England culture, a woman whose character is a direct expression of her powerful sexuality. Her very existence is rooted in the community's recognition of her sexual independence. She is a "Fallen Woman"—a "Dark Lady"—who generates moral and intellectual strength from her defiant refusal to accept the masculine world's definition of her. She surrounds the stigmatizing "A" on the breast of her gown with the "gorgeous luxuriance of elaborate embroidery." "Gorgeous" in 1850 meant not only "dazzlingly beautiful or magnificent," as in today's usage, but in that chaster day it signified "overly sumptuous," with implications of sexual irregularity and sensual "indulgence."

Twice in the novel Ann Hutchinson is mentioned, and Hester walks in her "footsteps." Over twenty years earlier Hawthorne had written in his biographical sketch of Mistress Hutchinson, "In the midst, and in the center of all eyes, we see the woman. She stands loftily before her judges with a determined brow; and unknown to herself, there is a flash of carnal pride half-hidden in her eye, as she surveys the many learned and famous men whom her doctrines have put in fear." Such a description could go straight into *The Scarlet Letter* (with perhaps the exception of "doctrines," though even that is applicable by the end).

Hester "had in her nature a rich, voluptuous, oriental characteristic—a taste for the gorgeously beautiful" ("gorgeous" again, and this time "oriental"). Moreover, she is not just physically brilliant; she is "brilliant" in the sense of "bright"—she has an active, alert, imaginative mind. She may think wrongly at times, but she thinks more profoundly than anyone else. And most importantly Hawthorne sees her far more clearly than his other brilliant heroines; we don't sense any mystification about her sin, and she is not distorted by deep, unsolved secrets. She is a deep and unsolved secret. Hawthorne does not encumber her with gimmicky curses as he does Miriam and Beatrice or tacked-on charges as he does Zenobia.

Hester's first act in the story is one of rebellion; led out of the dark prison by the town beadle, "she repelled him by an act marked with natural dignity and force of character, and stepped into the open air, as if by her own free will." The book marks dramatic confrontations between Hester and those who would repress her. When the judges try to take her daughter away from her, she confronts "the old Puritan magistrate with almost a fierce expression" showing that "she felt that she possessed indefeasible rights against the world, and she was ready to defend them to the death." From the very beginning, when Hester not only bears the letter but brandishes it, "The world's law was no law for her mind." At the end, when Dimmesdale ascends the scaffold to make his public confession, Hester draws near "slowly, as if impelled by inevitable fate and against her strongest will." She is reluctant; she does not want him in the marketplace, she does not want him under terms of the "world's law."

For Hester, from the very start of the story, experience is over. It is not to have. The world has been turned around. The future is the past. The world has told her she is no longer allowed to be a woman. But she knows that what the world tells her is false; her love for Dimmesdale and for her daughter proves to her daily that she is a woman. On the scaffold, when she faces the multitude, "she was supported by an unnatural tension of the nerves, and by all the combative energy of her character, which enabled her to convert the scene into a kind of lurid triumph." That lurid triumph cannot last, for the intensity of the mad moment of public display must be borne out in dreary routine: "with the unattended walk from her prison-door began the daily custom; and she must either sustain and carry it forward by the ordinary resources of her nature, or sink beneath it." Hester endures the knowledge that no one will respond to her as Hester but "as the figure, the body, the reality of sin." Women are the only people who feel a common twinge, a sense of shame, when they see the scarlet letter. Men notice it and know what it stands for—although Indians and Governor Bellingham's manservant think that it stands for high rank. Hester comes to have a "dread of children" because "the utterance of a word that had no distinct purport to their own minds, but was none the less terrible to her as proceeding from lips that babbled it unconsciously. It seemed to argue so wide a diffusion of her shame, that all nature knew of it." In her walks with Pearl she has to face children and hear them say, "Come, let us fling mud at them."

From the beginning, when she tries to conceal the sign of adultery with the product of adultery, she fights back. In another sense, she simply takes the world on its own terms; she plays the role her culture assigns to her. And by behaving herself she becomes "Able." She is given "a part to perform in the world." Humble in that sense, at least, she continues to display her vibrant sexuality and deep inner resources. Anthony Trollope, in an article for *The North American Review*, wrote that in *The Scarlet Letter* "the reader is expected to sympathize with the woman—and will sympathize only with her." She has, as even Chillingworth says, "great elements."

When Hawthorne wrote of women, he usually tended to divide them, as has so often been remarked upon, into two groups: the blondes and the brunettes, the light snow maidens and the dark women of voluptuous nature and high passion. Of the snow maidens Emily Dickinson would later exclaim, "What soft cherubic creatures / These gentlewomen are!" In a little sketch, "The Canal Boat," Hawthorne indicates his distaste for the American idea of women; he speaks of "the pure, modest, sensitive, and shrinking women of America—shrinking when no evil is intended, and sensitive like diseased flesh, that thrills if you but point at it." Hawthorne does not always stick by this indictment; his creation of Phoebe and Priscilla and Hilda shows that he, too, was enamored of "the pure, modest, sensitive, and shrinking woman of America." But he did have a love of vitality and rich sexuality. "As a point of taste," he wrote that he would prefer his dove-ladies to the English matrons he described in *Our Old Home*, but, he said, "it is a pity that we must choose between a greasy animal and an anxious skeleton."

The interesting thing in *The Scarlet Letter*, in this regard, is the way he plays with the conventions of hero and heroine, suggesting in his play a criticism of the American stereotypes of sexual roles. In Old Boston the roles are reversed. T. Walter Herbert correctly calls Hester Prynne "a manly woman and Arthur Dimmesdale a womanly man." Dimmesdale's sin never really feels like seduction; Hester seems more the seducer than the seduced. Hester Prynne is the first real woman in American literature and still the greatest. Hawthorne piles superlatives about her: "none so ready as she is to give," "none so self-devoted as Hester," "unfailing to every real demand, and inexhaustible by the largest."

Dimmesdale, on the other hand, is not the dashing, decisive young pastor; he is constantly described in the language normally applied to the young maiden heroines of the sentimental novels. He compulsively holds his hand over his heart the way the persecuted dove-ladies compulsively put the backs of their white hands to their white brows. Dimmesdale is a damsel in distress. In the forest scene he begs Hester for help: "Be thou strong for me!" "Advise me what to do." "I am powerless to go!" "Think for me, Hester! Thou art strong. Resolve for me!" These are the words scattered out by snow maidens to their swashbuckling saviors in Brockden Brown and Cooper and the popular stage melodramas. In *The Scarlet Letter* Hawthorne has turned about completely not only the general nature of the hero–heroine conventions in mid-nineteenth-century fiction, but he also has turned around the whole complex of tags and devices and stock poses that went along with those conceptions.

Hester keeps asking, "What is this being which I have brought into the world!""Is that my Pearl?" Pearl, in turn, becomes a cameo of Hester; looking at herself in a salty pool of tidewater, she soon finds "that either she or the image was unreal." Hester asks Pearl what the A means. Pearl answers, "It is the great letter A. Thou hast taught me in the hornbook." "A" is the first letter the child learned, and she learned it in a context appropriate for understanding what it means on her mother's bosom:

A

> In Adam's fall
> we sinnéd all.

Language and sin are inseparable on Hester's breast. "A" is the first letter and the letter from which all others follow. On Hester's dress it signals sexual irregularity; it is thus associated with the first sin which forced man and woman out of the garden and from which all sins follow. The A, then, is at the beginning of things in our minds, the first sin which infects all subsequent society and the first verbal signal we learn in order to communicate in society.

The scarlet letter is a sign of the times. It covers and announces the bosom, standing on "that inward sphere." As the novel unfolds, the letter becomes what Richard Chase calls "the Hawthorne image: a cultural image of sexual love and moral community." It is that "Secret Thing In Public." Private impulse is given public articulation as a symbol of sexual shame.

While it is true that from its first publication *The Scarlet Letter* was hailed as an American classic, some of its earliest readers were dismayed. My own favorite is a scandalized custodian of culture who cried out, in *The Church*

Review, "Is the French era actually begun in our literature?" The influential Orestes Brownson declared that

> Hawthorne can hardly be said to pervert God's gifts, or to exert an immoral influence. Yet his work is far from being unobjectionable. It is a story of crime, an adulteress and her accomplice. Crimes like the one imagined are not fit subjects for popular literature, and moral health is not promoted by leading the imagination to dwell on them. There is an unsound state of public morals when the novelist is permitted, without a scorching rebuke, to select such crimes, and invest them with all the fascinations of genius and all the charms of highly polished style. No man has the right to love another man's wife, and no married woman has the right to love any man but her husband.

Nowadays we tend to think we've grown out of that prudery. What's all this fuss about Adultery? Big deal. Hester Prynne and Arthur Dimmesdale don't seem to modern readers to have "sinned," and to insist that they did only illustrates Mencken's wonderful definition of Puritanism as "the haunting suspicion that somewhere someone may be happy."

In any age, though, *The Scarlet Letter* is decidedly a gloomy book. Henry James said, "no story of love was surely ever less of a 'love-story.'" And Hawthorne himself complained that "it wears, to my eye, a stern and somber aspect, too much ungladdened by genial sunshine." He attributed that quality to "the still seething turmoil" he felt when he was writing it. He had been fired from his job in the Salem Custom-House, a victim of the spoils system, a Democrat turned out by the Whig victory of 1848. The loss of his position embittered him and created disorder in his professional and personal circumstances. His heart was broken by another, deeper loss: his beloved mother had just died. Her death caused him to break down—in public, on one occasion, the only time on record that Hawthorne experienced that kind of collapse. He wrote *The Scarlet Letter* in a desperate frenzy of sustained composition unmatched in his previous writing life.

In *Hawthorne, Melville, and the Novel,* Richard H. Brodhead remarks that "Chillingworth's free thinking is as a 'window thrown open' to Dimmesdale and shortly after this is said the two men look out of an actual open window." Brodhead argues cogently that such metaphors and actualities—side by side or fused into one—are typical of the book: "Hester embroiders robes for occasions of state, and official ceremonies like the Election Day pageant are called the 'brilliant embroidery to the great robe of state.' It is all but impossible to isolate an item in *The Scarlet Letter* that does not make both physical and metaphorical appearances." They are "manifest now as parts of an actual scene, now as features of the mind." Brodhead cites the great forest interview between Hester and Dimmesdale as an encounter in an actual geographical place and as metaphor: Hawthorne has already spoken of "the moral wilderness in which Hester had been so long wandering." The forest appears, Brodhead asserts, as "both a natural place and as an externalization of their mental states. Our experience in the world of this novel is akin to Hawthorne's own in the moonlit room." Ordinary boundaries become fluid so that "things are seen both as facts and as thoughts."

The letter itself is designed, first by the judges and then by Hester's elaborate needlework, to be seen. The name of the book asks us to see. The chapter titles—"Another View of Hester," "The Interview," "The Interior of a Heart," "The Minister in a Maze"—all of them constantly remind us that the important question in the novel is this: how can one know a fact and at the same time see its meaning? The images of mirrors and pools and spectators predominate. When he sees his wife and another man's child, Chillingworth says to his guide, "'Ah!'—'Aha!'—'I conceive you.'" Is that a pun on "conceive"? Michael Colacurcio is absolutely convincing when he reads what he calls "the heretical-idea-as-illegitimate-child conceit"; Colacurcio cries out, "behold the Puritan wit," in tracts that speak of an "erroneous gentlewoman herself, convicted of holding about *thirty* monstrous births at once" and "there were no more monstrous *births* than what is frequent for women laboring with *false conceptions* to produce." In these terms Hester Prynne *is* Ann Hutchinson.

A continuous theme in the book is the discrepancy between what Puritans design and the way nature refutes them. Where everything means, nothing is. For all its allegory, *The Scarlet Letter* enforces a world of anti-allegory. The elders try to locate sin, fasten it as a sign—that is their way of caging it. But like the grass growing back in the wheel tracks of the road, nature "refutes" man's arguments. The Puritans are more systematic and more intelligent than their Utopian great-grandchildren whom Hawthorne describes in *The Blithedale Romance*, but both communities, in their single-mindedness, fail. The world contradicts all schemes that do not reckon with its complexity. The Blithedalers attack evil by ignoring it; they try to reduce "the inward sphere" to an inane innocence. The Puritan community has a far deeper awareness of the power of human impulses, but the rigidity of their method fails to deal humanely with perceived error. We see the Puritan community "putting on, for ceremonials of pomp and state, the garments that had been wrought by Hester's sinful hands. Her needle-work was seen on the ruff of the Governor; military men wore it on their scarfs, and the minister on his band; it decked the baby's little cap; it was shut up, to be mildewed and moulder away in the coffins of the dead."

Hester's handiwork is in the clothes of all public and private ceremonies (except, of course, bridal veils). The "type of sin" leaves her mark on all the functions of the colony that had denied her her existence as a person. Although the letter is designed to estrange Hester from the community, it gives her a special sense of the secret sins of others, a kind of clairvoyance about the inner lives of the people around her. Thus, the stigmatizing element in sin becomes associated with increased knowledge, increased power of vision. "The tendency of her fate and fortune had been to set her free. The scarlet letter was her passport into regions where other women dared not tread." Thus, "the truth" of her situation is a language of travel complete with that prominent "passport" as she moves from state to state. In his portrait of Dimmesdale, Hawthorne repeats the figure and exclaims "A bitter kind of knowledge that!" A bitter kind for Hawthorne because the rhetoric of his book invites us to form the conclusion that sin acquaints the sinner with the knowledge that purity cannot have. *Felix culpa*! Hester wonders whether "if the truth were everywhere to be shown, a scarlet letter would blaze forth on many a bosom besides Hester Prynne's." She could, indeed, cry out a modulation of Minister Hooper's dying wail: Lo, everywhere, on every breast, a red A. In this sense the scarlet letter signifies a collapse of meaning. It is a social sign designed to perform a single function. When Hawthorne writes that it "had not done its office" he is referring, specifically, to the state of Hester's unrepentant mind. But in a more general sense the statement can be applied to the inability of the signs devised by the Puritans to perform their offices. Hawthorne continually refers to the way in which all acts reverberate in the public mind; the story is full of phrases like "no sensible men, it was confessed, could doubt" and "a widely diffused opinion" and "the vulgar idea." Hawthorne keeps showing us that although these signs are continually interpreted, the result is not density of meaning but accumulation of contrary meanings.

The quest is spelled out in agony. At the very beginning, when Hester clutches the baby to her, it screams; we are pulled into that instinctive grasp: our eyes are not down on the ground with the onlookers. Hawthorne pulls us up onto the scaffold to share the agony of Hester when she realizes "Yes!—these were her realities,—all else had vanished!" What Hester plays out publicly on the scaffold, Dimmesdale plays out in private at his mirror. He asks, "Then, what was he?—a substance?—or the dimmest of all shadows?" The search for identity is articulated in the pain of self-inquisition. "I, your pastor, whom you so reverence and trust, am utterly a pollution and a lie!" Dimmesdale is lost between what he appears to the community and what he knows is true of himself. Consequently, "the whole universe is false,—it is impalpable,—it shrinks to nothing within his grasp. And he himself, in so far as he shows himself in a false light, becomes a shadow, or, indeed, ceases to exist." These were his realities—all else had vanished.

Calvinism, Hawthorne suggests in "Young Goodman Brown," forced on its adherents the kind of morbidity and fascination with sin that made them peculiarly susceptible to temptation. And, as Hawthorne presents it, the Puritan mind is incapable of making a crucial distinction: the sinner becomes reducible to the sin. Hester is a perfect "example." The community tries to shut Hester up in a dark closet and stamp a label on the door, to obliterate herself behind her sin. That is what happens literally and allegorically in one of the finest images of the book: in Governor Bellingham's manse she sees herself reflected in a suit of armor: "the scarlet letter was represented in exaggerated and gigantic proportions, so as to be greatly the most prominent feature of her appearance. In truth, she seemed absolutely hidden behind it." Mission accomplished. The community makes of the errant woman a hideous and intolerable allegory. Denied her right to be, everywhere she must mean, must signify her sin, must be "absolutely hidden behind it."

Hester looks at her bodice and asks herself: by *these* signs you shall know me? No one is supposed to know her as a person. She must present herself to the community with a kind of doubleness (red letter and gold thread) but never as her richly various self. She can stand on the scaffold as an adulteress enduring punishment or as a prideful refutation of her judges, but she is not allowed to stand there as Hester Prynne. When she comes out of prison, the townspeople note the "desperate recklessness of her mood, by its wild and picturesque peculiarity." What they mistake is her extreme state of mind for the woman herself—all eyes focus on "the letter."

Hester is a great refutation of the Puritan mind; she brings into the community a kind of vitality which Puritanism is too narrow to contain. They refuse to express sexual passion; she incarnates it. She stands like a queen facing a mob: "tall," with "perfect elegance," "on a large scale with dark and abundant hair, so glossy that it threw off the sunshine with a gleam." She is "beautiful from regularity of feature and richness of complexion." She is "lady-like" with "feminine gentility," possessing "a certain state and dignity." She is Elizabethan largesse. The Puritans have had to delimit human variety and vitality to the point where they refuse to recognize the power of the passions which Hester incarnates. She is too much for them. What they have gained in narrowing for control they have lost in being able to cope with the most richly endowed member of the community. Thoreau wrote that the Puritans were unable to worship in the vibrant colors of an autumn forest; when the Puritans made their churches they cut down any riotous trees that would distract them from grey piety.

A second indication Hawthorne gives us of the Puritan mind's incapacity to deal with transgressors is that the mind is, in one sense, promiscuous. Why are the townspeople's eyes "fastened" on the prison door? What expectations have the public officials created in the citizenry? From the assemblage one knows that "some awful business is at hand." But, Hawthorne tells us, the members of that assemblage did not know whether they were there to see the punishment of "an undutiful child," or the driving into the forest of a "riotous Indian," or the censure of a "witch" who will "die upon the gallows," or the correction of "a sluggish bond-servant," or "an Antinomian," or a "Quaker." The Puritan mind is profoundly aware of evil, but it is incapable of discriminating among types and degrees of evil. Whatever may happen, "there was very much the same solemnity of demeanor on the part of the spectators." The Puritan does not solve a moral problem; he stamps it out.

As the beadle leads Hester onto the pillory, he shouts, "A blessing on the righteous colony of Massachusetts, where iniquity is dragged out into the sunshine!" The Puritans turn a merciless, brilliant light on sin, but the sun shines indiscriminately on all sins alike.

> Out of the whole human family, it would not have been easy to select the same number of wise and virtuous persons, who should be less capable of sitting in judgment on an erring woman's heart, and disentangling its mesh of good and evil, than the sages of rigid aspect towards whom Hester Prynne now turned her face.

Nowhere else does Hawthorne more fully explore the causes and consequences of the rigid mind than in *The Scarlet Letter*, where he makes it stand for the way society as a whole conducts its business of dealing with the isolated, mutinous individual.

The dismal severity of "the Puritanic code" is, for Hawthorne, in some sense good: it gives a coherent and deep meaning to every human act. The Puritan community takes sin with admirable seriousness. Hawthorne admires the dignity the Puritans give to human life. He finds greatness in the Puritan community: "They had fortitude and self-reliance, and, in time of difficulty or peril, stood up for the welfare of the state like a line of cliffs against a tempestuous tide." In "Main Street" he said that the Puritans "were stern, severe, intolerant, but not superstitious, not even fanatical; and endowed, if any men of that age were, with a far seeing worldly sagacity."

While Hawthorne indicts the Puritans for their errors, he knows that their mind accomplished "so much, precisely because it imagined and hoped so little." They were facing almost impossible odds in a new, savage land, with little protection and little skill to fight the elements. In many cases they had to act as "one man" because the alternative was death. Hawthorne is especially attracted to Governor Bellingham, who, while he is a stern magistrate, is also able to wear a "loose gown and easy cap," to surround himself with "appliances of worldly enjoyment." The Governor's house had "a very cheery aspect; the walls being overspread with a kind of stucco, in which fragments of broken glass were plentifully intermixed; so that, when the sunshine fell aslant-wise over the front of the edifice, it glittered and sparkled as if diamonds had been flung against it by the double handful. The brilliancy might have befitted Aladdin's palace, rather than the mansion of a grave old Puritan ruler." Hawthorne says that "it is an error to suppose that our grave forefathers" simply "made it a matter of conscience to reject such means of comfort, or even luxury, as lay fairly within their grasp." The Reverend Wilson "never taught" such a creed; he "had a long-established and legitimate taste for all good and comfortable things." Hawthorne quickly points out that Wilson's "professional contemporaries" did not display with such "genial benevolence" this fullness of being. Nevertheless, Hawthorne provides us with these figures of Bellingham and Wilson so as not to reduce his portrait of the society to caricature. And, while the Puritans lacked the ability to address "the whole human brotherhood in the heart's native language," they did establish civilization on a savage continent; they did order that civilization so that it could endure. And that, surely, is the reason the setting of the book is of such stark necessity for a story of conflict between the individual and society. It was in the Puritan settlement that American society exacted its highest price; if the community was going to live at all, it would live at tremendous cost to the individual. *The Scarlet Letter* embodies Hawthorne's ambivalence about the Puritans as he expressed it in "Main Street": "Let us thank God for having given us such ancestors; and let each successive generation thank Him, not less fervently, for being one step further from them in the march of ages." The statement is a poised declaration of the attitude that informs *The Scarlet Letter*, in the novel there is a careful division of allegiances.

One prominent sign of that division is a series of cross-cultural references. Hawthorne compares the Puritan community of the past to his own present. The Puritans usually win the laurels. In a little review of Bunyan's "The Life and Death of Mr. Badman," which Hawthorne wrote for *The American Magazine of Useful and Entertaining Knowledge*, he says, "We doubt whether the present generation has not lost more than it has gained, by the philosophy which teaches it to laugh, rather than tremble, at such tales as these." In *The Scarlet Letter* Hawthorne frequently asks if the Puritans were not, far from being merely cruel, more honest and serious about human problems than his own contemporaries. Some of his commentary may seem ambiguous: the punishment of Hester Prynne was "a penalty, which in our days would infer a degree of mocking infamy and ridicule, might then be invested with almost as stern a dignity as the punishment of death itself." Is mocking infamy better or worse than the stern dignity associated with the death penalty? Hawthorne answers when he says that the scene of Hester's punishment "must always invest the spectacle of guilt and shame in a fellow-creature, before society shall have grown corrupt enough to smile, instead of shuddering, at it." Constantly these cultural cross-references appear in *The Scarlet Letter*, of a popular superstition about Hester's letter, Hawthorne says that there was "more truth in the rumor than our modern incredulity may be inclined to admit." "The discipline of the family, in those days, was of a far more rigid kind than now." Hawthorne does not dismiss the Puritans as a gloomy band; they were still invested with the old spirit of Merry England, "the offspring of sires who had known how to be merry." They were, Hawthorne suggests, capable of more merriment than his own contemporaries. Only the immediate posterity of the first settlers, "the generation next to the early emigrants," was the generation which "so darkened the national visage" that "we have yet to learn again the forgotten art of gayety."

In public places we see men of iron rigidity and women as rotundity. "The women who were now standing about the prison-door stood within less than half a century of the period when the man-like Elizabeth had been the not altogether unsuitable representative of the sex." The sun shines on "broad shoulders and well-developed busts, and on round and ruddy cheeks, that had ripened in the far-off island, and had hardly yet grown paler or thinner in the atmosphere of New England." In these cross-cultural references, we see Hawthorne indicating that the Puritan community, whatever its great errors, still had a vitality that was missing from the New England world of his own day. One female spectator to the punishment of Hester Prynne asks, "What think ye, gossips?" Another answers that the magistrates are "merciful overmuch" and "at the very least, they should have put the brand of a hot iron on Hester Prynne's forehead. Madam Hester would have winced at that, I warrant me." From the other wing of the crowd, a frightened man cries out, "Mercy on us, goodwife, is there no virtue in woman, save what springs from a wholesome fear of the gallows?" Of course there is. In the syrupy fiction of Hawthorne's contemporaries, the virtuous woman was always in bed, her single one.

There are no social situations in *The Scarlet Letter*. Relationships between people are driven to two extremes. On one hand, there are large public or ceremonial confrontations in the marketplace or the governor's manse where people are forced into categories (as the object lesson of sin or the defendant in a formal trial). On the other, there are scenes between just two or three persons, scenes in which private life becomes unbearable, since language has to carry between the two people all the emotion that has been submerged and can find release only in meetings that occur at wide intervals in time. There is no possibility for the development of a tradition of manners, for manners are not needed in this world. How could anyone say or do anything in "bad taste"? You are right or wrong, saved or damned. The one great release and efflorescence of submerged emotion in the book comes in the single, primitive social scene where the family has a brief, heretical reality: Hester, Dimmesdale, and Pearl in the forest.

In such a world Hawthorne worked confidently. He explored the region that Emerson, in *Society and Solitude*, located "underneath our domestic and neighborly life," where some "tragic necessity" is at work "driving each adult soul as with whips into the desert, and making our warm covenants sentimental and momentary." Through that place one goes down, Emerson says, "to a depth where society itself originates and disappears; where the question is, Which is first, man or men? where the individual is lost in his source." The Prison Door opens the book. Hawthorne calls the prison "the black flower of civilized society." In the opening chapter the war of Hawthorne's roses is between this "black flower" of civilization and the "wild rose-bush" of untamed nature. Symbolically, these flowers represent, respectively, the planned social order and the visible assertion of natural forces. The colors used in the description of the flowers impel the reader to identify the dismal flower with the soberly dressed community and the red rose with the fancifully embroidered A on Hester's bosom. When The Reverend Wilson asks Pearl who made her, the girl replies "that she had not been made at all, but had been plucked by her mother off the bush of wild roses that grew by the prison door." Pearl is usually right about these matters; in the economy of *The Scarlet Letter* she is metaphorically correct that she was born out of the passions that Hawthorne symbolizes by the red flower. The tension in the novel is between red flower and black prison, between natural impulse and repressive social force.

In exploring how this tension was organized in a people for whom "religion and law were almost identical," Hawthorne concentrates not on the theology but on its social manifestations. Hawthorne had not studied Edwards; he had read the Mathers more for history than theology. If religion and law are identical, our only way of apprehending that identity is in the way social organization expresses religious conviction. There is little disputation in the book about religious matters, no description of a church, no scene staged in one. It is the scaffold, not the church, that stands in the center of Boston. At the scaffold, where punishments are borne, we find the "congregation." Hawthorne is explicit about his charge against this congregation: "There can be no outrage, methinks, against our common nature—whatever be the delinquencies of the individual—no outrage more flagrant than to forbid the culprit to hide his face for shame, as it was the essence of this punishment to do so." The scarlet capital A is a verdict which Hawthorne issues against the community: it is the most "flagrant outrage that civilization can employ."

After noting in a newspaper that an opera was being based on *The Scarlet Letter*, Hawthorne wrote in his English notebooks that he thought "it might possibly succeed as an opera, though it would certainly fail as a play." This seems to me a remarkably keen insight into the nature of his work and its formal properties. Hawthorne knew he worked best with the isolated big scene, not with an accumulation of little scenes. His characters do not speak in the cut and thrust of actual dialogue; rather, they have arias, formal set-speeches in a formal setting.

The plot works that way, too. In *American Renaissance* F. O. Matthiessen says of *The Scarlet Letter* that "its symmetrical design is built around the three scenes on the scaffold of the pillory." True enough: there is a scene at the beginning, in the middle, and at the end; the three scaffold scenes rise up as the actual scaffold of the plot, giving it symmetry and formal poise. But that is something we recognize retrospectively; it is impossible for someone reading the book for the first time to say after reading the first two appearances on the pillory, "Two down, one to go."

Of equal structural importance is the way Hawthorne leads us to expect a private meeting between Hester and Dimmesdale. A discussion solely of the scaffold scenes in the novel's structure cannot account for our sense that the retreat into the forest is, as Hawthorne tells us it is, "the point whither their pathway had so long been tending." Since the novel centers on what happened when Hester and Dimmesdale were together privately, it builds a necessity for them to meet privately again, to meet and take up together what they had lived with separately. There is a prolonged postponement of this inevitable confrontation.

It is accurate to say that the three scaffold scenes are exactly half of the novel's design. The scaffold marks the necessity for public recognition, a place where that recognition must sooner or later be made. The other half of the picture is the forest where the private recognition must be made. Glade and pillory, these are the two ends of the road down which the novel moves.

A helpful question here is: where does the following sentence occur in the novel—near the beginning, the middle, or the end? Hawthorne writes that the face of Hester Prynne "was like a mask; or, rather, like the frozen calmness of a dead woman's features; owing this dreary resemblance to the fact that Hester was actually dead, in respect to any claim of sympathy." The answer to this question may tell us a good deal about the way the plot of *The Scarlet Letter* operates.

The sentence could come, of course, at the very beginning of the book when Hester is forced to stand alone facing the townspeople, when they point out to her that she is "actually dead" so far as their capacity to treat her as a woman instead of a "type of sin" is concerned. The sentence could also come in the middle section of the book when Hawthorne is describing the daily terms of Hester's new life, when on her errands through the city to the darkened sick rooms she must drop her eyes and assume a coldness of expression so that she will not have to endure the townspeople staring at her letter.

But the sentence describing Hester's aspect comes in chapter XXI, "The New England Holiday." Coming there, near the bitter end, it shows us that Hawthorne's descriptions remain, in one very important sense, static. Over and over again Hawthorne repeats the same device or provides a different context for the same meaning. There is a continual alternation between demands for speech ("Speak out the name!") and demands for silence ("Hush, hush.") Repeatedly Hester hushes Pearl when Pearl pesters her mother about who made her or cries for a rose. When Hester says to Dimmesdale that what they did "had a consecration of its own," Dimmesdale replies, "Hush, Hester." When at the end she asks him what he seeks in eternity, Dimmesdale again sighs, "Hush, Hester, hush." With the hushing there is also a pattern of great, startling sounds. Dimmesdale screams at midnight and hears his voice echoing about the hills; Pearl's shriek at the brookside "reverberated on all sides." The sighing wind in the forest, the far-off sound of Dimmesdale's voice, which Hester hears from her position outside the church, and, most dramatically, Pearl's continual laughing indicate the great auditory resonance of the book. In "Ethan Brand" Hawthorne wrote that "Laughter, when out of place, mistimed, or bursting forth from a disordered state of feeling, may be the most terrible modulation of the human voice." It was so in "My Kinsman, Major Molineux"; it is so in *The Scarlet Letter*. While Hawthorne works extremely hard to elaborate the A—even flashing it across the cope of Heaven—there are far more convincing and successful reverberations in the laughter of Pearl at what are, for her parents, all the wrong places.

The central sin of the book, adultery, is a close analogue to Original Sin; Hester gives Dimmesdale the apple of sexual knowledge; they are forced out of Paradise (the soul-saving, repressive paradise that Boston, the City of Man, represents). The plot tells, in one sense, the story of exile; there are, throughout the book, many journeys. Hester walks from prison to scaffold, and later through the streets; Chillingworth plods around the forest looking for medicinal herbs; Dimmesdale, near the end, wanders from the forest to the town. The book emphasizes these casual and formal motions—"A Forest Walk" and "The Procession"—to show how paths meet and cross in public and in private. In *The Scarlet Letter* the minds of the central figures fall in and out of their "accustomed tracks."

Hester pays in public and expiates her sin in private; Dimmesdale pays in private and expiates his sin in public. Evil is emblazoned on Hester, and she keeps her sanity; Dimmesdale loses his sanity by keeping his evil a secret. At the opening of the novel the people stand in rigid censure, motionless; at the end, there is a pageant of Indians and sailors, and Pearl spinning through them. In this counterpoise the narrative power accumulates through a series of static scenes separated by long stretches of time. That power does not fully gather itself and burst into action until the entire story veers off into another direction, when the two stories—Hester–Pearl and Dimmesdale–Chillingworth—come together. The first half of the novel oscillates between the two histories. On the one hand we see Hester and Pearl, enduring together the stings of the community. The emphasis is on Hester's life; the few encounters between her and the others suggest her loneliness. When she meets Dimmesdale she meets him in public (Governor Bellingham's manse) where she must operate on his ability to apprehend what she is saying as something radically more than what her public voice indicates: "Thou wast my pastor, and hadst charge of my soul, and knowest me better than these men can." But Dimmesdale did not only beget Pearl; he begot Chillingworth as well; thus, the first half of the novel is also the story of the two men and how they live together.

Compare a chapter in the first half, "The Interview," with one in the second half, "A Flood of Sunshine." They belong to different fictive planes. The first is a scene of temptation; Hester wonders if Chillingworth is "The Black Man." It is an encounter which sets the work in motion; it is done in the rhetoric of formal speech. But "A Flood of Sunshine" shows Hawthorne's attempt to escape the formal emblematic picture and to attain the condition of fiction as a realistic portrayal of the psychological play of two characters. The first half of the book, in which "The Interview" occurs, covers seven years. The second half deals with time in measured hours, just a few days. Between the first and the second scaffold scenes Hawthorne goes over the elapsed time once in terms of Hester and Pearl, then again in terms of Dimmesdale and Chillingworth. Between the second and third scaffold scenes the narrative moves straight ahead, no backtracking.

The difference between the time of the first and second halves of the book lies not solely in the length of the elapsed time but rather in the conception of the way time itself operates. In the first section time is all there for Hawthorne; it exists as a stable and completed unit to be taken up, deployed, shifted, and manipulated. The people are as they are; they are presented in significant, emblematic moments. But in the later chapters, time carries people with it. The characters do not exist in extratemporal moments when Hawthorne can lift them off the continuous screen of time. Time rushes on; there is no time to go back over. People exist not just as they are but as they are becoming.

Now we are better prepared to come to terms with a central question: does *The Scarlet Letter* move toward the forest scene in chapters XVII, XVIII, and XIX or toward the final scaffold scene in chapter XXIII? The book leads us to expect that Hester and Dimmesdale will meet in private before the story is done. Hawthorne gives us, as a place of privacy where antisocial meetings are consummated, the forest. It is the domain of Mistress Hibbins, the "dark recess" from community control. The forest is the amphitheater of the "wild rose-bush." It is the place where the outsider knows "that the deep heart of Nature could pity and be kind to him." In the first chapter Hawthorne plucks a flower from his rose bush and presents it to the reader. "It may serve," he says, "to symbolize some sweet moral blossom, that may be found along the track, or relieve the darkening close of a tale of human frailty and sorrow." In the forest scene he offers the blossom again, in all its vitality, to relieve the darkening tale.

Hester, who has repeatedly been identified as a wanderer of "desert places," meets Dimmesdale, literally, on her own ground. We know they cannot meet in town. Hawthorne makes it impossible for them to meet there. "Hester never thought of meeting him in any narrower privacy than beneath the open sky." It is a personal transaction. As Hester later explains to Pearl, "We must not always talk in the market-place of what happens to us in the forest." "Kisses," she explains, "are not to be given in the market-place."

The tie between Hester and Dimmesdale "like all other ties ... brought along with it its obligation." "Having cast off all duty towards other human beings, there remained a duty towards him." Hester recognizes human responsibility as a primitive social contract, the most primitive possible. She thinks of herself as "playing a part," a social role in the world. But with Dimmesdale, she feels that the part is generated entirely from within, not stamped upon her by public power.

In preparation for the meeting Hawthorne gives us two chapters dealing with Hester and Pearl together, domestic scenes, which develop a familiar intimacy. Dimmesdale in his nocturnal vigils before his looking glass, has asked the same question Hester has in her lonely walks through the city streets and out in the wilderness—Who am I? Am I the being I privately know myself to be, or am I the person this formidable community insists on my being? Why is secrecy and shame the reward for engaging my deepest energy?

The most dramatic scene in the book answers these questions with imaginative generosity. This scene has always seemed to me—in spite of the usual attention paid to the three great pillory scenes—the finest thing in the novel and its true center. One day, by chance Arthur Dimmesdale and Hester Prynne meet on the outskirts of town. They talk only a bit, but their conversation manages to release all their original passion. The first question when the adulterers meet is about each other's "bodily existence." This far apart they have come. They had been "intimately connected in their former life, but now stood coldly shuddering." After all the proliferation of meaning, "The soul beheld its features in the mirror of the passing moment." It is, for me, the most beautiful sentence Hawthorne ever wrote. The entire book has raised the question: how and where does a soul behold its features? No speeches. "Without a word more spoken" the two of them in a dream-like state "glided back into the shadow of the woods." The richness of the prose indicates that what is occurring is a re-efflorescence of their original sin; they respond to each other as private persons rather than as official personages and "now felt themselves, at least, inhabitants of the same sphere."

"When they found a voice to speak, it was, at first, only to utter remarks and inquiries such as any two acquaintances might have made, about the gloomy sky, the threatening storm ..." We wait and wait and what happens? Very simply, Hester Prynne and Arthur Dimmesdale talk about the weather. Which is entirely right: we see the characters meeting each other with the customary social awkwardness. The great jar of the scene is that suddenly, in the midst of categorical punishment and the proliferation of symbolic significance, two sinners emerge from behind their social disguises to expose their humanity.

In "The Pastor and His Parishioner," the roles are reversed; Hester gives her pastoral counsel and takes off her cap; the whole scene vibrates with her released sexuality. "Her sex, her youth, and the whole richness of her beauty, came back from what men call the irrevocable past, and clustered themselves, with her maiden hope, and happiness before unknown, within the magic circle of this hour."

Holmes said of Hawthorne that "talking with him was almost like love-making." In the forest scene of *The Scarlet Letter*, talking becomes a kind of love-making. Since this is the only scene where the lovers privately come together, their long separation produces extreme richness of feeling in the smallest word.

"Alone, Hester!"
    "Thou shalt not go alone!" answered she, in a deep whisper.
    Then all was spoken.

The tongue of flame is resonant silence. It is Hawthorne's moment of terrible simplicity—the novel, the huge super-structure of multiplying allegorical signs splinters down to all that needs, for the time, to be said—all that, for this time, can be said. It is an arresting declaration; the form of the great work almost seems to catch its breath, for its central point has just been laid bare in small words. Hawthorne accomplishes in silence what he could not in great sound, for the point of *The Scarlet Letter* is to subvert the resonance of public speech. Hester cries out for forgiveness, admitting that Chillingworth is her husband; when Dimmesdale is staggered, "With sudden and desperate tenderness, she threw her arms around him, and pressed his head against her bosom; little caring though his cheek rested on the scarlet letter." The image is as powerful as anything in our literature. Hester whispers, "What we did had a consecration of its own." That line is justly celebrated as the finest in the book. But what I cherish are the next two short sentences: Hester says, "We felt it so! We said so to each other!"

But the heretical reality of the scene is brief. Hester urges flight to Europe; Dimmesdale knows he can not run away. When I first began teaching *The Scarlet Letter* to Cornell students in the late 1960s, the scene in the forest was what most appealed to them. The imaginative power of the real encounter felt right; that was their Hawthorne—the "*real*" Hawthorne—as if the rest of the book was just the time he lived in. When the catchphrases on campus were "Make Love, Not War" and "Flower Power," young readers tended to sentimentalize the book for their own radical and visionary purposes. Now, however, students are more inclined to accept the forest scene for what it is, a "flood of sunshine" that is by definition only momentary. The right reading comes at great cost—sometimes I long for the days when enthusiasm got it wrong. But Hawthorne himself placed his great scene of escape in a stern context of return.

The Scarlet Letter has for its subject the tension between personal desire and community solidarity. In the forest scene we have been presented with the first; now, at the end of the book, the energy released in the forest is poured into the old context, the brutalizing categories of the Puritan state. Dimmesdale achieves what Hawthorne calls "the tongue of flame"; his congregation senses a power and humanity in him that they had never known before. But when he emerges from the church and totters to the pillory, the book begins to falter. In the forest scene Hester had pleaded, "Do anything, save to lie down and die." On the scaffold Dimmesdale lies down and dies. Hawthorne seems to indicate that Dimmesdale has thus saved his immortal soul. The problem is that in throwing himself on God's mercy, Dimmesdale abandons Hester and Pearl. As Michael Colacurcio puts it: "fleeing from the arms of Hester Prynne to those of the heavenly bridegroom his own (rather too feminine) nature finally manages to prefer." Dimmesdale has never been Hester's husband, Colacurcio insists, "and it would only be a little cruel to suggest that he is dying to evade that very role." D. H. Lawrence puts it aptly: the ending shows Dimmesdale "dodging into death, leaving Hester dished."

At the end of the book Hawthorne retreats into Phoebe-talk: "The angel and apostle of the coming revelation must be a woman, indeed, but lofty, pure, and beautiful: and wise, moreover not through dusky grief, but the ethereal medium of joy and showing how sacred love should make us happy." Sacvan Bercovitch has it backwards when he writes of these lines that "the entire novel tends toward this moment of reconciliation." Bercovitch says "this is not some formulaic Victorian ending." I think it is: the critical necessity is to see that Hawthorne certainly does mean this, and at the same time to see that it is a violent contradiction of the most serious motive in the novel. We must not mistake the statement at the end of the book for anything other than what it is—a pious retraction.

There is, however, on the very last page, a partial recovery. Dimmesdale has celebrated in his dying sermon the great America to be; what we know of the future is that Hester returns. She knows her fate. In chapter 14 she had protested that "it lies not in the pleasure of the magistrates to take off this badge." She returns to bear that out. Finally the A is Hester and Hester knows it. "There was more real life for Hester Prynne, here in New England than in that unknown region where Pearl had found a home." The A becomes her. Hester belongs in Boston precisely because she is the single person who has not been allowed to belong there. She has turned a badge of shame into a coat of arms.

A NOTE ON SOURCES

For the convenience of the reader, not to mention my own, I have used Norton Critical Editions wherever possible. For three reasons: first, the texts are impeccable; second, several critical essays from which I quote appear as afterwords in those editions; third, each edition has an extremely helpful "Selected Bibliography." I recommend the Modern Library edition of *The Bostonians* (1956) and the Penguin Classic *What Maisie Knew* (1985); for all the rest, the reader can rely confidently on the Nortons: *The Scarlet Letter, Nathaniel Hawthorne's Tales, The Blithedale Romance, Tales of Henry James, The Portrait of a Lady* (2d. ed.), *The Ambassadors, The Turn of the Screw* (2d. ed.), and *Emerson's Poetry and Prose*. I have also made rather free use of the *Henry James Review*, especially the issue devoted to *Portrait* (Winter-Spring, 1986). Other works—some old, some new, some brilliant, some awful, all interesting if only by negative example are briefly noted here in the order in which they are cited in my book.

Stephen Donadio, "Emerson, Christian Identity, and the Dissolution of the Social Order," in *Art, Politics, and Will: Essays in Honor of Lionel Trilling* (1997) and *Nietzsche, Henry James, And the Artistic Will* (1978).

Lionel Trilling, "Our Hawthorne" in *Hawthorne Centenary Essays* (1964).

Millicent Bell, *Meaning in Henry James* (1991).

James R. Mellow, *Nathaniel Hawthorne in His Times* (1980).

Michael J. Colacurcio, "The Woman's Own Choice," in *New Essays on "The Scarlet Letter"* (1985).

Sacvan Bercovitch, "Hawthorne's A—Morality of Compromise," in the St. Martin's Press ed. of *The Scarlet Letter* (1991).

David Van Leer, "Hester's Labyrinth" in *New Essays* (1985).

Darrel Abel, *American Literature*, especially volumes 2 and 3 (1963).

David B. Davis, *Homicide and American Fiction* (1957).

Irving Howe, *Politics and the Novel* (1957) and *The American Newness* (1978).

Judith Fetterley, *The Resisting Reader: A Feminist Approach to American Fiction* (1978).

J. Hillis Miller, *Hawthorne and History* (1991).

Caroline Gordon and Allen Tate on "Young Goodman Brown" in *The House of Fiction* (1954).

Philip Horne, *Henry James and Revision* (1990).

Eve Kosofsky Sedgwick, "The Beast in the Closet: James and the Writing of Homosexual Panic," in *Sex, Politics, and Science in the Nineteenth-Century Novel* (1986).

Shoshana Felman, "The grasp with which I recovered him," in *Henry James, The Turn of the Screw: Studies in Contemporary Criticism* (1995).

Stanley Penner, "Red hair, very red, close-curling," in ibid.

Joseph Wiesenfarth, "A Woman in *Portrait of a Lady*," *HJR*, special *Portrait* issue (1986).

Cheryl B. Torsney, "The Political Context," ibid.

Tony Tanner, "The Fearful Self" in *Henry James: Modern Judgments* (1968).

Dorothea Krook, *The Ordeal of Consciousness in Henry James* (1962).

Peter Buitenhuis, "Introduction," *Twentieth-Century Interpretations of "The Portrait of a Lady"* (1968).

Fred Kaplan, *Henry James: The Imagination of a Genius* (1992).

Alfred Habegger, *Henry James and the "Woman Business"* (1989).

DAVID B. KESTERSON

Hawthorne's *"Mad, Merry Stream of Human Life"*: *The Roman Carnival as Apocalypse in* The Marble Faun

The Roman Carnival that Hawthorne wrote about in his letters and Italian notebooks of 1858 and 1859 and used strategically as the climactic scene in his last completed novel, *The Marble Faun* (1860), boasts a storied and colorful past.

The origins of the famous Carnival at Rome associated with pre-Lenten activities were in the pagan rites of the pre-Christian era. From early times pagan communities in Babylonia, Egypt, Greece, Rome, and perhaps others unrecorded, staged "parades, masquerades, pageants, and other forms of revelry" whose origins lay in fertility rites associated with the arrival of spring and the rebirth of vegetation.[1] Early examples of such festivals were celebrations of Osiris in Egypt and of Dionysus in the Athens of the sixth century B.C., the latter of which, as historical record reveals, saw the first use of floats for spring festivals.[2] During the era of the Roman Empire, the main carnivals in Rome, whose origins were folk celebrations and the Greek Mysteries of Dionysis, were the Bacchanalia, honoring the god of wine and revelry; the Saturnalia, in honor of the god of agriculture; and the Lupercalia, a festival of fertility rites held to celebrate the pastoral god Lupercus.

Since all of these carnivals were the outgrowth of folk and pagan traditions, when Christianity gained a foothold in the Roman Empire, the

From *Value and Vision in American Literature: Literary Essays in Honor of Ray Lewis White*, ed. Joseph Candido, pp. 95-114. © 1999 by Joseph Candido.

Catholic church was powerless to stop them and ultimately had to adopt them, especially the Saturnalia, as part of Christian religious celebrations, albeit in reformed modes. Immediate church influence was seen in the Feast of Fools, which included a mock mass, and the Feast of the Ass, which "retained pagan rites and was at times very bawdy."[3] Gradually, however, the church's influence overtook many of the Carnival proceedings, and they were transformed into a single extended celebration closely associated with Lent, the eight-day celebration beginning the Tuesday before Shrove (or Fat) Tuesday and concluding on that notable day before Lent itself began. In fact, the word *carnival* itself possibly derives from Medieval Latin *carnem levare* or *carnelevarium* (*caro* meaning flesh and *levare* to put aside), thus referring to abstinence from meat during the forty days of the Christian Lenten season each year.[4]

During medieval times the church so controlled the Roman Carnival that it lost much of its festive flavor, but fifteenth-century Renaissance Rome saw the return of carnival "high jinks and horrors of ancient times."[5] Pietro Barbo, or Pope Paul II (1464–71), took such delight in the celebration that he set up horse races and other varieties of races in the spirit of good, clean fun: races for children, young Christians, middle-aged men, senior citizens, buffaloes, and donkeys. These races, or *corsi*, extended from the pope's Palazzo Venezia at the south end and proceeded north along the city section of the Via Flaminia, which in time assumed the name Via del Corso. The Corso is the longest and straightest street in old Rome, extending about a mile from the Palazzo Venezia to the Piazza del Popolo; thus despite its narrowness, it was most suited to the prolonged races. As the festival continued over the years, however, Pope Paul II allowed the races to degenerate into what Sir Rennell Rodd calls "unseemly contests" that included races by hunchbacks and other disabled persons, Jews (who were tormented by the crowd along the route), and naked old men—all of whom were pursued by mounted troopers. In later years the horse races became riderless.[6]

After the Renaissance, the Carnival began to decline in magnitude and deviltry. It was only up to the time of the mid-seventeenth century, Mikhail Bakhtin observes, that people "were *direct participants* in carnivalistic acts and in a carnival sense of the world."[7] As the city of Rome expanded, rowdiness prevailed to the extent that it grew "impossible any longer to abandon the main thoroughfare of the capital city to a week of misrule."[8] As we know from Hawthorne's remarks in 1858–59, the Carnival was long past its prime then, and it continued to decline until by the beginning of the twentieth century it hardly resembled its storied past. Present-day remnants exist mainly on Shrove Tuesday, which is the day carnival-goers in costume flock to the city's piazzas as part of pre-Lenten activities.

Along with Hawthorne's extensive commentary on the Carnival in the late 1850s, other writers have recorded their observations of the spectacle. John Evelyn, while in Rome in the winter and spring of 1645, took in the "impertinences" of the Carnival, finding the area "swarming with whores, buffoones & all manner of rabble."[9] Goethe, who lived along the Corso from November 1786 to April 1788, comments extensively on the Carnival in his *Italian Journey* of 1788. He lambastes the Carnival for its inability to "make an altogether agreeable impression: it will neither please ... [the] eye nor appeal to ... emotions"; moreover, "the noise is deafening, and the end of each day unsatisfactory."[10] Closer to Hawthorne's time, and reacting much less negatively to the event, Charles Dickens describes the Carnival in *Pictures from Italy* (1846), focusing on the "bewitching madness" of the costumes and painting a graphic picture of the balconies on almost every house decked out as viewing boxes for the parade—the balconies so haphazard in their architectural placement that, Dickens says, "if year after year, and season after season, it had rained balconies, hailed balconies, snowed balconies, blown balconies, they could scarcely have come into existence in a more disorderly manner.[11]

Shortly after Hawthorne's Italian sojourn, in 1873, Henry James witnessed the Carnival and, in *Italian Hours*, discusses it more in a political context. He states that the Carnival was a more joyous occasion before the recent political unification of Italy.[12] "The fashion of public revelry has woefully fallen out of step.... Now that Italy is made the Carnival is unmade.[13] He says that a traveler, once used to the fully papal Rome and returning now, "must have immediately noticed that something momentous had happened—something hostile to the elements of picture and color and style" (136–37). The Carnival scene, in a Corso always well trafficked but now "a perpetual crush" (137), is not pretty—it's "degenerated" (139): the women wear ugly masks of wire, and flour and lime shower down on celebrants and bystanders alike, tossed by people on the balconies above. James himself experienced the dumping of a "half a bushel of flour on my too-philosophic head" (139). Leaving the scene and attempting to skirt around the perimeter of Rome to avoid the Corso, "his ears full of flour," he discovers that "do what you will you can't really elude the Carnival" (139–40). James concludes that "the Carnival had received its death-blow in my imagination" (139).

Generally sharing James's views some thirty-five years later, William Dean Howells witnessed the Carnival in 1908 in its twilight years. He remarks, "It was the eve of the last sad day of such shrunken and faded carnival as is still left to Rome," and notices a few children in holiday costumes and young girls in a cab "safely masked against identification and venting in the sense of wild escape, the joyous spirits kept in restraint all the rest of the year."[14]

Francis Wey describes the Carnival of the 1880s in detail, including the political background of recent events when Rome was annexed to the rest of Italy. His depiction of the scene in the Corso, with "hailstones of plaster" pelting the revelers, is vivid. He echoes James's lime- and flour-covered image, and his elaborate description of the gaiety, especially on Shrove Tuesday, is one of the most detailed in print. In a meaningful comment that embraces to some degree the feelings of both Hawthorne and Kenyon in *The Marble Faun*, and more certainly the philosophy of Carnival voiced by Mikhail Bakhtin, Wey concludes, "If you were alone, you would lose your sense of isolation, for everybody accosts you, and, making merry with you or at you, offers himself as a butt for your whims."[15]

Finally, Sir Rennell Rodd in *Rome of the Renaissance and Today* (1932) describes the Carnival of the 1870s as follows: "All the Balconies were draped and filled with merry companies. Elaborately decorated cars with allegorical groups and carriages filled with masqueraders drove up and down in continuous procession." Everyone in the streets was costumed, "and the prudent provided themselves with wire masks because not only were flowers and sweetmeats thrown from the balconies, but a lively battle was maintained with little pellets of lime-whitened day about the size of a pen, called coriandoli, which gave a stinging blow on the face." At the end of the week of revelry, "everyone lighted a taper and the whole length of the Corso glittered with little flames. The revel continued till midnight. Then the church bells rang. The sound of merriment died away. It was Lent, and weeks of abstinence and penitence ensued."[16]

Following his service as U.S. consul to Liverpool, England, Nathaniel Hawthorne and Sophia, their three children, and governess Ada Shepard visited France briefly and then traveled on to Italy, where they were to live for a total of seventeen months. They resided in Rome from January to June 1858, in Florence from June to October, then back in Rome for a second sojourn that extended from October until May of 1859. Thus Hawthorne was in Rome during two of the annual pre-Lenten Carnivals, and he availed himself of both of them.

In keeping with his ambivalent feelings about Rome in general, Hawthorne unsurprisingly developed a like–dislike attitude toward the Carnival, as reflected in his letters, notebooks, and *The Marble Faun* itself.

His negative reaction to the first Carnival he witnessed, in 1858, was caused in large part, it seems, by the wet, gloomy weather that held for the duration of the celebration.[17] On February 9, 1858, Hawthorne comments in his notebooks on the preparation for the Carnival, noting "bouquets ... bounteously for sale, in the shops and at the street corners ... and reservoirs of ammunition in the shape of sugar-plums and little pellets of paste or chalk." But he questions "whether the Romans themselves take any great interest in the Carnival: The balconies along the Corso are almost entirely taken by English, Americans, or other foreigners."[18] A few days later (February 13, 1858) he writes a long, detailed description of the Carnival and all its trappings. He records being hit in the eye with a sugarplum "made up of lime—or bad flour at best—with oats or worthless seeds as a nucleus" (64). Disappointed with the whole affair, he comments dispiritedly that the Carnival has simply grown old and tiresome and seems to appeal more to foreigners (especially Americans and the British) than to Italians themselves. He notes that the Roman bystanders were not even smiling and appeared to be having anything but a good time. He quips, "The whole affair is not worth this page or two," concluding, "I never in my life knew a shallower joke than the Carnival of Rome" (70).

The next day, February 14, 1858, he takes younger daughter Rose with him along the fringes of the Carnival vicinity up on the Pincian Hill's "safe heights" above the Piazza del Popolo, where they watch the festivities before descending to the Corso. He sees revelers arrested for throwing lime at will and observes that the jollity of the Carnival "does not extend an inch beyond the line of the Corso," where it "flows along in a narrow stream." Beyond that one sees "nothing but the ordinary Roman gravity" (76). The day following, February 15, he notes that several people were killed in the Corso, either trampled by the racing horses or by the dragoons clearing the racecourse (78–79). Two days later, on the last afternoon and evening of the Carnival, he and Rose again attend the festivities together and stand at the edge of the crowd, while Sophia, Una, and Julian occupy a hired balcony above the Corso. In the midst of showers of falling confetti, Rose catches a bouquet while Hawthorne is hit with a cabbage-like object, undoubtedly informing his comment in the *Notebooks* that the Carnival is most enjoyed by those under twenty (83). However unimpressed is he with the event, however, he nevertheless muses over the possibility that "I could make quite a brilliant sketch of it, without widely departing from truth" (83).

Interestingly, the next year, 1859, after his several months in Florence, Hawthorne's reactions to the Carnival are much more sanguine.[19] Describing preparations for the Carnival on February 27, he remarks in his notebook about the bright sunshine as opposed to the rain and gloom of the previous year. After enumerating all the necessary supplies for the Carnival that fill the shops (especially the "masks of wire, pasteboard, silk, or cloth, some of beautiful features, others hideous; fantastic, currish, asinine, huge-nosed, or otherwise monstrous" (496–97), he concedes, getting caught up in the spirit of it all, "I could have bandied confetti and nosegays as readily and riotously as any urchin there. But my black hat and grave Talma would have been too good a mark for the combatants" (499). A few days later, March 4, in a letter to his publisher William D. Ticknor, he writes with surprising levity: "We are now in the height of the Carnival, and the young people find it great fun. To say the Truth, so do I; but I suppose I should have enjoyed it still better at twenty."[20] In the remaining days of the 1859 Carnival he records in his *Notebooks* that he enjoys the festivities "better ... than could have been expected" and witnesses the events "principally in the street, as a mere looker-on (which does not let one into the mystery of the fun) and twice from the balcony whence I threw confetti and partly understood why the young people like it so much" (499). Yet he is also puzzled by something elusive about the spirit and gist of the Carnival—something about its mystery: when he tries to isolate and focus on any one humorous masquerader for detailed description and comment, the figure tends to slip out of his hands and vanish; still, he remarks that "there really was fun in the spectacle as it flitted by" (500).

In a similar observation, when he and Una attend the next day, March 8, and sit in Mrs. (Mary Elizabeth Benjamin) Motley's balcony in the Corso, he writes that the passing "spectacle is strangely like a dream, in respect to the difficulty of retaining it in the mind and solidifying it into a description" (501). But he still enjoys it enough that he does his part "to pelt all the people in cylinder hats with handfulls of confetti" (501). He is also complimentary of the behavior of the throng, as opposed to the unruly way similar crowds would act in England or America. He marvels at "how people can let loose all their mirthful propensities without unchaining their mischievous ones" (502).

On the closing day of the 1859 festival, after eight "playdays," as he designates them, Hawthorne again observes the celebration from both the street level and Mrs. Motley's balcony. Standing on the street among the crowd, he takes pains to describe the lower-class bystanders around him: the women, "generally broad and sturdy figures," wearing large silver or steel bodkins in their hair (503). This last day, ominously, is sunless, rendering the costumes and decorations drab and shabby looking. Yet Hawthorne's appraisal of the event remains positive: it might appear a depressing spectacle to the bystander, but even if one should take "the slightest share in it, you become aware that it has a fascination" (503–4). He then describes in detail the closing ritual of the last night—the "Mocollo"—as the revelers crowd the Corso with lighted tapers, or Roman candles, in hand shouting, "Senza Moccolo," and the participants try hard to extinguish the candles of those around them.[21] As the lights flicker and die, gaslights, which Hawthorne refers to as the "fixed stars" of the "transitory splendors of human life," are illuminated and overpower the scattered mocolli (504). So the Carnival ends, with Hawthorne curiously admitting that he is "glad that it is over" (504). His journal entry on the next morning reads, ironically, "but, to-day, we have waked up in the sad and sober season of Lent" (505).

Carnival, then, was a phenomenon that played on Hawthorne's mind and creative imagination while he was in Italy, as indeed it did over his entire career as a writer. We recall the carnivalized revelers in "The May-Pole of Merrymount," the unruly spectacle of the "parade" that rides Major Molineaux out of town to waves of raucous laughter in "My Kinsman, Major Molineaux," the boisterous, grotesque Black Sabbath celebration in "Young Goodman Brown," the joyous political parade passing along Pyncheon Street under the arched window in *The House of the Seven Gables*, the colorful election day festivities in *The Scarlet Letter*, and the pastoral frolics of the main characters in the bucolic fields of Blithedale Farm in *The Blithedale Romance*—all instances of what Nina Baym refers to as the "Walpurgisnacht" scenes that appear throughout Hawthorne's fiction.[22]

It was thus out of an act of self-effacement or calculated understatement that Hawthorne wrote to his publisher and friend James T. Fields from Leamington on February 11, 1860, "received your letter from Florence, and conclude that you are now in Rome, and probably enjoying the Carnival—a *tame* description of which, by the by, I have introduced into my Romance."[23] Hawthorne's denoting the Carnival scenes of *The Marble Faun* a "tame" description, of course, has to be taken with a grain of salt, for chapters 48 and 49, "A Scene in the Corso," and "A Frolic of the Carnival," are the key climactic chapters of the novel in which we discern the fates of all four major characters: the two Americans, Kenyon and Hilda, and the two Italians, Donatello and Miriam. Further, there are significant foreshadowings of the Carnival chapters in the novel, episodes in which the main characters are caught up in rare displays of joy and abandon in this otherwise dark tale.

Such instances include three chapters early in the novel and two just before the Carnival scene. Chapters 8, "The Suburban Villa," 9, "The Faun and Nymph," and 10, "The Sylvan Dance," all take place in the woods of the Villa Borghese and depict Donatello and Miriam caught up in lighthearted frolicking and sporting repartee until, in the midst of their mirthful sylvan dance, Miriam is suddenly confronted by the sinister figure of the model. Then late in the book, just before the Carnival episode, chapters 46 and 47 depict Kenyon's pleasant stroll on the Campagna and an unexpected happy encounter with Miriam and Donatello, both of whom are already dressed in costume for the Carnival: Donatello as a young peasant in "short blue jacket, the small-clothes buttoned at the knee, and buckled shoes" and Miriam "in one of those brilliant costumes, largely kindled up with scarlet, and decorated with gold embroidery, in which the contadinas array themselves on feast-days."[24] It is a significant scene in which Kenyon finds the fragmented statue of the Venus figure that Miriam and Donatello had discovered two days earlier. In a fleeting moment, before the weight of Miriam's and Donatello's fates settles on them oppressively, Miriam exhorts, "Ah, Donatello, let us live a little longer the life of these last few days! It is so bright, so airy, so childlike, so without either past or future! Here, on the wild Campagna, you seem to have found, both for yourself and me, the life that belonged to you in early youth; the sweet, irresponsible life which you inherited from your mythic ancestry, the Fauns of Monte Beni. Our stern and black reality will come upon us speedily enough. But, first, a brief time more of this strange happiness!" (428).

For the last time, it appears to Kenyon that Donatello has regained "some of the sweet and delightful characteristics of the antique Faun.... There were slight, careless graces, pleasant and simple peculiarities, that had been obliterated by the heavy grief" incurred by hurtling the model to his death off the Tarpeian Rock, with Miriam's tacit consent (433–34). This scene on the Campagna, of course, with its lighthearted yet soon chastened emotions directly presages the Carnival scene, which follows immediately. And it is here that Miriam instructs Kenyon how to become reunited with Hilda, who has been ominously missing for several days (and we know is being held for questioning by authorities about the murder of the model/monk). Miriam advises Kenyon, "The day after tomorrow ... an hour before sunset, go to the Corso, and stand in front of the fifth house on your left, beyond the Antonine Column. You will learn tidings of a friend!" (435). And then the "happy ... flitting moment" on the Campagna passes and Miriam and Donatello—momentarily having been "sylvan Faun" and "Nymph of grove or fountain"—depart, a "remorseful Man and Woman, linked by a marriage-bond of crime," setting forth "towards an inevitable goal" (435).

Thus many elements of *The Marble Faun* lead into chapters 48–49, set during the Carnival itself. On the appointed day during the celebration, Kenyon shows up on the Corso an hour earlier than Miriam instructed, hoping to find Hilda. He discovers the "merriment of this famous festival ... in full progress." The Corso "was peopled with hundreds of fantastic shapes, some of which probably represented the mirth of ancient times, surviving through all manner of calamity, ever since the days of the Roman Empire. For a few afternoons of early Spring, this mouldy gayety strays into the sunshine; all the remainder of the year, it seems to be shut up in the catacombs or some other sepulchral store-house of the past" (436).

Briefly, what happens in these two chapters, "A Scene in the Corso" and "A Frolic of the Carnival," is that Kenyon becomes caught up in the throng of revelers and all the trappings of the festival as he awaits sight of Hilda. In contrast to his state of anxiety and melancholy, the scene about him is resplendent with gay colors and beautiful flowers and other decorations. Hawthorne tells us that had Kenyon been of lighter mood and able to see it all with his "clear, natural eye-sight, he might have found both merriment and splendour in it" (438). Bushel baskets of bouquets were for sale at every street corner, the Corso itself a "spectacle ... picturesque" as from every window and many balconies along "that noble street, stretching into the interminable distance" hung "gay and gorgeous carpets, bright silks, scarlet cloths with rich golden fringes, and Gobelin tapestry, still lustrous with varied hues" (438), and in every window were "the faces of women, rosy girls, and children, all kindled into brisk and mirthful expression by the incidents in the street below" (439). Fake sugar plums of lime and oat kernel were thrown up from the streets and sometimes down from the balconies, while "a gentler warfare of flowers was carried on, principally between knights and ladies." These bouquets, we are told, in former times were pretty and fresh; however, the present nosegays, hastily bundled by "sordid hands," are made up chiefly of ordinary flowers. Further, the current-day flowers are recycled, being picked up out of the streets wilted and muddy and quickly resold, "defiled as they all are with the wicked filth of Rome" (440). Originally gathered by young people out of the nearby fields or their own gardens, they were "flung ... with true aim, at the one, or few, whom they regarded with a sentiment of shy partiality at least, if not with love.... What more appropriate mode of suggesting her tender secret could a maiden find than by the soft hit of a rosebud against a young man's cheek" (440).

While waiting and watching amid the hurly-burly of the day, Kenyon catches sight of Miriam and Donatello, in their costumes worn on the Campagna, but this time each with face concealed behind "an impenetrable black mask" (443). Shortly afterward, the two figures, hand in hand, reappear out of the crowd and all three clasp hands momentarily in forming an ephemeral "linked circle of three" before they part, uttering "Farewell" in unison (448). Donatello and Miriam are almost immediately detained by

Roman officials, and at the same time, symbolically, Kenyon is hit by two
missiles—a cauliflower, "flung by a young man from a passing carriage"
(451), and a rose-bud "so fresh that it seemed that moment gathered" tossed
by Hilda, dressed all in white domino, from a balcony occupied by an
English family. Hilda smiles down on Kenyon with "a gleam of delicate
mirthfulness in her eyes," which Kenyon "had seen there only two or three
times, in the course of their acquaintance, but thought it the most bewitching
and fairy-like of all Hilda's expressions" (451). That night, Hilda returns to
her quarters in her "Virgin's shrine," relights the lamp that had been
extinguished during her absence and now which "burned as brightly" as if it
had never been cold, and the next morning is greeted by the one faithful dove
that had not deserted her ethereal mistress during her absence (454). The
Carnival scene, in short, is one of joy and gloom, as Rita Gollin has observed:
"The moment of Donatello's arrest is the moment Hilda is released from
confinement."[25]

When approaching the meaning of these two chapters that constitute
the crucial Carnival scene in the novel, it is fruitful to look closely first at the
language that Hawthorne uses in describing the dynamic of the Carnival.[26]
His phrases are very telling, many of them reflecting on Kenyon's mixed
attitude toward the festivities occurring all around him. Hawthorne writes of
the "merriment of this famous festival" (436) in which some of the "fantastic
shapes represented the mirth of ancient times" (436). The present Carnival,
however, exudes a "mouldy gayety" and is an institution of mere "shallow
influence" with "flagging mirth," a "worn-out festival" (436–37). It is a
"grotesque and airy riot" (437) to be enjoyed by youth, but to Kenyon it
seems but "the emptiest of mockeries" (437). It is "a spectacle ... fantastic and
extravagant" (441), a "wild frolic" (451), "the tumult of life" (453), "a crowd
of masquers rioting" (453), and an "obtrusive uproar" (454). The engulfing
water images are especially pertinent to Kenyon's character and immediate
situation: the Carnival is a "mad, merry stream of human life" (439), "a
tempestuous sea," as the crowd sweeps over the spot where Kenyon,
Donatello, and Miriam hurriedly exchanged their few parting words—(448),
a "turbulent stream of wayfarers" (448), a "whirlpool of nonsense" (450), and
an "eddying throng" (450). The Carnival, then, is as a stream or confluence
of forces that threatened to engulf Kenyon but appear to divide and flow
around him rather than pull him into their vortex. Kenyon is only partially
the "active participant" that Bakhtin identifies as essential to the nature of
carnival.[27]

Much of the Carnival scene is imbued with a surrealistic aura, as
Kenyon, described by Udo Natterman as a "sullen outsider in the
Carnival,"[28] with his dark mood and what Hawthorne describes as a

"troubled face" (445), is accosted by the swarming revelers. The irony and juxtaposition of the conflicting images is striking. We are told:

> Fantastic figures, with bulbous heads, the circumference of a bushel, grinned enormously in his face. Harlequins struck him with their wooden swords, and appeared to expect his immediate transformation into some jollier shape. A little, long-tailed, horned fiend sidled up to him, and suddenly blew at him through a tube, enveloping our poor friend in a whole harvest of winged seeds. A biped, with an ass's snout, brayed close to his ear, ending his discordant uproar with a peal of human laughter. Five strapping damsels (so, at least, their petticoats bespoke them, in spite of an awful freedom in the flourish of their legs) joined hands and danced around him, inviting him by their gestures to perform a horn-pipe in the midst. Released from these gay persecutors, a clown in motley rapped him on the back with a blown bladder, in which a handful of dried peas rattled horribly. (445)

As if there were not sufficient harassment, Kenyon finds that his "merry martyrdom was not half over":

> There came along a gigantic female figure, seven feet high, at least, and taking up a third of the street's breadth with the preposterously swelling sphere of her crinoline skirts. Singling out the sculptor, she began to make a ponderous assault upon his heart, throwing amorous glances at him out of her great, goggle-eyes, offering him a vast bouquet of sunflowers and nettles, and soliciting his pity by all sorts of pathetic and passionate dumb-show. Her suit meeting no favour, the rejected Titaness made a gesture of despair and rage; then suddenly drawing a huge pistol, she took aim right at the obdurate sculptor's breast, and pulled the trigger. The shot took effect, (for the abominable plaything went off by a spring, like a boy's pop-gun,) covering Kenyon with a cloud of lime-dust, under shelter of which the revengeful damsel strode away.
>
> Hereupon, a whole host of absurd figures surrounded him, pretending to sympathize in his mishap. Clowns and parti-colored harlequins; orang-outans; bear-headed, bull-headed, and dog-headed individuals; faces that would have been human, but for their enormous noses; one terrific creature with a visage right

in the center of his breast, and all other imaginable kinds of monstrosity and exaggeration. These apparitions appeared to be investigating the case, after the fashion of a coroner's jury, poking their pasteboard countenances close to the sculptor's, with an unchangeable grin that gave still more ludicrous effect to the comic alarm and horrour of their gestures. Just then, a figure came by, in a gray wig and rusty gown, with an ink-horn at his button-hole, and a pen behind his ear; he announced himself as a notary, and offered to make the last will and testament of the assassinated man. This solemn duty, however, was interrupted by a surgeon, who brandished a lancet, three feet long, and proposed to him to let him blood. (446)

The phantasmagoric scene is not unlike scenarios found in modern and postmodern writers such as Franz Kafka, Kurt Vonnegut, Robert Coover, Donald Barthelme, and John Barth, especially in contrasting the joyous masquerading to Kenyon's soul-struck despair and disjointed presence from the whole mad scene. "The affair was so like a feverish dream," we are told, that "Kenyon resigned himself to let it take its course" (446). Earlier, before Kenyon had been personally bombarded, the scene of the "spectacle so fantastic and extravagant" is said to affect him "like a thin dream, through the dim, extravagant material of which he could discern more substantial objects, while too much under its control to start forth broad awake" (441–42). Kenyon is also said to react with "dreamy eyes" to the "riotous interchange of nosegays and confetti ... while the procession passed" (443). Gollin has already perceptively identified and explained the dreamlike nature of Kenyon's experience. She writes that more "explicitly dream-like" than the earlier "sylvan dance" scenes of chapter 9, the Carnival scene "is a trope for the dance of life."[29] Gollin also observes that throughout the novel "dreams define the way characters respond to experiences and the way they appear to others. Miriam, Donatello, and the model all appear to be as strange and ambiguous as dream phantoms that go through metamorphoses yet remain recognizable." Kenyon's getting struck by the cauliflower, Gollin avers, "suggests [his] summons by mundane reality, and the rosebud his opportunity for love."[30]

Does the Carnival process hold out any hope for Kenyon?[31] Many scholars think not. Baym refers to "the end of Kenyon's feverish season in purgatory." Reading *The Marble Faun* as an "elegy for art," she interprets the ending as "a gesture of heartsickness and despair, of hopes denied, effort repudiated." The novel is like the Venus statue that three of the main characters discover in the Campagna, "created by Hawthorne's imagination, then discolored, disfigured, and shattered by his prudence, his conscience, his fatigue, his sense of futility."³² Natterman dwells on Kenyon's (and Hilda's) inability to adapt to the foreign environment, commenting that for both of the American characters there is the reality of the "slightly hostile quality of the foreign environment"; fittingly, at the Carnival "Kenyon is symbolically shot with lime dust and hit by a cauliflower used as a missile."³³ Gollin is one of the few who is less pessimistic in her interpretation, concluding that in Hilda's presence, despite the noise and confusion of the Carnival, Kenyon finds his "perplexing dream is dispelled."³⁴ But if we reflect on *The Marble Faun* in the mode of carnivalized literature, as defined and articulated by Mikhail Bakhtin, Hawthorne does indeed (as in Gollin's reading) imply some hope. To Bakhtin the basic elements of carnivalized experience as reflected in novels informed by that tradition are that everyone participates in the carnival act, normal laws, prohibitions, and restrictions are suspended, and "a free and familiar attitude spreads over everything."³⁵ Moreover, as is evident in the distorted, costumed figures milling along the Corso in *The Marble Faun*, Bakhtin emphasizes the role of ambivalent images in carnivalized literature: there are dualities, polar opposites, paired images, opposites, everything seemingly in reverse appearance and order (126), all of which prompt him to observe that because "a carnivalistic" life is "life drawn out of its *usual* rut, it is to some degree 'life turned inside out,' 'the reverse side of the world'" (122). Marty Roth amplifies Bakhtin's statement by observing that "the distinctive markers of carnivalesque art are less likely to be intoxication and drunkenness than the trope of the world upside down, destructive laughter, feasting, or the image of the grotesque body."³⁶ Indeed, except for the feasting, these traits certainly characterize the Carnival scene in *The Marble Faun*.

　　This is not to say, however, that *The Marble Faun* as a whole is what Bakhtin categorizes as "carnivalized literature." For one thing, while the world of the Roman Carnival is one of dualities, opposites, and reversal of mores and norms, the same does not fully apply to life outside the frame of this annual revelry. Hawthorne, in contrast to Bakhtin, does not advocate a topsy-turvy world order that overturns the accepted "official" values system, or else we would find Kenyon giving himself wholeheartedly to his pursuit of art rather than yielding to Hilda's influence and the comforts of the hearth. Another major feature of Bakhtinian carnival is not so evident in Hawthorne's novel either—or at best is only selectively applicable in what occurs. Bakhtin speaks of carnivalized literature, through the inversions mentioned above, as evoking a dialogized rather than a monologized dynamic. In his view, "All *distance* between people is suspended, and a special carnival category goes into effect: *free and familiar contact among people*. This is a very important aspect of a carnival sense of the world. People who in life are separated by impenetrable hierarchical barriers enter into free familiar contact on the carnival square."[37] The differences between Bakhtin and Hawthorne are, of course, obvious. What Bakhtin describes may be true of Rabelais's as well as Dostoevsky's works, the two writers about whom Bakhtin has mainly written and holds up as examples of carnivalization, but it does not ring true of Hawthorne in the overall context of his fiction despite certain carnivalized scenes and episodes scattered throughout his works. Again, we think of the scene Hawthorne describes in his *Notebooks* of standing on the pavement of the Corso among the working-class people, whom he describes in restrained uncomplimentary terms: the dowdy women with "generally broad and sturdy figures."[38] This is not to insist that there is no measure of "togetherness" in *The Marble Faun*. Carnival does suggest influences that can be lasting. Miriam and Donatello are caught up together in what Norris Yates describes as the "wild Bacchic dance of the Carnival,"[39] but it is a tragic dance after all. And Kenyon is drawn into the melee whether he desires it or not and refuses to give himself over to it wholeheartedly.[40] Whereas Bakhtin's idea of carnival is one of exhilarating, liberating experience, Hawthorne's "American Carnival," as Roth astutely points out, "usually has dark and forbidding features."[41] Further, it offers no true, lasting alternative for monologism. As Roth says, "One condition of Carnival is a release of oceanic feeling, a suspension of the sense of self."[42] In the carnival of Hawthorne's novel we see Kenyon momentarily "linked" to a "circle of three" (448) with Donatello and Miriam; he is so passive overall in the midst of this "mad, merry stream of life" (439) that he simply "resign[s] himself" to "let it take its course" (446). The "eddying throng of the Corso" (450), the "whirlpool of nonsense" (450), the "tempestuous sea," the "turbulent stream of wayfarers" (448) may engulf almost everyone in their way, including Donatello and Miriam and even in a sense Hilda, who appears in her white domino costume on the balcony above Kenyon "full of tender joy" and with "a gleam of delicate mirthfulness in her eyes" (451). Meaningfully, Hawthorne writes of Hilda, "That soft, mirthful smile," which Kenyon had seen only two or three times since he has known her, "caused her to melt, as it were, into the wild frolic of the Carnival, and become not so strange and alien to the scene, as her unexpected apparition must otherwise have made her" (451). But not so the "distant," dreamy-eyed Kenyon standing below, who largely eludes immersion in the scene.

As Roth emphasizes, however, "Carnival is unthinkable without mood alteration,[43] and although Kenyon's mood remains unaltered until the end of the scene, when he is hit by Hilda's rose, it is obviously changed at that juncture and appears to be sustained, as we see a few days later, when he jests to Hilda about a tabby cat lying on an altar in the Pantheon assuming that she is "an object of worship" (458). The "anxious and unquiet spectator" of a "darker mood," with the "sad and contracted brow" and "troubled face," is released from his doldrums by the appearance of the carnivalistic figure of Hilda clad in white domino. And while in chapter 50 Kenyon capitulates on his notion of the fortunate fall and asks Hilda to be his "guide... counsellor ... [and] inmost friend" and to "guide... [him] home," they both will return to that home at least somewhat transformed by their experiences.[44] And all of their experiences, like those of Donatello and Miriam, appear to coalesce in the apocalyptic (in the sense of revelatory) Carnival chapters. Carnival took a front and center position among Hawthorne's own associations with Rome and thus ineluctably became an integral, climactic part of *The Marble Faun*, his last finished novel.

NOTES

1. *New Columbia Encyclopaedia*, 4th ed., *s.v.* "carnival."

2. Ibid.

3. Ibid.

4. See *New Encyclopaedia Britannica*, 15th ed., *s.v.* "carnival"; *The Encyclopedia Americana: International Ed., 1997 s.v.* "Carnival."

5. Hsio-Yun Chu and Jan Z. Pervil, *Let's Go Rome: 1998* (New York. St. Martin's Press), 13.

6. Rennell Rodd, *Rome of the Renaissance and Today* (London. Macmillan, 1932), 40–41. It was not until some two hundred years later, in 1688, that Pope Clement IX ended the Jew races, but the horse races continued until the end of the nineteenth century. See John Varriano, *Literary Companion to Rome* (New York: St. Martin's Griffin, 1991), 126.

7. Mikhail Bakhtin, *Problems of Dostoevsky's Poetics*, ed. and trans. Carl Emerson (Minneapolis: University of Minnesota Press, 1984), 131.

8. Rodd, *Rome*, 41.

9. *The Diary of John Evelyn*, ed. E. S. de Beer (London: Oxford University Press, 1959), 196.

10. J. W. Goethe, *Italian Journey (1786–1788)* (New York: Pantheon Books, 1962), 445–46. See also Goethe, *Das Romische Carnival* (Berlin: Weimar and Gotha, 1789).

11. Charles Dickens, *Pictures from Italy* (Oxford: Oxford University Press, 1987), 371, 372.

12. In 1870, after a plebiscite, Rome was annexed by the Kingdom of Italy. In 1871 the capital was transferred from Florence to Rome, and the government "set about transforming the city into a modern metropolis" (*New Catholic Encyclopedia*, 1967, *s.v.* "Rome").

13. Henry James, "A Roman Holiday," in *Italian Hours* (Boston: Houghton Mifflin, 1909), 136. James's parting shot, interestingly, was somewhat more positive: viewing the Carnival on the climactic Shrove Tuesday, he pronounces the Corso "altogether carnivalesque" (151). Subsequent references are noted parenthetically in the text.

14. William Dean Howells, *Roman Holidays and Others* (New York: Harper & Brothers, 1908), 167,

15. Francis Wey, *Rome* (New York: D. Appleton, 1888), 428–29.

16. Rodd, *Rome*, 41.

17. Julian Hawthorne later confirmed that "the weather was bad nearly all the time, and my father's point of view was correspondingly unsympathetic." Julian's own description of both Carnivals that occurred while the Hawthornes were in Italy is informative. See *Hawthorne and His Circle* (New York: Harper & Brothers, 1903), 277–91; the quotation appears on p. 277.

18. Nathaniel Hawthorne, *The French and Italian Notebooks*, ed. Thomas Woodson. *The Centenary Edition of the Works of Nathaniel Hawthorne*, ed. William Charvat et al. (Columbus: Ohio State University Press, 1980), 14:64. Hereafter cited as *Notebooks*, or by page numbers, in the text.

19. Again, see Julian Hawthorne, who observes: "This mood [in 1859], we see, is far more gentle and sympathetic than the former one; there is sunshine within as well as without; and, indeed, I remember with what glee my father took part in the frolic, as well as looked on at it, he laughed and pelted and was pelted; he walked down the Corso and back again; he drove to and fro in a carriage; he mounted to Mr. [John Lothrop] Motley's balcony and took long shots at the crowd below. The sombre spirit of criticism had ceased, for a time, to haunt him" (*Hawthorne and His Circle*, 286–87).

20. Nathaniel Hawthorne, *The Letters, 1857–1864*, ed. Thomas Woodson, *Centenary Edition*, 17.164.

21. This is the night of the Carnival that Bakhtin describes as the embodiment of the ambivalent "image of fire" in carnival. It is a fire that "simultaneously destroys and renews the world" (*Problems of Dostoevsky's Poetics*, 126). At the end of the carnival "hell"—a special structure such as a vehicle covered with carnival trappings—was "triumphantly set on fire." Each participant, as he or she tries to put out the candle, cries "*Sia ammazzato*" ("Death to thee").

22. Nina Baym, "*The Marble Faun*: Hawthorne's Elegy for Art," *New England Quarterly* 44 (1971): 374,

23. Hawthorne, *Letters*, 229 (emphasis added).

24. Nathaniel Hawthorne, *The Marble Faun, The Centenary Edition*, 4:426. All citations of the novel are to this edition and are noted parenthetically in the text.

25. Rita Gollin, *Nathaniel Hawthorne and the Truth of Dreams* (Baton Rouge: Louisiana State University Press, 1979), 184.

26. Bakhtin's summation of the nature, or "problem," of carnival is that "its essence, its deep roots in the primordial order and the primordial thinking of man, its development under conditions of class society, its extraordinary life force and its undying fascination ... is one of the most complex and most interesting problems in the history of culture" (*Problems of Dostoevsky's Poetics*, 122).

27. Ibid., 122.

28. Udo Natterman, "Dread and Desire: 'Europe' in Hawthorne's *The Marble Faun*," *Essays in Literature* 21 (Spring 1994):61.

29. Gollin, *Nathaniel Hawthorne*, 183.

30. Ibid., 184. Baym and Natterman interpret the cauliflower incident differently. Baym reads it as perhaps Hawthorne himself casting the blow on Kenyon as an "expression of contempt for the sculptor's pitiful weakness" ("*Marble Faun*," 375). To Natterman Kenyon's being hit by both the cauliflower and lime dust is a sign of the "slightly hostile quality" of the foreign country toward travelers ("Dread and Desire," 62).

31. The psychological dimensions of Kenyon's Carnival experience are the focus of Nina Baym's article "*The Marble Faun*: Hawthorne's Elegy for Art." Baym's point is that

Donatello and Miriam become such "figures of fantasy" in the last third of the book (almost always appearing in costumes) that "they are not 'themselves' any longer, but rather are phantoms in Kenyon's consciousness." They become "less whole characters than fragments of Kenyon's suddenly exploded psyche" (372). The Carnival, according to Baym, "represents the final capitulation" of Kenyon, for without Hilda he "will surely go mad," so "ludicrously inadequate" is he for the profession of artist that he has chosen to pursue. Baym insightfully interprets the grotesqueness of the Carnival: "The psyche in a state of anarchic turbulence throws up into the light of consciousness a myriad of horrible fears and fantasies, grotesque and terrifying figures out of the world of dreams, mostly with sexual import" (374).

Norris Yates, the first scholar to pursue the masked dance trope in Hawthorne's fiction, refers to the masked dance in *The Marble Faun* as "both an escape and a penitential rite" ("Ritual and Reality: Mask and Dance Motifs in Hawthorne's Fiction," *Philological Quarterly* 34 [1955]: 70). Certainly in their "final celebration [during the Carnival], Miriam and Donatello are whirled along in a saturnalia of penitence" (69).

32. Baym, "*Marble Faun*," 375, 376.

33. Natterman, "*Dread and Desire*," 62.

34. Gollin, *Nathaniel Hawthorne*, 184.

35. Bakhtin, *Problems of Dostoevsky's Poetics*, 122, 123.

36. Marry Roth, "Carnival, Creativity, and the Sublimation of Drunkenness," *Mosaic: A Journal for the Interdisciplinary Study of Literature* 30 (1997): 8.

37. Bakhtin, *Problems of Dostoevsky's Poetics*, 123.

38. Hawthorne, *Notebooks*, 503.

39. Yates, "Ritual and Reality," 69.

40. As John Wegner points out, Kenyon is the only character who, by the novel's end, associates freely with all three of the other major characters. See "Contemporary Inspiration for Kenyon in *The Marble Faun*," *Nathaniel Hawthorne Review* 23 (1997): 26–38.

41. Roth, "Carnival, Creativity," 14.

42. Ibid., 4.

43. Ibid.

44. Thus I believe Baym goes too far in stating that the Carnival "fail[s] utterly" in providing a catharsis for Kenyon ("*Marble Faun*," 374).

RICHARD KOPLEY

A Poem by Lowell

Arthur Dimmesdale may be linked with the objects of the various possible Chillingworth figures, including Robert Carr's Thomas Overbury, Caleb Williams's Mr. Falkland, Dr. Chillingworth's Sir Francis Varney, Richard Crowninshield and the Knapp brothers' Joseph White, and the narrator's sleeping foe in Poe's famous tale, but, of course, other historical and literary connections may be mentioned, as well. One of these is the biblical David, the adulterous king depicted in the tapestry of Dimmesdale's apartment (1:126). Others, suggested by scholars, include Nathaniel Manning, a maternal ancestor of Hawthorne, who had committed incest with his two sisters Anstiss and Margaret; Michael Wigglesworth, the Puritan poet; Jean-Jacques Rousseau's Saint-Preux, the former lover of a now-married woman; J. G. Lockhart's Adam Blair, a remorseful adulterous widowed minister; and James K. Paulding's Walter Avery, the seducer of beautiful young Phoebe Angevine. John Cotton, the minister of the heroic woman with whom Hawthorne links Hester Prynne, Anne Hutchinson, has also been proposed. Once again, we may infer that Hawthorne was working from a catalog of sources—once again, we may see that he relied on an array of matching threads.[1]

Dimmesdale's Election Sermon, concerning the "high and glorious destiny for the newly gathered people of the Lord" (1:249), has naturally

From *The Threads of* The Scarlet Letter: *A Study of Hawthorne's Transformative Art*, pp. 36–63. © 2003 by Rosemont Publishing & Printing Corp.

attracted much attention. Some scholars have sought links to prior writing: Reiner Smolinski notes that Hawthorne withdrew from the Salem Athenaeum the *Election Sermons* (and other books of sermons) in 1828, Thomas F. Walsh shows that Dimmesdale's Election Sermon features a vocabulary typical of election sermons, and Frederick Newberry relates the characterization of Dimmesdale's delivery of that sermon to the "rushing mighty wind" of Acts 2:2.[2] It is precisely Hawthorne's characterization of Dimmesdale's delivery of the Election Sermon—as well as the response to that sermon—that warrants further attention here, attention that will lead to a new and important source.

Dimmesdale's voice is sensitively elaborated throughout *The Scarlet Letter*. Hawthorne first describes Dimmesdale's plaintive speech to the condemned Hester:

> The young pastor's voice was tremulously sweet, rich, deep, and broken. The feeling that it so evidently manifested, rather than the direct purport of the words, caused it to vibrate within all hearts, and brought the listeners into one accord of sympathy. (1:67)

The implicit sorrow in Dimmesdale's voice is owing to his love for Hester, his guilt for his adultery, and his failure to acknowledge his part. As the narrative proceeds, Hawthorne writes that Dimmesdale's voice was "sweet, tremulous, but powerful" (1:114), that "though still rich and sweet, [it] had a certain melancholy prophecy of decay in it" (1:120), that it became "more tremulous than before" (1:122), and that, if not for Dimmesdale's sin, his voice might have been "listened to and answered" by "the angels" (1:142). Then, for the Election Sermon passage, Hawthorne describes Dimmesdale's "very peculiar voice" (1:243) with exceptional fullness. Hawthorne's allusion to the extraordinary preaching on the day of Pentecost in Acts is altogether fitting, as Newberry shows, but an allusion to another work may be identified, as well. We may best understand Hawthorne's rendering of Dimmesdale's voice here by considering a critically informing text, a narrative poem by Hawthorne's friend James Russell Lowell, a work once acclaimed, but long since neglected: "A Legend of Brittany."

Lowell's first book of poetry, *A Year's Life*, was published in January 1841. Although Lowell later wrote to Poe that it was "a volume of rather crude productions (in which there is more of everybody else than of myself)" (Poe, *Complete Works* 17:144) and to Longfellow that it was "crude and immature," it did elicit numerous positive reviews, often for its perceived elevated sensibility.[3] Poet Elizabeth B. Barrett wrote to Lowell, encouragingly, on 31 March 1842, "I hope that you will write on, and not suffer your 'Year's Life' to be only *one* year's life."[4] Lowell continued to write poetry (including "Rosaline," concerning a man's murder of his beloved), contributed essays to the *Boston Miscellany*, and prepared for his new journal, *The Pioneer*. Only a few months after *The Pioneer* ceased publication—due, in large part, to an unworkable agreement with its distributors—Lowell found himself particularly excited about a poem that he was writing, one with a thematic affinity with "Rosaline."[5] He stated in a letter of 15 June 1843 to his friend George B. Loring,

> I am now at work on a still longer poem in the *ottava rima*, to be the first in my forthcoming volume. I feel more and more assured every day that I shall yet do something that will keep my name (and perhaps my body) alive. My wings were never so light and strong as now. So hurrah for a niche and a laurel![6]

Indebted for the form of "A Legend of Brittany" primarily to previous works written in *ottava rima*—such as Lord Byron's *Don Juan* (1819–24), John Keats's "Isabella; or the Pot of Basil" (1820), and Percy Shelley's "The Witch of Atlas" (1824)—Lowell was vitally indebted for the poem's story to a fourteenth-century French ballad, "Les Trois Moines Rouges" ("The Three Red Monks").

Charles Oran Stewart, who discovered this source, notes that young Lowell was taught French by his mother Harriet and his older sister Mary. Indeed, when he was not yet eight years old, Lowell wrote to his brother Robert, "I read french stories." Lowell continued to develop his skills in French, reading Old French volumes when he was at Harvard. He would have found the seminal French ballad, "Les Trois Moines Rouges," most probably in the 1839 or 1840 volume *Chants Populaires de la Bretagne*, translated by Theodor Hersart de la Villemarqué.[7] The background for the ballad involved the belief that Knights Templar would anoint an idol with the fat of a child produced by the union of a Templar and a virgin. According to the ballad, three Knights Templar kidnap a young woman, get her pregnant, and, months later, bury her and her baby alive beneath the altar of the church. Before her burial, she seeks only baptism for her baby and extreme unction for herself. A knight who witnesses the digging of her tomb tells the bishop, and the woman and her baby are disinterred. The mother is dead or dying, having done violence to herself in her despair. But, amazingly, the baby, in three days' time, identifies the murderers, who are then burned alive.[8] Lowell adapted this horrific tale for his purposes, crafting a long narrative poem about a love affair, a terrible crime, and the attainment of an otherworldly peace. His elaborate reshaping and expansion of the French ballad might well be compared to Washington Irving's reshaping and expansion of the German folktale, "Peter Klaus the Goatherd," for "Rip Van Winkle." But while Irving's debt was known by his contemporaries, Lowell's debt does not seem to have been known by the readers of his time.[9] Lowell's friend Charles F. Briggs asked in a 22 January 1845 letter, "Pray do you never write a story? It strikes me that you might, if you invented the Legend of Brittany."[10]

Lowell did not invent the story of "A Legend of Brittany," but he did fully transform "The Three Red Monks" for his poem. "A Legend of Brittany" was published by Christmas 1843 in Lowell's second volume of poetry, titled simply *Poems*.[11] Hawthorne would have read his friend's book and would have been aware of some of the considerable critical response that its featured poem prompted.

Hawthorne had a growing relationship with Lowell in the period before the publication of *Poems*. Edward Everett Hale wrote that "Lowell probably met [Hawthorne] for the first time at Elizabeth Peabody's" (at 13 West Street) and that "Hawthorne soon after married her charming sister [Sophia Peabody]." Accordingly, Lowell and Hawthorne would have first met shortly before 8 July 1842, the date of the wedding of Sophia and Nathaniel, an event that also took place at the West Street house. Lowell's fiancée since November 1840, Maria White, had been a "childhood friend" of Sophia's—indeed, according to Rose Hawthorne Lathrop, "had long been an intimate friend" of hers. On 6 November 1839, the two women had attended the first class of Margaret Fuller's "Conversations," also at West Street.[12]

On first meeting Hawthorne, Lowell would have been well aware of the distinguished reputation of the author of *Twice-Told Tales*; in fact, in April 1851, Lowell wrote to Hawthorne, "I became a disciple [of yours] in my eighteenth year" (in 1837, when *Twice-Told Tales* first appeared).[13] Of Hawthorne's most recent work, Lowell certainly knew the short story "A Virtuoso's Collection," which had appeared in the May 1842 issue of the *Boston Miscellany*, preceding the second number of Lowell's series, "The Old English Dramatists." Lowell mentioned that short story in his own (unsigned) short story, "The First Client," appearing later in the same issue.[14] Similarly, Hawthorne would have known of Lowell's rising reputation, especially with regard to the poet's first book of poems, *A Year's Life*, published only eighteen months before the first Hawthorne–Lowell meeting and reviewed by Hawthorne's friend George S. Hillard, as well as by Orestes Brownson, William Wetmore Story, Margaret Fuller, and by

Charles J. Peterson in the same issue of *Graham's Magazine*—that of April 1842—in which Poe first reviewed Hawthorne.[15] And, of course, of Lowell's most recent work, Hawthorne would have known the aforementioned series in the *Boston Miscellany*, "The Old English Dramatists." When Lowell undertook *The Pioneer* in the fall of 1842, he naturally turned to Hawthorne for a contribution, and Hawthorne readily obliged.

Lowell's fiancée Maria White wrote to her friend "Kiddy"—Caroline King, of Salem—on Tuesday, 4 October 1842, "James has gone to Portland today to engage John Neill [Neal] as a contributor [to *The Pioneer*] and will go this week to Concord to see Hawthorne and obtain his services." Possibly, Lowell, by himself, did then visit Hawthorne in Concord—perhaps this is when, according to Sophia Hawthorne, "[Lowell] offered Mr. Hawthorne *any* price for his articles."[16] Her husband later suggested the rate that was provided by editor Epes Sargent, five dollars per page (15:663). Perhaps, too, it was during this visit that Lowell and Hawthorne talked at a Revolutionary War gravesite near Hawthorne's home, as mentioned in "The Old Manse" (10:9). Possibly, too, at this time, Lowell spoke of his planned work, which might have included the long poem that he would soon be writing, "A Legend of Brittany"—the piece that would commence his next volume, *Poems*. However, the conversations may also have taken place during Lowell's visits with Maria to the Hawthornes.

Shortly after Sunday, 2 October 1842, Mary Peabody reported to her sister Sophia Hawthorne what Maria White's brother William White had said: "James Lowell & Maria are going up to see you in about a fortnight." On Sunday, 9 October 1842, Sophia Hawthorne requested that her mother, Mrs. Elizabeth Palmer Peabody, invite James Russell Lowell and Maria White to visit the Hawthornes in Concord "*next week,*—not this week."[17] It was to be several weeks, in fact, before the visit took place—the Hawthornes were in Boston and Salem from 23 October through 31 October (8:363)— but Lowell and his fiancée did call on the Hawthornes in Concord on Wednesday, 2 November. On Friday, 4 November, Maria wrote to family friend Sarah Shaw, "I went on Wednesday with James to spend the day with Mr. & Mrs. Hawthorne. They seemed very blissful and our time passed delightfully."[18]

Some time after that visit, Hawthorne completed his sketch "The Hall of Fantasy," which he sent to Lowell on 17 December (15:663). Hawthorne described Lowell in that work as "the poet of the generation that now enters upon the stage" (10:636). (The story appeared in the second issue of *The Pioneer*; Hawthorne's story "The Birth-mark" [sent on 1 February 1843 (15:669)] appeared in the third issue.) Lowell, in turn, would write by mid-December his admiring review of Hawthorne's *Historical Tales for Youth* (for the first issue of *The Pioneer*), identifying Hawthorne as "a man of acknowledged genius."[19]

The two writers became more friendly as time passed: Hawthorne closed his 17 December 1842 letter "Yours truly, Nath. Hawthorne." (15:663), and he closed his (circa) May 1843 letter—one about his inability to fulfill Poe's request for a story for the *Stylus*—"I shall not forget your promised visit," and signed it (despite problems in receiving payment for his *Pioneer* work), "Truly your friend, Nath. Hawthorne." (15:684).[20] Apparently the Lowells again visited the Hawthornes some time during 1844 after 3 March since they saw the baby girl, Una. In December 1844, the soon-to-be-married (or lately married) Lowell—who wed Maria White on 26 December—arranged to have Hawthorne sent a copy of his new volume, *Conversations on Some of the Old Poets*, "with author's love." (And that book offered two references to Hawthorne, who, Lowell wrote, "has a right in any gathering of poets.") Then, on 16 January 1845, Lowell's wife Maria wrote to Sophia Hawthorne from Philadelphia, "James desires his love to Mr. Hawthorne and yourself and sends a kiss to Una, for whom he conceived quite a passion when he saw her in Concord."[21]

In light of the increasing friendship between Hawthorne and Lowell in 1842, 1843, and 1844, Hawthorne was sure to have read "A Legend of Brittany" soon after it appeared as the first and longest work in Lowell's *Poems*. Perhaps Lowell even gave Hawthorne one of the twenty copies of the book that he had received from his publisher.[22] And certainly Hawthorne would have been much engaged by the story of "A Legend of Brittany." Mordred, a Knight Templar, loves the beautiful young Margaret, whom he makes pregnant, but he loves power more. He controls her, and then, concerned about his vow of celibacy and his ambition to become grand master, he kills her and hides her body beneath the altar of the church. After the townspeople have gathered at the church for a festival, and after extraordinary organ music is heard in the church, and then the chant of the responding choir, Margaret's spirit, come from heaven, speaks. Although she is still in love with Mordred and hopes to be reunited with him in the hereafter, Margaret's spirit reveals the crime that has been committed so that she may ask that her dead infant be baptized. Finding Margaret's body, the priests baptize the unborn infant, whose spirit, with his mother's, ascends to heaven. Mordred, hearing Margaret's spirit and witnessing the baptism, is relieved; he then dies, with an amaranth flower upon his chest, a token of eternal life—perhaps, by implication (after penance is done and faith has grown), with the murdered Margaret. (As a reader of *The Faerie Queen* and *Paradise Lost*, Hawthorne might well have recalled Spenser's treatment of the amaranth as the flower to which the grieving lover Amintas was transformed [bk. 3, canto 6, st. 45] and Milton's description of the amaranth as a flower of Eden, "but soon for man's offense / To heav'n removed" [bk. 3, lines 353–56]. Lowell had earlier treated the amaranth in "The Ballad of the Stranger," and he later employed it in *Conversations on Some of the Old Poets*.)[23]

Hawthorne would have encountered in Lowell's poem a reminder of the beginning of one of his own early notebook entries: "A man, to escape detection for some offence, immures a woman whom he has loved in some cavern or other secret place" (23:153). Furthermore, Hawthorne would have encountered in that poem some of his own great themes: human passion, one individual's violation of another, secret guilt, penance, and ultimate redemption. He would have recognized a tale of the Fall and its consequences. And he would have encountered familiar language—in light of his March 1843 story, "Egotism, or the Bosom Serpent" (written, according to John J. McDonald, between 2 February and 15 February 1842), Hawthorne would probably have been intrigued to read that a desire for power, prompting a man's murder of his lover, was characterized by Lowell as "a serpent in his breast," "the black serpent ... round his heart." And even as the poem would have interested him for its story, themes, and language, it would also have interested him simply because it was by his friend Lowell. We should recall here the comment of Hawthorne's son Julian about his father's attitude toward the writing of his friends:

> we may concede, too, in general, that Hawthorne was human enough to love best the literature which, other things being equal, or nearly so, had for him the warmest personal associations. If he loved a writer, he was apt to read some of his liking into that writer's productions.[24]

Hawthorne's attention to Lowell's "A Legend of Brittany" would very likely have been heightened because of the critical response it elicited. Most notable was the unsigned laudatory review in the March 1844 issue of *Graham's Magazine*, a piece that Hawthorne would not have missed. He would have been following *Graham's* because he awaited publication there of the story that he had completed by 9 January 1844, "Earth's Holocaust," and had sent on to the magazine.[25] Unfortunately, the work remained unpublished (and presumably unpaid for) for several months. On 24 March 1844, Hawthorne wrote to his friend George S. Hillard, "Unless he [George R. Graham] publishes it ["Earth's Holocaust"] next month, I shall reclaim it—having occasion for it elsewhere" (16:23). (The tale was published, probably in late April 1844, in the May 1844 issue of *Graham's* [10:579].) Looking for "Earth's Holocaust" in the March 1844 issue of *Graham's*,

Hawthorne would have come upon the very favorable review of Lowell's *Poems*.

This unsigned review was by Poe. Writing to Lowell on 19 October 1843, Poe had promised a review: "I am seeking an opportunity to do you justice in a review, and may find it, in 'Graham,' when your book [*Poems*] appears." Three years later, in response to an astute query from George W. Eveleth, Poe acknowledged having found that opportunity in *Graham's*: "The notice of Lowell's 'Brittany' *is* mine."[26] Poe began his review of *Poems* with a strong encomium:

> This new volume of poems by Mr. Lowell will place him, in the estimation of all whose opinion he will be likely to value, *at the very head* of the poets of America. For our part, we have not the slightest hesitation in saying, that we regard the "Legend of Brittany" as by far the finest poetical work, of equal length, which the country has produced. (*Complete Works* 11:243)

Poe's high opinion of "A Legend of Brittany" here seems all the more striking in light of the fact that, in responding to Lowell's uncertainty about his as-yet-unpublished narrative poem, Poe had warned against writing narrative poetry.[27] (But, of course, Poe's greatest success, coming in early 1845, would be one of his own narrative poems, "The Raven.") Poe followed two paragraphs of introduction in his review of *Poems* with a paragraph of plot summary for "A Legend of Brittany" and a paragraph on the "*sublimity* of human love" as illustrated by extracts from the second part of Lowell's poem, six stanzas of Margaret's otherworldly plea. And then Poe offered an exceptional paragraph of intense and focused tribute to ten stanzas appearing before these extracts, the first four stanzas of which concern an extraordinary church organ:

> The description of the swelling of the organ—immediately preceding these extracts—surpasses, in all the loftier merits, any similar passage we have seen. It is truly magnificent. For those who have the book, we instance the forty-first stanza of the second book, and the nine stanzas succeeding. We know not where to look, in all American poetry, for anything more richly ideal, or more forcibly conveyed. (*Complete Works* 11:246)

Here is the peak of Poe's commendation. With the phrase "richly ideal," Poe appears to imply what he had termed in his 1836 Drake-Halleck review "the beautiful ... the sublime ... the mystical" and "the beautiful ... the mystical ...

the august" (*Complete Works* 8:282–83, 301; see also 10:64)—a suggestive undercurrent intimating to the reader "the Hope of a higher Intellectual Happiness hereafter" (*Complete Works* 8:283), "a far more ethereal beauty *beyond*" (*Complete Works* 10:65–66). And this undercurrent is produced by "the sentiment of Poesy," "the Poetic Sentiment" (Complete *Works* 8:282, 284). The remaining paragraphs of Poe's review of *Poems* offer some additional praise of "A Legend of Brittany," a caution with regard to its didacticism and smaller faults, very brief comment on other poems in the book, and brief summary (*Complete Works* 11:249). This review would have compellingly focused Hawthorne's attention on "A Legend of Brittany," and, particularly, on its remarkable church organ passage.[28]

And some of the other reviews might have also called his attention to the poem and its church organ passage. The anonymous and mixed review in the 30 January 1844 issue of the New York *Tribune* noted the "great sweetness, beauty and ease of style" of "A Legend of Brittany," objected to the poem's familiar account of seduction and its unfamiliar language, and identified the organ music passage as "original" and "full of truth," quoting from "Part Second" stanzas 41 and 42 (the first two of the four stanzas in the passage).[29] A positive, anonymous review in the February 1844 issue of the *Knickerbocker* described the poem as "a romantic story, fringed with rhyme," and quoted the second part's stanzas 39 and 41, terming them and the treatment of the choir "equally beautiful." Charles J. Peterson's highly praising review in the March 1844 issue of the *Ladies' National Magazine*—a review resembling the *Graham's* review of *Poems* by Peterson's former colleague on that magazine, Poe—stated that "A Legend of Brittany" "displays a genius of the very highest order" and that "[w]e know no sustained poem by an American author equal to it." The Peterson review quoted "Part Second"'s stanzas 41 through 49, asserting that the nine stanzas constitute "the finest passage in the poem," and that "[h]ere is the highest imagination combined with a graphic power rarely equalled."[30] An anonymous review in the March issue of the *New Jerusalem Magazine* (a review not cited by Alvan R. McFadyen) quoted five early stanzas of "A Legend of Brittany" and then stanzas 41, 43, and 44 in the poem's second part; the writer for this Swedenborgian periodical praised Lowell's "pure and elevated affections." Another anonymous review in the 15 April 1844 issue of *The Critic* of London quoted the same stanza 41 and observed its "power." And an additional anonymous review, appearing in the London *Inquirer* and reprinted in the November 1844 issue of *Littell's Living Age*, described "A Legend of Brittany" as "full of beauty, lavished on a repulsive subject," an old story "clothed ... with fresh interest and beauty," and this piece quoted the second part's stanzas 41 through 44, a passage considered "almost perfect in its way."[31] Hawthorne would assuredly have seen Poe's appreciative comments regarding "A Legend of Brittany" and its church organ passage, and he may well have seen one or more of these other instances of such comments, with reprintings of that passage.

One review that praised "A Legend of Brittany" but did not focus on the church organ passage was especially likely to have come to Hawthorne's attention: the extended analysis in the April 1844 issue of the prestigious *North American Review*, an assessment written by C. C. Felton, the distinguished Harvard professor and member of the "Five of Clubs" (with Hawthorne friends and acquaintances George Hillard, Henry Wadsworth Longfellow, Charles Sumner, and Henry Russell Cleveland [15:82]). Suggesting various possible improvements for Lowell's poems—including "compression"—and not quoting from "A Legend of Brittany" because "we prefer to leave it to be read as a whole," Felton did comment, "The first poem, 'A Legend of Brittany,' is written with great beauty and pathos."[32]

Lowell's *Poems* sold well—indeed, Lowell wrote to Poe on 6 March 1844, "It will please you to hear that my volume will soon reach a third edition. The editions are of five hundred each, but 'run over,' as printers say, a little so that I suppose about eleven hundred [copies] have been sold" (Poe, *Complete Works* 17:159–60). Poe responded on 30 March 1844, "I sincerely rejoice to hear of the success of your volume. To sell eleven hundred copies of a bound book of American poetry, is to do wonders."[33] And Poe continued to acknowledge the virtues of "A Legend of Brittany": he offered additional praise of the poem in the 11 January 1845 issue of the New York *Evening Mirror*, in his first identifiable book review in that newspaper, a review of Lowell's *Conversations on Some of the Old Poets*:

> We have few men among us of any kind, who think or write at once so earnestly, so purely, and so originally as Lowell; and certainly we have no man among us who can do all this, in prose, as well as he, and at the same time compose a "Legend of Brittany."

Probably in large part because of the considerable critical regard expressed for "A Legend of Brittany"—and especially its church organ passage—Rufus Wilmot Griswold excerpted the second section's stanzas 41 through 48 for the eighth edition of his popular anthology, *The Poets and Poetry of America*, a book that appeared between 24 April and 22 May 1847.[34] And these stanzas would be included in subsequent editions, as well.

Poe returned to his acclaim of "A Legend of Brittany" in his March 1849 *Southern Literary Messenger* review of Lowell's *A Fable for Critics*, the volume that features the oft-quoted couplet, "There comes Poe, with his raven, like Barnaby Rudge, / Three fifths of him genius and two fifths sheer fudge." Lowell had not remained Poe's friend: genial relations had ended because of Poe's drinking, Poe's alienating Lowell's friend Charles F. Briggs (of the *Broadway Journal*), and Poe's accusing Lowell of plagiarism (*Collected Writings* 3:211). Poe wrote, nonetheless, in the context of a highly negative review, that "A Legend of Brittany" is "decidedly the noblest poem, of the same length, written by an American" (*Complete Works* 13:168).[35] Finally, Griswold added a fuller biographical introduction to the Lowell section of the tenth edition of *The Poets and Poetry of America*—a volume that was available on 15 December 1849—and that introduction discussed "A Legend of Brittany." Griswold wrote, "'A Legend of Brittany,' is without any of the striking faults of [Lowell's] previous compositions, and in imagination and artistic finish is the best poem [Lowell] has yet printed." After recounting the narrative, Griswold commented, "The illustration of this story gives occasion for the finest of Mr. Lowell's exhibitions of love, and the poem is in all respects beautiful and complete."[36]

Although it is unclear whether Hawthorne knew of Poe's continuing praise for "A Legend of Brittany," it certainly seems probable that he would have known of the inclusion of a passage from that poem in Griswold's *The Poets and Poetry of America* in 1847. Hawthorne had sent Griswold a copy of *Mosses from an Old Manse* in 1846 (16:158, 167), and his work was reprinted and excerpted in Griswold's prose anthology, *The Prose Writers of America*, in 1847.[37] If Hawthorne did not own or borrow a copy of the eighth, ninth, or tenth edition of *The Poets and Poetry of America*—all of which included the church organ passage from "A Legend of Brittany"—then perhaps he saw a copy at Elizabeth Peabody's West Street bookshop or the Old Comer Bookstore or the Boston Athenaeum's Reading Room or the Salem Athenaeum or the Salem bookstores. And perhaps, too, Lowell might have mentioned to Hawthorne the growing reputation of "A Legend of Brittany."

Hawthorne and Lowell continued their friendship in the period from the publication of Lowell's *Poems* through Hawthorne's writing *The Scarlet Letter*. The two writers' mutual regard is evident in their occasional writings about one another. Hawthorne, in his April 1845 tale "P's Correspondence," referred to Lowell as one of the "most fervent and worthiest worshippers" of Keats (10:375). And Hawthorne wrote in his introduction to the 1846 *Mosses from an Old Manse*, "The Old Manse," that Lowell had told him a "deeply impressive" story at the Concord grave of two British soldiers (10:9). Indeed,

Hawthorne wrote that Lowell's story of a Concord youth's axing to death a wounded British soldier (a story prompting Hawthorne's inference that the youth's "soul was tortured by the blood-stain") "has borne more fruit for me, than all that history tells of the fight" (10:10).

Lowell wrote in his 1848 satirical poem *A Fable for Critics* an unsatirical appreciation of Hawthorne:

> There is Hawthorne, with genius so shrinking and rare
> That you hardly at first see the strength that is there;
> A frame so robust, with a nature so sweet,
> So earnest, so graceful, so lithe and so fleet,
> Is worth a descent from Olympus to meet![38]

Also, Lowell gave to Hawthorne a copy of his two-volume *Poems* of 1849, the first volume of which began with the revised "A Legend of Brittany." The poet inscribed that volume, "Nathaniel Hawthorne from the author." Presumably Lowell presented this set at the time of its publication, December 1849—when Hawthorne was writing *The Scarlet Letter*.[39] Lowell, responding to Poe's criticism of the didacticism of "A Legend of Brittany," had eliminated some of the preachiness for this new edition, and, responding to C. C. Felton's criticism in the *North American Review*, had compressed the work. He must also have considered the response of Elizabeth B. Barrett "a woman whose genius I admire," Lowell had written. She offered her criticism of the poem in an 1844 letter (the mutilations in which necessitate occasional ellipses):

> Your "Legend of Brittany" is full of beautiful touches, ... to go no farther,—and the whole of the cathedral scene presents signs of no ordinary power.... that your object is (a noble one!) to teach not merely the holiness but hallowingness of love, I still shrink a little at the sudden escape from guilt & its results, which you confer on Mordred.

One imagines that Barrett's reservation may have led Lowell to delete the promised redemption of Mordred in the revised version of "A Legend of Brittany" for the 1849 *Poems*.[40] However, he let the church organ passage stand—not surprisingly, in light of the critical recognition it had received.

Finally, on 13 January 1850, as Hawthorne approached his writing the final three chapters of *The Scarlet Letter*, Lowell wrote letters to friends soliciting financial support for Hawthorne.[41] Lowell addressed one of the editors of the New York *Literary World*, Evert A. Duyckinck, noting that money for Hawthorne had already been raised "in this neighborhood" and asking, "Could not something be also done in New York? I know that you appreciate him, and that you will be glad to do anything in your power. I take it for granted that you know personally all those who would be most likely to give." The letter to Duyckinck indicates that Lowell was writing, as well, to the former editor of the *Democratic Review*, John O'Sullivan. And Lowell penned a letter to the president of the Eastern Pennsylvania Anti-Slavery Society, Edward M. Davis, of Philadelphia, asking if he could provide money for Hawthorne (through writer and theologian William Henry Furness)— after all, Lowell wrote, "Hawthorne is a man of rare genius and we all owe him a debt."[42] The irony is that Hawthorne was then incurring a debt to Lowell—specifically for "A Legend of Brittany," another "deeply impressive" story that had "borne ... fruit" for Hawthorne.

The edition of "A Legend of Brittany" that we may most profitably rely on here is that of the 1844 *Poems*—it is longer and more suggestively detailed than the later version in the 1849 *Poems*. Clearly Hawthorne would have known both versions, but he would have had six years to muse about the first of these, and only days and weeks to consider the second. Furthermore, neither the first version's didacticism (which irked Poe), nor its length (which seems to have troubled Felton), nor its redemption of Mordred (which disturbed Barrett) would have been very likely to bother Hawthorne.[43]

Before examining the church organ passage in Lowell's poem and the rendering of Dimmesdale's voice in the Election Sermon passage, we should note correspondences between the story of Mordred and Margaret in "A Legend of Brittany" and that of Arthur Dimmesdale and Hester Prynne in *The Scarlet Letter*. In Lowell's poem and in Hawthorne's novel, an innocent young woman has a love affair with a man of religious station, a love affair that results in pregnancy or the birth of a child. The unborn infant or child imbibes the sorrow of its mother. In both narratives, the man, anxious about others' disapproval and about his possible loss of professional standing (for breaking a vow of celibacy or committing adultery), tries to hide the love affair (through murder or silence) and consequently feels great guilt. In both narratives, the woman continues to love the man and seeks reunion with him in heaven. During a festival at which the townspeople have gathered at the church, the man's crime (of murder or adultery) is revealed to the awestruck crowd, and the unborn infant is released to heaven or the child is released to the world.[44] Relieved that all is now known, the guilty man dies, with a supernatural amaranth or *A* on his chest. The man will do penance or has done penance and will probably be reunited with his beloved in the next world.

Although significant differences exist between the two stories—clearly the manipulative and murderous Mordred possesses some of the diabolical qualities of Chillingworth—the parallels in plot are sufficient to warrant consideration. Hawthorne had been gripped by Lowell's Revolutionary War tale of violence and implicit guilt; he would again have been gripped by Lowell's medieval tale of violence and explicit guilt. The correspondences observed suggest the influence of the poem on the novel and invite attention to correspondences between the poem's celebrated passage about the music of the church organ and the response to that music, and the novel's treatment of Dimmesdale's voice in his final sermon and the response to that voice.

Leading to the climactic church organ passage in "A Legend of Brittany" are Margaret's meeting Mordred in "a little dell" that was "[d]eep in the forest" (16) and her returning home with him, where "Her summer nature felt a need to bless, / And a like longing to be blest again" (22). Leading to the climactic Election Sermon in *The Scarlet Letter* is Hester's meeting her former lover Arthur in "a little dell" that is "deep into the wood," where the minister witnesses Hester's provocative casting off of the scarlet letter, her release of her confined hair, and her "smile, that seemed gushing from the very heart of womanhood," her "crimson flush," and the return of "[h]er sex, her youth, and the whole richness of her beauty" (1:202–3). Furthermore, like Margaret in the forest, who "would have gone, / Yet almost wished it might not be alone" (19), Hester says to her beloved, "Thou shalt not go alone!" (1:198).[45]

The church organ passage in "A Legend of Brittany" is introduced by two stanzas concerning the gathering of the people to the church on the occasion of a festival (50–51); the passage about Dimmesdale's "vocal organ" in *The Scarlet Letter* is introduced with the procession of gentlemen soldiers (linked by Hawthorne to "Knights Templars") and civic and religious leaders to the church on the occasion of a holiday, Election Day (when the new governor will be installed) (1:236–40). The concluding action of each work is imminent. In "A Legend of Brittany," the music of the church organ will lead to the music of the choir and the speech of the murdered Margaret, followed by the performance of the baptism, the release of the unborn infant, and the death of Mordred; in *The Scarlet Letter*, Dimmesdale will give the Election Sermon in the church, and the people will respond with much talk and a great shout; then, on the scaffold, supported by Hester, he will confess his guilt for adultery, acknowledge Pearl, and die.

Verbal parallels begin to be evident on comparison of the much-hailed stanza 41 of the second part of "A Legend of Brittany" with a portion of the passage about Dimmesdale's voice in the church in *The Scarlet Letter*. These parallels concern the rising and sinking of a majestic sound in (or from) a church:

"A Legend of Brittany"
Part Second, Stanza 41

Then swelled *the organ*: up through choir and nave
    The *music* trembled *with an* inward thrill
Of bliss at its own *grandeur*: wave on wave
    Its flood of mellow thunder *rose, until*
The hushed air shivered with the throb *it* gave,
    Then, poising for a moment, *it* stood still,
And *sank* and *rose* again, to burst in spray
That wandered into silence far away.
                (51; emphasis added)

The Scarlet Letter
Chapter 22

This vocal *organ* was in itself a rich endowment.... Like all other *music*, it breathed passion and pathos, and emotions high or tender, in a tongue native to the human heart.... Now she [Hester Prynne] caught the low undertone, as of the wind *sinking* down to repose itself; *then* ascended with it, as *it rose* through progressive gradations of sweetness and power, *until its* volume seemed to envelop her *with an* atmosphere of awe and solemn *grandeur*.
                (1:243; emphasis added)

The verbal parallels about the noble ascent of the "music" become more marked in stanza 42 (and lines in stanza 43) and the subsequent portion of the Election Sermon passage. Comparison reveals in both texts the music's filling the church and "bursting" the walls:

"A Legend of Brittany"
Part Second, Stanza 42
(and lines from Stanza 43)

Like to a *mighty heart* the music seemed,
    That yearns with melodies it cannot speak,
Until, in grand despair of what it dreamed,
    In the *agony* of effort it doth break,
Yet triumphs breaking; on it rushed and streamed
    And wantoned in its might, *as when* a lake,

Long pent among the mountains, *bursts its walls*
And in one crowding *gush* leaps forth and falls.

Deeper and deeper shudders shook *the air*,
    As the huge bass kept gathering heavily,
. . . .
It *grew up* like a darkness everywhere,
    Filling the vast *cathedral*....
                    (52; emphasis added)

The Scarlet Letter
Chapter 22

And yet, majestic as the voice sometimes became, there was for
ever in it an essential character of plaintiveness. A loud or low
expression of *anguish*,—the whisper or the shriek ... that touched
a sensibility in every bosom! ... But even *when* the minister's voice
grew *high* and commanding,—*when* it *gushed* irrepressibly
upward—*when* it assumed its utmost breadth and power, so
overfilling the church as to *burst its* way through the solid *walls*, *and*
diffuse itself in the open *air*,—still, if the auditor listened intently,
and for the purpose, he could detect the same cry of pain. What
was it? The complaint of a human *heart*, sorrow-laden, perchance
guilty, telling its secret, whether of guilt or sorrow, to the *great
heart* of mankind.
                    (1:243; emphasis added)

The correspondences between the passage regarding the church organ and
that concerning the "vocal organ" conclude with the similar rendering of the
music's effect. In the poem, the church organ prompts the "rich chant" of the
"full-toned choir," and *"fifty voices in one strand* did twist / Their varicolored
tones" (52–53; emphasis added). In the novel, Dimmesdale's voice prompts
in his listeners both rapturous speech (1:248) and "that more impressive
sound than the organ-tones of the blast, or the thunder, or the roar of the
sea; even that mighty swell of *many voices, blended into one great voice*" (1:250;
emphasis added).

The verbal correspondences are evident. The "music" of the church
"organ," music of some "grandeur," music that "rose" and "sank," that "grew
up," "filling the vast cathedral," music like a lake that "leaps forth" "in one
crowding gush," having "bursts its walls," causing "fifty voices" to form "one
strand," in "A Legend of Brittany," resonates with the "music" of
Dimmesdale's "vocal organ," a sound of some "grandeur," that "rose" and

sank, that "grew high," "gushed irrepressibly upward," "over-filling the church as to burst its way through the solid walls," causing "many voices" to form "one great voice," in *The Scarlet Letter*. Having read his friend Lowell's "A Legend of Brittany"—the lead poem in both the 1844 and 1849 editions of Lowell's *Poems* and a work frequently acclaimed—Hawthorne drew upon its plot and its setting, and, with regard to its most admired passage, some of its language as well. Even as Hawthorne had fashioned a passage concerning a spiritual murder by relying, in part, on Poe's account of a literal murder, he shaped a passage concerning a climactic speech in a church by relying, in part, on Lowell's treatment of similarly climactic organ music in a church. Perhaps in turning to Lowell's treatment, Hawthorne sought for his Election Sermon passage the "richly ideal" quality that Poe had mentioned in his review of "A Legend of Brittany" in *Graham's Magazine*—or the "almost perfect" rendering that a British critic had noted in a reprinted appraisal in *Littell's Living Age*—or the "great beauty and pathos" that Felton had observed in his critique in the *North American Review*. Clearly, by alluding to Lowell's church organ passage, Hawthorne provided an added dimension to Dimmesdale's presentation of his Election Sermon, subtly imbuing one impassioned triumph with another.

The notable pattern of correspondences plainly argues against mere coincidence, but a reader might propose that Hawthorne need not have been aware of his debt to Lowell—he could have relied on what Henry James termed "the deep well of unconscious cerebration," so honored by John Livingston Lowes in *The Road to Xanadu*.[46] This view cannot be definitively disproved—unquestionably Hawthorne's imaginative process involved unconscious, as well as conscious workings. Yet the considerable critical attention to "A Legend of Brittany" in the 1840s, Hawthorne's growing friendship with Lowell in that period, and the degree of correspondence between "A Legend of Brittany" and *The Scarlet Letter*—including verbal parallels—tend to indicate that more probably Hawthorne was aware of his borrowing. While his unconscious no doubt did exert some influence over the reworking of the church organ passage, in all likelihood Hawthorne knowingly relied on "A Legend of Brittany" for his novel.

Not surprisingly, even as Hawthorne modified his source passage in Poe for *The Scarlet Letter*—and, as scholars have shown, other source passages for the novel, as well—so, too, did he modify his source passage in Lowell. Through Hawthorne's imaginative reformulation, the despair of the organ music over its ever attaining full expression, in "A Legend of Brittany," became the despair in Dimmesdale's voice over his ever attaining relief from his guilt, in *The Scarlet Letter*. Serving the theme and characterization in his novel, Hawthorne replaced a sense of frustration with a more abiding sense of sin. Furthermore, the erotic energy that seems suggested by Lowell's passage—evident in such language as "swelled," "trembled," "inward thrill," "bliss," "shivered," "throb," and "burst in spray"—is diminished in Hawthorne's passage. Still, that energy remains present in the gushing, bursting organ. As with the violent in Poe, with the erotic in Lowell, Hawthorne refined and preserved at the same time. We shall return to this point later in this chapter.

The correspondences between the denouement of Lowell's poem and that of Hawthorne's novel may be briefly stated. In "A Legend of Brittany," the music of the church organ and the choir ceases suddenly as "a nameless fear ... leapt along from heart to heart"—a fear that causes all, with "a dark, freezing awe," to look to the altar—where Margaret is buried (53–54). In *The Scarlet Letter*, "The shout died into a murmur, as one portion of the crowd after another obtained a glimpse" of the "feeble and pale" Dimmesdale. As the minister pauses at the foot of the scaffold, "The crowd ... looked on with awe and wonder" (1:252). The great quiet in both works leads to the revelation: Margaret's spirit, come from heaven, reveals Mordred's responsibility for her unborn infant and intimates his guilt for her murder, and Dimmesdale reveals his own guilt for adultery.

And then comes the release. After Margaret's spirit asks for baptism for her infant to allow him to enter heaven, the priests perform the rite, the crowd hears "A sigh, as of some heart from travail sore / Released," and the spirits of mother and son, singing "*Misereatur Deus*" ("God have mercy"), rise to heaven (62). Dimmesdale asks for his daughter Pearl's kiss, so long denied; she kisses him on the lips, and "A spell was broken": her tears on her father's cheek are "the pledge that she would grow up amid human joy and sorrow, nor for ever do battle with the world, but be a woman in it" (1:256). In both poem and novel, the revelation of a secret passion yields redemption for the consequence of that passion—for Margaret's unborn infant and for Pearl. Furthermore, Margaret's spirit says to Mordred, "Yes, ages hence, in joy we yet may meet, / By sorrow thou, and I by patience, tried" (61); Hester, less certain, asks the dying Dimmesdale, "Shall we not meet again? Shall we not spend our immortal life together?" (1:256).

After Margaret's speech and the baptism, Mordred dies, and "Upon his breast a little blossom lay / Of amaranth, such as grows not in earth's mould" (63); Dimmesdale, having acknowledged God's mercy, dies with the scarlet letter *A* upon his breast (1:258). And while Margaret's spirit said to Mordred, "If thou wast false, more need there is for me / Still to be true" (57), Hawthorne comments on the story of Dimmesdale by advising his reader to allow his or her worst to be inferred: "Be true! Be true! Be true!" (1:260).

"A Legend of Brittany" was a particularly important thread for Hawthorne in his composition of *The Scarlet Letter*. It offered suggestive plot detail, characterization, setting, and language. There are, of course, major differences: for example, Lowell offers a medieval tenor, Hawthorne a Puritan one; Lowell offers a manipulative lover, Hawthorne a manipulative cuckold; Lowell treats murder, Hawthorne adultery; and Lowell tells of an unborn boy, Hawthorne a little girl. Still, as has been noted, the two tales share much. The issues in both works that require further consideration here are sex, love, and religion.

Sex is clearly a critical element in both "A Legend of Brittany" and *The Scarlet Letter*. In both works, sexual passion, although never explicitly described, is the catalyst for subsequent events. Lowell's language is sometimes romantic and sentimental—Margaret's "long dreamed-of ecstasy" (26), the "[b]right passion of young hearts" (27), and the "dewy dawn of love" (28), for example. Yet the church organ passage in "A Legend of Brittany"— one that elaborates lines that appeared in Lowell's "The Church"—invites at least consideration of suggestiveness.[47] The swollen, rising, throbbing, trembling organ that bursts in spray does seem to warrant attention in this regard. We should recall Lowell's words in *Conversations on Some of the Old Poets*:

> To be a sensualist in a certain kind and to a certain degree is the mark of a pure and youthful nature. To be able to keep a just balance between sense and spirit, and to have the soul welcome frankly all the delicious impulses which flow to it from without, is a good and holy thing. But it must welcome them as the endearments of a wife, not of a harlot.

And we should note that an older Lowell, arguing in an 1874 letter against licentiousness in literature, did allow that the erotic might find a place in poetry: "Shelley almost alone (take his 'Stanzas to an Indian air,' for example) has trodden with unfaltering foot the scimitar-edged bridge which leads from physical sensation to the heaven of song."[48] The strong evidence of Lowell's church organ passage—evidence reinforced by his critical comments— argues that this passage of spiritual ascent possesses, too, a quality of physical joy.

Certainly Hawthorne does write suggestively (as Frederick Crews has shown): the minister, returning from his forest meeting with the beautiful and vibrant Hester, "leaped across the plashy places, thrust himself through the clinging underbrush, climbed the ascent, plunged into the hollow" (1:216).[49] Emboldened by his encounter with Hester, Dimmesdale imagines violating the faith and innocence of parishioners he meets—including a "maiden" whose "field of innocence" he feels "potent to blight" (1:219–20). Moreover, the minister returns home no longer fearful of Roger Chillingworth, and, with "an impulsive flow of thought and emotion" (1:225), he writes the Election Sermon. The source of Dimmesdale's "impulsive flow" is his newly aroused libidinal energy, as Crews first noted; the minister's sexual excitement will prompt his writing a prophetic sermon that will provoke excitement in his community.[50] But Dimmesdale does not fully recognize the origins of his seeming inspiration, his sublimation: "he ... only wondered that Heaven should see fit to transmit the grand and solemn music of its oracles through so foul an organ-pipe as he" (1:225).[51]

For his passage on Dimmesdale's voice in the church, surely Hawthorne would have recognized the physical joy in Lowell's church organ passage. Hawthorne did noticeably reduce that passage's suggestiveness in his reworking. However, appropriately (for a sermon prompted by the speaker's libidinal awakening), he did not wholly remove it.[52] Regarding its erotic tones, the thread that Hawthorne borrowed from Lowell was only moderately faded. Perhaps with regard to the bursting organ in the Election Sermon passage in *The Scarlet Letter*, we may conclude that, in terms of the balance of subtlety and accessibility, the figure of consummation is consummately figured.

It is true that the regard of Lowell's fiancée Maria White for "A Legend of Brittany" prompted Charles F. Briggs to term the poem "proper reading for pure-minded loving creatures." But we may remember that Sophia Hawthorne was moved by and admiring of Hawthorne's *The Scarlet Letter*, though it also has evident sexual resonance.[53] (Whether she denied or missed the resonance is not clear.) Both Lowell's poem and Hawthorne's novel have a subtle but strong physical passion.

And that physical passion is an expression of love. Of Margaret, Lowell writes:

> All beauty and all life he was to her;
>   She questioned not his love, she only knew
> That she loved him, and not a pulse could stir
>   In her whole frame but quivered through and through
> With this glad thought ... (28)

And of her beloved, the murderous Mordred, Lowell acknowledges, "At first he loved her truly" (34).

Hawthorne writes that, after seven years, Arthur was the man whom Hester had "once,—nay, why should we not speak it?—still so passionately loved" (1:193). And the writer reinforces this view with a touching biblical allusion—a small portion of what Michael J. Colacurcio calls Hawthorne's "vast store of twice-told words."[54] Chapter 3 of The Song of Solomon begins with a description of a woman bereft of her lover:

> By night on my bed I sought him whom my soul loveth: I sought him, but I found him not.
>
> I will rise now, and go about the city in the streets, and in the broad ways I will seek him whom my soul loveth: I sought him, but I found him not. (3:1–2)

When Hester sees the minister in the marketplace as he passes her and ignores her altogether, she sorrowfully concludes that "there could be no real bond between the clergyman and herself"—and, Hawthorne adds, "she groped darkly, and stretched forth her cold hands, and found him not" (1:239–40). Thus, Hawthorne delicately and aptly intimates the passionate love that animates the action of The Scarlet Letter. The bereft woman in the broad ways—Hester in the marketplace—the two are one—each sought her lover and "found him not." Hawthorne ably employs some of his "twice-told words"—artfully sews into his cloth a biblical thread—to hint at the passion that he must so often subdue.[55]

And Hester is herself loved. Although, as Ernest Sandeen has admitted, the minister, still so dependent on the rigid structure of Puritan orthodoxy, is "not a disciple of true love," he is nonetheless susceptible—as the occasion for Hester's punishment suggests. Torn between conscience and passion, Dimmesdale later admits to Hester that he has not been penitent (1:192)—arguably, as Sandeen has written, because "he is still in love and can no more regret this passion than Hester can regret hers." Indeed, Hester says to Arthur, "What we did had a consecration of its own. We felt it so! We said so to each other! Hast thou forgotten it?" And the minister responds, "Hush, Hester!" and then, "No; I have not forgotten!" (1:195). In further support of his view, Sandeen adduces the tremulous voice of Dimmesdale as he addresses Hester in the first scaffold scene, the joy he feels as he senses the warmth of Pearl and Hester in the second scaffold scene, the passion of his writing the new Election Sermon, the emotional delivery of that sermon, and his public confession in the third and final scaffold scene—a confession that reveals both conscience and pride and that redeems the minister's passion. Sandeen writes of Dimmesdale, "we like him most when he is most the lover." And Sandeen fittingly quotes Hawthorne on the appearance of sunshine in the forest when Hester's "radiant and tender smile" and "crimson flush" return: "Love, whether newly born, or aroused from a deathlike slumber, must always create a sunshine, filling the heart so full of radiance, that it overflows upon the outward world" (1:203). Sandeen argues that here Hawthorne comes as close as he will to revealing love to be "the deep force which moves through the story."[56]

It is relevant to recall here the concluding motto of Hawthorne's novel and that motto's source. As Robert L. Brant first noted, "ON A FIELD, SABLE, THE LETTER A GULES" was drawn from the final line of Andrew Marvell's poem, "The Unfortunate Lover," "In a field sable a lover gules."[57] Hawthorne's black field with a red letter was originally a black field with a red lover. The complete final stanza from Marvell's poem reads:

> This is the only banneret
> That ever Love created yet:
> Who though, by the malignant stars,
> Forced to live in storms and wars;
> Yet dying leaves a perfume here,
> And music within every ear:
> And he in story only rules,
> In a field sable a lover gules.[58]

Perhaps Hawthorne is suggesting with his allusion that the two who are marked by the letter A (and who rule only in his novel), the lovers Hester Prynne and Arthur Dimmesdale, though undoubtedly unfortunate, leave behind them, after their deaths, a gladness in those who know their story. Through allusion, Hawthorne subtilized and enriched the romantic passion in his novel, thereby providing a guide, an insight into his own perception of his characters.

Finally, there is assuredly also a strong religious element in both "A Legend of Brittany" and *The Scarlet Letter*. Lowell writes in "A Legend of Brittany" that Art's "fittest triumph is to show that good / Lurks in the heart of evil evermore" (32), and he later asserts that "God doth not work as man works, but makes all / The crooked paths of ill to goodness tend" (37). (The poet thus recalls Milton's Adam in *Paradise Lost* [bk. 12, lines 469–78].) And he suggests in his poem both Satan and an innocent Eve. Lowell writes of Mordred—he with "a serpent in his breast" (35)—"He fell as doth the tempter ever fall, / Even in the gaining of his loathesome end" (37), but he writes of the still-innocent Margaret after the love affair, "Though tempted much, her woman's nature clings / To its first pure belief, and with sad eyes / Looks backward o'er the gate of Paradise" (38). (Mordred's eventual redemption seems later implied by the immortal amaranth flower, which departed Eden for heaven at the time of the Fall.) A Catholic element emerges as the poem proceeds. After Margaret has been killed by Mordred and gone to heaven, she comes to believe that with the help of the Virgin Mary, Mordred may eventually join her: "And thou, dear Mordred, after penance done, / By blessed Mary's grace may'st meet me here" (60). And she asserts that she has been able to plead for her infant's baptism "in Christ's dear name" (59) only through Mary's intercession: "For she it was that pitied my sad moan, / Herself not free from mother's pangs whilere, / And gave me leave to wander forth alone / To ask due rites for him I hold so dear" (60). Although the original fourteenth-century ballad, "The Three Red Monks," offered Catholic detail, it did not feature the marian emphasis of "A Legend of Brittany"; that element was Lowell's addition.

With *The Scarlet Letter*, Hawthorne also offers a providential tale with Catholic elements. The act of adultery constitutes the Original Sin, as Roy R. Male first noted, and Hester and Dimmesdale, repeatedly termed "fallen" (1:73, 110, 117, 118, 159, 195–96, 259), have a child who was "worthy to have been brought forth in Eden"—indeed, "worthy to have been left there, to be the plaything of the angels, after the world's first parents were driven out" (1:90).[59] Pearl comes "by the inscrutable decree of providence" (1:89) to bring her mother's soul to heaven—"to remind [Hester]," as Dimmesdale argues, "at every moment, of her fall,—but yet to teach her, as it were by the Creator's sacred pledge, that, if she bring the child to heaven, the child will also bring its parent thither!" (1:115). Hester comes to see her daughter as evidence of Providence's "design of justice and retribution" and "purpose of mercy and beneficence" (1:180). And, as mentioned in chapter 1, Roger Chillingworth is the providential afflicter of Dimmesdale—the satanic figure who has "the Divine permission ... to burrow into the clergyman's intimacy" to help the minister achieve salvation (1:128).[60] The minister, confessing all on the scaffold, recognizes Chillingworth's providential role and sees it as evidence of divine mercy (1:256–57). God's providence is intimated, too, in the message of the Election Sermon—the "high and glorious destiny for the newly gathered people of the Lord" (1:249). Like "A Legend of Brittany," *The Scarlet Letter* affirms what Hawthorne termed "celestial guardianship" (1:155). That guardianship is developed further, through the form of the novel, as will be seen in chapter 4.

The Catholic elements in Hawthorne's novel are well known. In the first of the three scaffold scenes that are so crucial to the structure of the novel, Hester holding her baby Pearl is said to resemble, for "a Papist," "the image of Divine Maternity" (1:56). As scholars have noted, the subsequent scaffold scenes also have a Catholic resonance: the second scaffold scene, involving Hester, Pearl, and Dimmesdale, may suggest Mary, Mary Magdalene, and Jesus; the final scaffold scene, involving Hester holding the dying Dimmesdale, suggests Mary and the dying Jesus—the Pietà.[61] Hawthorne later writes about the generous Hester, "She was self-ordained a Sister of Mercy" (1:161), and he asserts that her scarlet letter came to have "the effect of the cross on a nun's bosom" (1:163). In contrast, the minister, still hiding his guilt, beat himself with "a bloody scourge" in his "secret closet"—a practice "more in accordance with the old, corrupted faith of Rome, than with the better light of the church in which he had been born and bred" (1:144). The faith of Rome, both respected and faulted, holds a prominent place in *The Scarlet Letter*.[62]

It is not surprising that Hawthorne considered an additional Catholic element for *The Scarlet Letter*—and confided that fact to Lowell. The poet wrote, in a 12 June 1860 letter to Charles Eliot Norton's sister Jane Norton, about his conversation with Hawthorne in Liverpool: "He said ... that it had been part of his plan in 'The Scarlet Letter' to make Dimmesdale confess himself to a Catholic priest." And Lowell added, "I, for one, am sorry he didn't. It would have been psychologically admirable."[63]

It is noteworthy that the Catholic motif in Lowell's "A Legend of Brittany" is markedly different from that in *The Scarlet Letter*. Never directly depicted, Mary nonetheless takes a part in the events of Lowell's poem—she permits Margaret to leave heaven and make her plea on earth. Lowell uses the Madonna in a straightforward and dramatic way—she is a part of the providence that the story reveals. On the other hand, Mary takes no part in Hawthorne's novel, providential or otherwise—rather, she is the standard of nurturing motherhood with which Hester is compared—and of innocence, with which Hester is contrasted. Hawthorne employs the Madonna image to intensify his characterization of Hester—even as he writes of the "bloody scourge" in the "secret closet" to intensify his characterization of the guilt-wracked Arthur. The final image of the Pietà intensifies the characterization further, highlighting Hester's maternal strength and Arthur's long suffering and his ultimate triumph.

We may here consider the significance of the presence of the erotic in the church passage in "A Legend of Brittany" and its modulated presence in the church passage in *The Scarlet Letter*. There could well be an aesthetic purpose—the hinted sexual passion in each of these passages effectively balances the original undescribed sexual passion, providing a satisfying symmetry. Perhaps, too, there is a dramatic purpose. Both the poem and the novel are accounts of family lost and recovered, and the erotic tension returns us to the beginning of the family and thus fittingly anticipates the coming recovery of the family: the reunion of Margaret, her baby, and eventually Mordred, in heaven; and the reunion of Hester, Pearl, and

Dimmesdale on the scaffold, and, presumably, again in heaven. But beyond the aesthetic and dramatic purposes, there seems to be a religious purpose. We may infer that the presence of a hint of sexual love in each church passage suggests—to adapt a phrase of Elizabeth Barrett's—a hallowing of sexual love. In "A Legend of Brittany," such treatment is not surprising since it was not the sexual love but the will to power that led to the tragedy. But in *The Scarlet Letter*, the hallowing of sexual love may seem remarkable since that love, in the context of an adulterous affair, did lead to the tragedy and was considered, by the minister and the townspeople, sinful. However, with the erotic energy in the church, helping to shape prophecy, Hawthorne provides a counter-balance to the scarlet letter, the badge of the sin of adultery. That the erotic energy occurs within this religious setting and situation may well covertly confirm that the love of Hester and Arthur did indeed have "a consecration of its own" (1:195); that "the whole relation of man and woman" in the case of these two did involve "sacred love" (1:263); that while their union was "unrecognized on earth," it would be recognized at "the bar of final judgment," which would be, as Hester had hoped, "their marriage altar" (1:80). It is surely true that, as Sophia Hawthorne wrote to her sister Mary Mann, *The Scarlet Letter* "shows that the Law cannot be broken" (16: 313 n), but, like the claims of law in the novel, the claims of love in this work are also compelling. And certainly the presence of a hint of physical passion in the church passage tends to strengthen these claims. The tension between law and love in *The Scarlet Letter* is unresolvable, but the artistry that created that tension seems clear and beyond challenge.

Providence in both "A Legend of Brittany" and *The Scarlet Letter* is merciful. Lowell's murderous Mordred may well be reunited with Margaret in heaven after he has done his penance. And Hawthorne's adulterous Dimmesdale—granted the opportunity to do penance for his sin (enduring Chillingworth and the scarlet letter) and to confess—achieves salvation. And, despite his doubts, he may be reunited in the afterlife with Hester, who has been brought there through her love of Pearl and, presumably, through her good works for the community. In the poem and in the novel, the sinner is punished, but not damned. Even the satanic Chillingworth is given a qualified reprieve (1:260–61). Both Lowell and Hawthorne reprise the story of the Fall of Man, honoring the human and the divine—and perhaps thereby managing to approach Milton's goal in *Paradise Lost*—to "assert Eternal providence, / And justify the ways of God to men" (bk. 1, lines 25–26).

The parallels observed here argue for the likelihood of additional parallels between Lowell's writing and *The Scarlet Letter*. And one additional correspondence may indeed by noted, involving again Dimmesdale's Election Sermon.

We know that Hawthorne would have encountered Lowell's "The Old English Dramatists," which appeared in the April 1842, May 1842, and August 1842 issues of the *Boston Miscellany*. Nathan Hale Jr., the editor of the *Boston Miscellany* (and former coeditor, with Lowell, of *Harvardiana*), had sent Hawthorne a copy of the January 1842 issue, and Hawthorne had responded on 6 December 1841, "I have read it with great pleasure, and like it very much indeed, both as to its external and material aspect, and its intellectual and spiritual being" (15:598). Hawthorne would surely have seen a review of the new edition of his *Twice-Told Tales* in the February 1842 issue of the *Boston Miscellany*, and, on 28 March 1842, Hawthorne submitted to Hale "A Virtuoso's Collection" (15:619), a work that was published in the May 1842 issue.[64] Furthermore, Lowell reworked the material in "The Old English Dramatists," giving it a conversational form, and this material was a significant portion of his 1845 book, *Conversations on Some of the Old Poets*— a copy of which, as already noted, Lowell gave to Hawthorne, "with author's love."

The first installment of "The Old English Dramatists" was placed prominently as the lead article in the April 1842 *Boston Miscellany*. If we recall Hawthorne's writing that Dimmesdale's Election Sermon culminated with a prophecy of the "high and glorious destiny for the newly gathered people of the Lord," we may well find the opening of the second paragraph of that first installment to be familiar and significant: "It is the high and glorious vocation of poesy to make our daily life and toil more beautiful and holy by the divine ministerings of love." Modified to address the fitness for poetry of a concern with slavery (perhaps because of Maria Lowell's influence), the line appears in *Conversations* thus: "It is the high and glorious vocation of Poesy as well to make our own daily life and toil more beautiful and holy to us by the divine ministerings of love, as to render us swift to convey the same blessing to our brethren."[65] In either version, the key adjective phrase "high and glorious" is present. Hawthorne's use of that phrase—a phrase appearing in two different Lowell works, both of which Hawthorne would have read— suggests another borrowing from Lowell for *The Scarlet Letter*. Although one could assert that the borrowing was only a coincidence, it seems likelier, in light of the Hawthorne–Lowell pattern already demonstrated, that the borrowing is a significant one—whether consciously or unconsciously made—and that it may clarify the Election Sermon itself.

The "high and glorious vocation of Poesy" takes us back to Poe's comment that the church organ passage in "A Legend of Brittany" was "richly ideal," for the ideal is the consequence of "the sentiment of Poesy"

(*Complete Works* 8:282). If we read the first paragraph in the first installment of "The Old English Dramatists," we note, in particular, Lowell's assertion that "under the thin crust of fashion and frivolity throb the undying fires of the great soul of man, which is the fountain and center of all poesy, and which will one day burst forth, and wither like grassblades all the temples and palaces which form and convention have heaped over it." And so I offer a tentative inference: the throbbing bursting organ in "A Legend of Brittany," which refers literally to the church organ and its music, suggests figuratively not only a sexual dimension, but also a larger dimension, which the sexual shadows forth: that of the poetic enterprise itself. According to this view, that throbbing bursting organ, like the throbbing bursting "fires of the great soul of man," is the genius of the poet. (In this regard, we should recall Lowell's assertion, in *Conversations*, regarding Wordsworth's Intimations Ode, "The grand symphony of Wordsworth's Ode rolls through me, and I tremble, as the air does with the gathering thunders of the organ." Again, for Lowell, the organ is a figure for poetic genius.) We encounter in the third paragraph of the first installment of "The Old English Dramatists" an analogy between the poet, whose work is the expression of love, and the "angel of love," who leaves Eden, behind Adam and Eve, holding the eternal amaranth—the very flower that Lowell associates with Mordred in "A Legend of Brittany." According to Lowell, the seed of the amaranth "gives a higher hope to the soul or makes life nobler or more godlike" (recalling Poe on the suggestive undercurrent), and this seed is nourished by "the overarching sky of poesy."[66] Lowell's phrase "high and glorious" is both applied to the "vocation of poesy" and embedded in an encomium for the power of poesy. Accordingly, in light of the use of that phrase with reference to the Election Sermon in *The Scarlet Letter*, the minister seems to suggest the poet; Dimmesdale seems to suggest Hawthorne.

It would seem likelier than not that Hawthorne deliberately borrowed Lowell's phrase "high and glorious" and its association. Poe had written that Hawthorne was "a prose poet" (*Collected Writings* 3:225). And, as already noted, Lowell himself had written in *Conversations* that Hawthorne "has a right in any gathering of poets."[67] And Hawthorne wrote to Longfellow on 5 June 1849, "I do not claim to be a poet; and yet I cannot but feel that some of the sacredness of that character adheres to me, and ought to be respected in me" (16:270). That Hawthorne associated the organ with poetry is evident from his narrator's mentioning, in the 1845 piece "P.'s Correspondence," having heard "scraps of poetry ... a few as grand as organ-peals" (10:379). Perhaps, even as Dimmesdale's prophecy concerns the "high and glorious destiny" of Puritan New England, it also suggests the "high and glorious vocation" of the writer. And perhaps, with this allusion to the "high and glorious vocation of poesy" in his climactic church sermon, Hawthorne was subtly asserting "the sacredness" of the writer's effort—indeed, "the sacredness" of his own vocation.

James Russell Lowell's "A Legend of Brittany"—like *The Scarlet Letter*, a story of secret sin—is yet another source in Hawthorne's catalog of secret sources. Or, to shift to the thread that is worked throughout this study— that is, the figure of threads—"A Legend of Brittany" is one of the preeminent matching threads that Hawthorne employed for exciting his imagination and enhancing his art. And even as the angry hue in the Poe thread (the physical murder) was modulated in *The Scarlet Letter*, so, too, was the brilliant hue in the Lowell thread (the sexual suggestiveness) diminished in Hawthorne's novel. That is, the borrowed threads were, in certain ways, allowed to fade. Although Hawthorne's "wonderful skill of needlework" may be "a now forgotten art" (1:31), if it is studied, that skill may well be partly recovered.

We should recall that, on 9 December 1853, Hawthorne repaid the financial debt that he had earlier incurred by accepting funds raised for him so that he could write *The Scarlet Letter*. He sent to George Hillard "a draft on [George] Ticknor for the sum (with interest included) which was so kindly given me by unknown friends, through you, about four years ago" (17:154). And even as he repaid his financial debt to these "unknown friends," he had earlier repaid his literary debt to Lowell by masterfully transforming—and thereby paying tribute to—"A Legend of Brittany" in *The Scarlet Letter* (even as he had repaid Poe with his transformation of "The Tell-Tale Heart"). It seems very likely that Lowell would have recognized Hawthorne's literary debt to him and Hawthorne's repayment. And in view of Lowell's own borrowing from "The Three Red Monks" for "A Legend of Brittany," the poet would surely have understood well Hawthorne's borrowing. Lowell's thinking about that borrowing may be clarified by a comment that he made later with regard to Edmund Spenser: "It is not what a poet takes, but what he makes out of what he has taken, that shows what native force is in him." Ultimately, Lowell's judgment of what Hawthorne had made of what he had taken was extremely high. Indeed, on 26 February 1862, Lowell wrote to Hawthorne, "It is a pure delight to me to admire any man's work as heartily as I do yours."[68] Lowell's "pure delight" in admiring Hawthorne's first novel would surely have involved his understanding that Hawthorne's "native force" had rendered in *The Scarlet Letter* a beautiful reworking of elements of Lowell's "A Legend of Brittany." Accordingly, Lowell would have had an enormous pride—both in Hawthorne and in himself.

NOTES

1. For further information on the historical and literary connections, consult the following references. For Nathaniel Manning, see Loggins, *Hawthornes*, 87–95, 278–79; Fiedler, *Love and Death*, 229–30; Ehrlich, *Family Themes*, 35–37; and Young, *Hawthorne's Secret*, 124–27, 165. For Michael Wigglesworth, see Claudia Durst Johnson, *Understanding "The Scarlet Letter,"* 57–64. For Rousseau's Saint-Preux, see Loggins, *Hawthornes*, 279–83; Fiedler, *Love and Death*, 228–29; and Hoffman, "Political Power," 18. With regard to Lockhart's Adam Blair, see Sir Nathaniel, Review of *The Scarlet Letter*, 52; James, *Hawthorne*, 111–13; and Stephenson and Stephenson, *"Adam Blair."* And for Paulding's Avery, see Owens, "Paulding's 'The Dumb Girl.'" John Cotton has been effectively put forth by Michael Colacurcio ("Footsteps of Ann Hutchinson," 462–66, 485–94). (See chapter 3 for more on the Antinomian Controversy.) Charles Wentworth Upham, a former minister who became Hawthorne's political enemy, has also been suggested as an influence on Hawthorn's creation of Dimmesdale (Woodson, "Hawthorne, Upham, and *The Scarlet Letter*"), but Hawthorne's sympathetic treatment of his fictional minister tends to argue against this view.

2. Smolinski, "Covenant Theology," 223; Thomas F. Walsh, "Dimmesdale's Election Sermon"; Newberry *Hawthorne's Divided Loyalties*, 191.

3. For the date of publication of *A Year's Life*, see Blanck and Winship, *Bibliography of American Literature*, 6:23–24. For Lowell's comments to Longfellow on *A Year's Life*, see James Russell Lowell, *Letters*, 1:98–99. For a discussion of reviews of *A Year's Life*, see McFadyen, "The Contemporaneous Reputation of James Russell Lowell" (23–35).

4. Barrett to Lowell, 31 Mar. 1842. Published by permission of the Houghton Library, Harvard University.

5. For the unworkable agreement, see Tucker, "James Russell Lowell and Robert Carter," 191. For further information on the early demise of Lowell's *Pioneer*, see his letter to Poe of 24 March 1843 (*Complete Works* 17:138–39); as well as Scudder, *James Russell Lowell*, 1:107–8; Sculley Bradley, Introduction, xxiv–xxvi, and his "Lowell, Emerson, and *The Pioneer*"; Howard, *Victorian Knight-Errant*, 129–34; Martin Duberman, *James Russell Lowell*, 52–53; and Lease, "Robert Carter."

6. James Russell Lowell, *Letters*, 1:71–72.

7. For discussion of the source for "A Legend of Brittany," "Les Trois Moines Rouges," see Charles Oran Stewart, *Lowell and France*, 23–26. For Lowell's reading French in his boyhood and youth, see 9–10. See also James Russell Lowell, *Letters*, 1:6. The Houghton Library holds the Charles Sumner copy of the 1840 *Chants Populaires* and a Lowell copy of the 1860 edition. By the time he was writing "A Legend of Brittany," Lowell certainly knew Sumner: when Lowell and his *Pioneer* co-editor Robert Carter took action against their publishers Leland and Whiting in March 1843, they provided a bond signed by lawyers Sumner and George S. Hillard (Howard, *Victorian Knight-Errant*, 130). It is relevant to note that Lowell drew from a book of Breton legends for his 1861 poem "The Washers of the Shroud"—a book that he had borrowed from Charles Eliot Norton (Pound, "Lowell's 'Breton Legend'").

8. "Les Trois Moines Rouges" was translated into English for me by Jill Landis, a Penn State graduate student in French.

9. For Irving's reliance on "Peter Klaus" for "Rip Van Winkle," see Pochmann, "Irving's German Sources," 489–97. For contemporary awareness of Irving's debt to "Peter Klaus," see "Peter Klaus: The Legend of the Goatherd—Rip Van Winkle."

10. Briggs to Lowell, quoted by permission of the Archives of American Art, Smithsonian Institution.

11. Blanck and Winship, *Bibliography of American Literature*, 6:25.

12. For the comment about Lowell's first meeting Hawthorne, consult Edward Everett Hale, *James Russell Lowell and His Friends*, 84. For the date of the wedding of Nathaniel Hawthorne and Sophia Peabody, see Mellow, *Nathaniel Hawthorne and His Times*, 175. For Sophia Peabody's early friendship with Maria White, see Mellow, 221, and Rose Hawthorne Lathrop, *Memories of Hawthorne*, 119. For the presence of Sophia Peabody and Maria White at the first class of Fuller's "Conversations," see Vernon, *Poems of Maria Lowell*, 10. For the date of that class, see von Mehren, *Minerva and the Muse*, 114.

13. Lowell asserts his early discipleship to Hawthorne in a letter to Hawthorne of 24 April 1851. (Quotation by permission of the Berg Collection of English and American Literature, The New York Public Library, Astor, Lenox and Tilden Foundations.) The letter is mentioned in Duberman, *James Russell Lowell*, 487 n.

14. Lowell, "The First Client," 230. "The First Client" was noted as Lowell's by E. E. Brown, 37–38; Underwood, *The Poet and the Man*, 22; Littlefield, "James Russell Lowell in 1842," xxv and xxix; and Cooke, *A Bibliography of James Russell Lowell*, 22. The short comic tale anticipates elements of both Poe's "The Man of the Crowd" and Melville's "Bartleby the Scrivener."

15. The reviews of *A Year's Life* are considered in McFadyen, "Contemporaneous Reputation," 23–35.

16. For the 4 October 1842 letter concerning Lowell's visiting Hawthorne, see Maria White Lowell to Caroline King. (The passage from this letter is published by permission of the Schlesinger Library, Radcliffe Institute, Harvard University.) See also chapter 1, note 6. Sophia Hawthorne made her statement about Lowell's offer to her husband in a letter to her mother, Mrs. Elizabeth Palmer Peabody, 28 February 1843. (Publication of the quoted passage from the letter of Sophia Hawthorne is by permission of the Berg Collection of English and American Literature, The New York Public Library, Astor, Lenox and Tilden Foundations.)

17. Publication of the quoted passages from the letters of Mary Peabody and Sophia Hawthorne is by permission of the Berg Collection of English and American Literature, The New York Public Library, Astor, Lenox and Tilden Foundations. The Mary Peabody letter, written after 2 October 1842, is mentioned in John J. McDonald, "Guide to Primary Source Materials," 272.

18. Publication of the quoted passage from the Maria Lowell letter (Lowell to Shaw, 4 Nov. 1842) is by permission of the Massachusetts Historical Society. Sarah Blake Sturgis Shaw was the beautiful and socially-conscious wife of the affluent Frank Shaw, who was a supporter of Brook Farm and a translator, for the *Harbinger*, of two novels by George Sand, *Consuelo* and *The Countess of Rudolstadt*. (See Milne, *George William Curtis*, 85; and Delano, "*Harbinger*," 36). A long-time friend of Maria Lowell's, Sarah Shaw was also a friend of both Elizabeth Peabody and Sophia Hawthorne. She and her sister-in-law Anna Blake Shaw visited the Hawthornes in Concord in June 1843 (15:696, 697 n). Frank Shaw evidently later provided some financial support to the Hawthornes (16:201; see also Rose Hawthorne Lathrop [117]). The Shaws' son, Robert Gould Shaw, was killed in 1863 at Fort Wagner while leading the famous black regiment, the Massachusetts 54th. His sister, Josephine Shaw, married Lowell's nephew Charles Russell Lowell, who, in 1864, was also killed in the Civil War.

19. For the various datings of Hawthorne's composition of "The Hall of Fantasy," see chapter 1, note 2. I contend that Hawthorne completed the work after the Lowells' visit

on 2 November 1842 because otherwise he would probably have handed the story to the editor of *The Pioneer* rather than mail it on 17 December. For Lowell's comment about Hawthorne's genius, see James Russell Lowell, Review of *Historical Tales for Youth*, 42. This comment may well allude to an earlier comment about Hawthorne's genius by Park Benjamin. (See chapter 1, page 27, and note 20.)

20. Lowell wrote to his partner Robert Carter on 19 January 1843, "Hawthorne should be paid, & Neal & Poe," and on 24 January 1843, "Tell H. [Hawthorne] why we do not pay him immediately, & that I am personally responsible for the debt." (See Tucker, "James Russell Lowell," 204, 208.) Hawthorne wrote to Carter on 1 February 1843, "I did not intend to make a demand for immediate payment of my last contribution," but Sophia wrote to her mother more bluntly on 28 February 1843, "James Lowell owes us seventy dollars I believe. I am sorry for him but we want it" (15:669, 669 n). Sophia Hawthorne, in Boston, informed her husband of the failure of *The Pioneer*, and Nathaniel Hawthorne responded on 16 March 1843, "It is queer news that thou tellest me about the Pioneer. I expected it to fail in due season, but not quite so soon. Not improbably we shall have to wait months for our money" (15:678). Leon Howard states, "All told, it is doubtful whether the editors [of *The Pioneer*] paid out more than seventy-five dollars to their authors while their magazine was alive" (*Victorian Knight-Errant*, 133). For an elaboration of Lowell's debts after the failure of *The Pioneer*, see Bradley's introduction to the magazine (James Russell Lowell, *Pioneer*, xxv–xxvi) and Robert Carter's 29 March 1843 letter in Lease, "Robert Carter."

21. The Lowells' visit to the Hawthornes in Concord after the 3 March 1843 birth of Una is evident from Maria Lowell's 16 January 1845 letter to Sophia Hawthorne. The letter is included in Julian Hawthorne, *Nathaniel Hawthorne and His Wife*, 1:283–84; and furnished in facsimile in Lowell, Maria White, *Letter*. For the date of the wedding of James Russell Lowell and Maria White, see Scudder, *James Russell Lowell*, 2:132; and Duberman, *James Russell Lowell*, 68. For Lowell's inscription to Hawthorne in *Conversations on Some of the Old Poets*, see Scudder, 2:419, and Tucker, "James Russell Lowell and Robert Carter," 217. The inscription appears in the "List of Copies of the 'Conversations' to be given away by the Don." ("The Don" is Robert Carter.) Carter dated this list of twenty copies "Dec. 1844." For a facsimile of the list, see Hale, *James Russell Lowell*, 92–93. For Lowell's reference to Hawthorne's "right in any gathering of poets" in *Conversations*, see 119. For the second reference to Hawthorne in *Conversations*, see 212.

22. The Houghton Library holds several first editions of *Poems*: one is inscribed by Lowell to William Henry Channing and features an original handwritten sonnet; another is inscribed by Lowell to Ralph Waldo Emerson and also features an original handwritten sonnet; a third is inscribed to E. H. Bartol (daughter of Lowell's friend Cyrus Augustus Bartol, who was the successor to Lowell's father Charles Lowell as minister of Boston's West Church); and a fourth is inscribed from publisher John Owen to Henry Wadsworth Longfellow. The Berg Collection of the New York Public Library has three large-print copies of the first edition of *Poems*; two of these are inscribed by Lowell—one volume to his friend G. W. Richardson, and the other to Ann A. Gray. The Berg also holds a standard first edition of the volume, inscribed by Longfellow to Emmeline Austin Wadsworth. The *National Union Catalogue* notes the Harvard College Library copy, presented by John Owen. The catalogue for the Stephen H. Wakeman Sale lists a copy that Lowell inscribed to "C. E. Briggs," Charlotte Briggs, the daughter of Lowell's friend Charles F. Briggs. See item 810. This copy is now held by the American Antiquarian Society. The *Bibliography of American Literature* mentions this inscribed copy, as well as another inscribed copy at the University of Virginia. Eva M. Chandler, cataloguing assistant at the Special Collections

Department of the University Library at the University of Virginia, adds that the inscribed copy was sold at auction (Swann Galleries, 21 Nov. 1974). The inscription is by Lowell's friend, Thomas Wentworth Higginson.

For information on Lowell's contract for the 1844 *Poems*, see note 33.

23. James Russell Lowell, "Ballad of the Stranger" (*The Token*, 136; *Uncollected Poems*, 27) and *Conversations*, 136.

24. The date of Hawthorne's writing "Egotism, or the Bosom Serpent" is offered in McDonald, "Old Manse Period Canon," 25. Lowell's figure for the desire for power, a serpent, appears in "A Legend of Brittany," *Poems*, 35, 44. Julian Hawthorne's judgment of his father's attitude toward a friend's work appears in *Hawthorne Reading*, 125.

25. Rufus Wilmot Griswold had solicited Hawthorne's contribution for *Graham's Magazine*, and Hawthorne had responded positively in his letter of 2 July 1843 (15:693–94). On 9 January 1844, Sophia Hawthorne wrote to her mother that Griswold had promised "five dollars per page, & the liberty of drawing for the money the moment the article was published, and the number of pages thus ascertained" (15:694 n; see also Rose Hawthorne Lathrop, *Memories of Hawthorne*, 69–73, and Sanborn, *Hawthorne and His Friends*, 31). For bibliographical information on "Earth's Holocaust," see 10:579. McDonald infers that Hawthorne had completed "Earth's Holocaust" by 9 January 1844 because of Sophia Hawthorne's stating, in the noted letter of that date, "My husband will dispatch a budget to Mr. Hillard's care, containing a paper which he is to send to Mr. Griswold, editor of 'Graham's Magazine'" (McDonald, "Old Manse Period Canon," 28; see also Rose Hawthorne Lathrop, 69).

26. For Poe's 19 October 1843 letter to Lowell, see *Letters*, 1:238. For Poe's 15 December 1846 letter to Eveleth, see *Letters*, 2:332. George W. Eveleth, a young correspondent of Poe's, had asked in a letter of 13 October 1846, "Also in 'Graham's' for March 1844, is the notice of Lowell's 'Legend of Brittany' by yourself?" (*Letters*, 8). Poe acknowledged his authorship in his 15 December 1846 response. Lowell may also have suspected that Poe had written the review: Lowell wrote to Poe on 6 March 1844 noting that he had inferred Poe's authorship in the "editorial matter (critical)" of *Graham's Magazine* but that Graham had denied Poe's hand (Poe, *Complete Works*, 17:160). If, as Dwight Thomas and David K. Jackson suggest, the March 1844 issue of *Graham's* appeared "before 22 February" (*Poe Log*, 452), then it is possible that Lowell was referring to Poe's review of *Poems*, a review that Poe had promised. (See *Letters*, 1:238.) If Lowell was referring to material in an earlier issue of *Graham's*, then his letter is still pertinent in that it indicates Lowell's inclination to try to identify Poe's authorship, an effort that he would likely have made again regarding the March issue, and surely successfully.

27. Poe, *Letters*, 1:238–39.

28. Some people in the Boston area would have been more than usually informed about the church organ when *Poems* was published because of a memorable lecture about the organ that Henry Russell Cleveland had given at the Odeon in Boston in the spring of 1841. (See the Hillard memoir in Henry Russell Cleveland, *Selection*, xxvi.) Although the lecture was never published, Cleveland's review of William Gardiner's *The Music of Nature*, appearing first in the *New York Review* and then in the memorial volume for Cleveland (who died in June 1843), featured considerable commentary on the organ, 157–97. While Hawthorne was responsive to Lowell's church organ passage, he seems to have had some reservations about the music of the organ itself. In October 1863 he declined James T. Fields's invitation to attend the dedication of a new organ, writing, "I have no ear for an organ or a Jews-harp, nor for any instrument between the two" (18:605). And his narrator in the 1837 sketch "Sunday at Home" writes that if he were within the nearby church, the

sound of the choir and "the massive melody of the organ" would fall "with a weight upon me" (9:24). But the narrator adds that, at a distance, the sound of choir and organ "thrills through my frame, and plays upon my heart-strings, with a pleasure both of the sense and spirit." He notes, as well, "Heaven be praised, I know nothing of music, as a science; and the most elaborate harmonies, if they please me, please as simply as a nurse's lullaby" (9:24).

29. The authorship of the *Tribune* review is not known; however, Lowell probably met with the *Tribune*'s editor, Horace Greeley, a year earlier. For Lowell's planned visit with Greeley in January 1843, see Tucker ("James Russell Lowell," 201). Greeley may have written the review.

30. Peterson, Review of *Poems*, *Ladies' National Magazine*, March 1844, 97. For Peterson's earlier short notice of *Poems*, see the February 1844 issue of the *Ladies' National Magazine*. The review of Lowell's *A Year's Life*, to which Peterson refers in his review of *Poems*, appeared in the April 1842 issue of *Graham's Magazine*. Peterson anticipated his March 1844 review's remarks on the church organ passage in "A Legend of Brittany" when he wrote to Lowell, on 10 January 1844, "I think, if one takes this portion of the poem, beginning with the festival day & that incomparable description of the music of a cathedral organ, that nothing can be found, in any American poet, at all approaching it." See Peterson to Lowell, and Prestwich, "Charles Jacob Peterson," 69–71. (This passage is published by permission of the Houghton Library, Harvard University) George R. Graham later told Lowell that he would have paid $150 to publish "A Legend of Brittany" (Tucker, "James Russell Lowell," 219).

31. Review of *Poems*, *New Jerusalem Magazine*, 253–54; Review of *Poems*, *The Critic*, 152; Review of *Poems*, *Littell's Living Age*, 161–62.

32. Felton, Review of *Poems*, 288, 291. For further information on the "Five of Clubs," see Horace William Shaler Cleveland, *Social Life and Literature*, 39–44; and Hale, *James Russell Lowell and His Friends*, 61. Another positive appraisal that did not quote from "A Legend of Brittany" was offered in the anonymous Review of *Poems*, Portland *Transcript*: this piece mentioned that "A Legend of Brittany" has a "freshness and vigor of thought." A third such appraisal appeared in Review of *Poems*, the *Boston Recorder*, where the unidentified critic refers to "the slower and statelier march of the Sonnets, and the Legend of Brittany." (Neither of these two reviews is collected in McFadyen.) On the other hand, W. A. Davis criticized "A Legend of Brittany" in the March 1844 issue of the *Christian Examiner*, stating, "We would not rest our author's fame on this so common-place performance. Were this his only work, he would offer no claim to a notice here; he would occupy no lofty place in the ranks of the sons of song" (Review of *Poems*, 174). However, Chandler Robbins, pastor of the Second Church of Boston, wrote to Lowell on 23 November 1844, "The Editor of the Christian Examiner sent me your Poems to notice for that periodical—but rejected what I prepared, because they could not consent to praise them so highly." (Lowell later sent Robbins a copy of *Conversations on Some of the Old Poets* [Tucker, "James Russell Lowell," 217].) And others privately indicated favorable responses to Lowell's work. William Henry Channing, liberal minister and editor of *The Present*, thought highly of Lowell's featured poem thanking Lowell for an inscribed copy of a first edition of *Poems*, Channing wrote on 27 February 1844, "In The Legend of Brittany, you appear to me to have reached a much unexpected success, for the subject was a very difficult one. Your picture of all confiding love in Margaret is as true as exquisitely beautiful" (Channing to Lowell). And Lydia Maria Child, author and abolitionist, wrote on 25 December 1844 to Maria White (who would be Maria Lowell when she received the letter), "Remember me most affectionately to your *husband*. I have been reading over his

last volume lately, and with fresh delight. It abounds with rare gems" (Child to Lowell). (Passages from the letters of Robbins, Channing, and Child are quoted by permission of the Houghton Library, Harvard University.)

Occasionally the church organ passage in "A Legend of Brittany" would be excerpted without a review—for example, *The Columbian* (of Hartford, CT) offered stanzas 41 and 42 ("The Organ") in its 2 March 1844 issue, with the brief introduction, "This powerful description of heavy organ music in a vast Cathedral, is by James Russell Lowell."

33. The contract for *Poems*, signed by Lowell and John Owen and dated 18 December 1843, stipulates that Lowell will receive "ten cents for every copy printed, & ten copies of each edition of five hundred copies" (Lowell and Owen, Contract). (Quoted with the permission of The Pierpont Morgan Library, New York. MA 648.) Accordingly, with 1,100 copies printed, Lowell would have earned at least one hundred dollars—perhaps one hundred and ten dollars—and received twenty copies of the book. For Poe's response to Lowell's letter about the sales of *Poems*, see *Letters*, 1:246.

34. For Griswold's excerpt of "A Legend of Brittany" in the eighth edition of *Poets and Poetry of America*, see 499. For the dating of the publication of this edition, see Blanck and Winship, *Bibliography of American Literature*, 3:290. Lowell denigrated an earlier edition of Griswold's anthology in August 1846, calling the volume, "Mr. Griswold's catacombs" (Tucker, *James Russell Lowell*, 226), but, nonetheless, he sought earlier that year the inclusion of Maria's poetry in Griswold's 1848 *Female Poets of America* (James Russell Lowell, *New Letters*, 16–17).

35. For Lowell's famous couplet on Poe, see *Writings*, 9:72. For Lowell on Poe's drinking, see Thomas and Jackson, *Poe Log*, 536. For Briggs on Poe and the *Broadway Journal*, see Thomas and Jackson, 542, 551, 554–55, 557. Poe does assert in this negative review that Lowell was an expert in "the poetry of *sentiment*," rather than the loftier poetry of "imagination" or "the passions"—but he does not clarify into which category "A Legend of Brittany" falls (*Complete Works* 13:168). For that work to be "the noblest poem, of the same length, written by an American," however, we may infer that Poe must have thought it to be, according to his own classification, one of the more elevated kinds of poetry.

36. The date of the availability of the tenth edition of *Poets and Poetry of America* is in Blanck and Winship, *Bibliography of American Literature*, 3:290. Griswold's comment on Lowell is in the tenth edition of *Poets and Poetry*, 485.

37. It is interesting to note that Griswold offered the primary text of the ballad "Bold Hawthorne," appearing in the October 1842 issue of *Graham's Magazine*. The work is about the involvement of Hawthorne's grandfather Daniel Hathorne, captain of the *True American*, in a sea battle. For Hawthorne's mention (in his 1853 autobiographical sketch) of the poem as it appeared in Griswold's *Curiosities of American Literature*, see 23:379. For analysis of Griswold's inaccurate text, see Dameron, *Bold Hawthorne*. It was also Griswold who first noted in print the existence of Hawthorne's early romance, *Fanshawe*. Griswold's 1851 mention of this work that Hawthorne preferred to ignore may have been indebted to Samuel Griswold Goodrich, once editor of *The Token* and publisher of Hawthorne's early fiction. For discussion of Griswold's comment and its likely source, see Robinson, "Rufus Wilmot Griswold."

38. James Russell Lowell, *Writings*, 9:59.

39. The inscription is quoted with the permission of the Berg Collection of English and American Literature, The New York Public Library, Astor, Lenox and Tilden Foundations. This copy of the 1849 *Poems* is mentioned by Cohen, "Hawthorne's Library," 137. For the time of the publication of Lowell's 1849 *Poems*, see Blanck and Winship, *Bibliography of American Literature*, 6:31.

40. Lowell's response in his revision of "A Legend of Brittany" to C. C. Felton's criticism is considered by Arthur W. M. Voss, "Lowell's 'A Legend of Brittany.'" Lowell's admiration for Elizabeth B. Barrett was expressed in *Conversation on Some of the Old Poets*, 37. Barrett's assessment of "A Legend of Brittany" may be found in Browning and Browning, *Browning to His American Friends*, 353.

41. Hawthorne would have been writing the final three chapters of *The Scarlet Letter* between 15 January 1850 and 3 February 1850. According to his 15 January 1850 letter to James T. Fields, "there are three chapters still to be written of 'The Scarlet Letter'" (16:305–6), and according to his 4 February 1850 letter to Horatio Bridge, "I finished my book only yesterday; one end being in the press in Boston, while the other was in my head here in Salem" (16:311–13). For an argument that Hawthorne inserted chapter 4 late in the composition of *The Scarlet Letter*, see Branch, "From Allegory to Romance." I am not persuaded by Branch's argument; I agree with Rita K. Gollin, who writes, "Branch's essay has the unintended effect of proving how tightly [the novel] is plotted," *American Literary Scholarship*, 32.

42. The Lowell letter to Duyckinck is quoted in Scudder, *James Russell Lowell*, 1:283–84. This letter and the letter to Davis are cited in Duberman, *James Russell Lowell*, 488 n. It should be noted that Duyckinck turned Lowell down: "In answer to your friendly letter with the Hawthorne suggestion I am compelled to conclude that little could be done here in the way you propose. Hawthorne is known best among those whose purses are no larger than his own." Duyckinck then goes on to suggest that Lowell propose that Hawthorne publish his collected works with George P. Putnam and thereby gain the needed funds. The passage from the Lowell letter to Davis and that from the Duyckinck letter to Lowell are quoted by permission of the Houghton Library, Harvard University.

We do not know what success Lowell had with Davis or Furness or O'Sullivan. (However, for elaboration of the Lowell–Davis friendship through Lowell's letters, see Hallowell, "Episode.") We do know that the money that was raised in New England was given to George S. Hillard, who, on 17 January 1850, sent it to Hawthorne on behalf of "those who admire your genius and respect your character." (See Julian Hawthorne, *Nathaniel Hawthorne and His Wife*, 1:354–55.) Hawthorne responded on 20 January 1850, admitting his tears at reading Hillard's letter, and adding "There was much that was very sweet—and something too that was very bitter—mingled with that same moisture. It is sweet to be remembered and cared for by one's friends—some of whom know me for what I am, while others, perhaps, know me only through a generous faith—sweet to think that they deem me worth upholding in my poor walk through life. And it is bitter, nevertheless, to need their support" (16:309).

43. Unless otherwise stated, the lines from "A Legend of Brittany" will be quoted from the 1844 edition of James Russell Lowell's *Poems*.

44. The relationship between the unborn infant in "A Legend of Brittany" and the young Pearl in *The Scarlet Letter* would have been strong for Hawthorne—Sophia had had a miscarriage in February 1843, and Una was born in March 1844 (Mellow, *Nathaniel Hawthorne*, 219–20, 239–40). Notably, in his 24 March 1844 letter about Una to his friend George Hillard, Hawthorne was sensitive to the fact that the Hillards had lost an infant— he closed by saying, "next to a child on earth, it is good to have a child in Heaven" (16:24). The release of Margaret's unborn infant to heaven is made possible by its baptism; Ernest W. Baughman has suggested a related point—according to Puritan practice, Pearl could not have been baptized until both her guilty parents had confessed ("Public Confession," 547–48). Whether Hawthorne knew this fact is uncertain.

45. Another item in Hawthorne's catalog of sources is also relevant here. The title of the chapter in which Hester releases her hair, "A Flood of Sunshine" (1:199), and the phrase in that chapter, "the sunshine, pouring a very flood into the obscure forest" (1:203), may owe a debt to Henry Wadsworth Longfellow's *Kavanagh, A Tale* (1849): "Mr. Churchill took occasion to make known to the company his long cherished purpose of writing a poem called 'The Song of the Saw-Mill,' and enlarged on the beautiful associations of flood and forest connected with the theme" (130). Commenting on Longfellow's relevant reading, Kent P. Ljungquist writes that "Longfellow must have just seen [William Cullen] Bryant's 'The Saw-Mill: From the German of Kerner,' which appeared in the February 1848 *Graham's Magazine*" ("Little War," 56 n). Hawthorne's phrases "the margin of the brook" (1:207, 211, 214) and "the mossy trunk" (1:195, 207, 217, 239) in the forest episode are also found in the forest episode in Longfellow, *Kavanagh* (128, 130). Longfellow sent an inscribed copy of his 1849 novel *Kavanagh* to Hawthorne on 19 May 1849 (16:271), and Hawthorne wrote to Longfellow on 5 June 1849 that the book was "a true work of genius, if ever there were one" (16:269). For further comment on the connection between *The Scarlet Letter* and *Kavanagh*, see Woodson ("Hawthorne," 185–86). A possible parallel with the forest scene in *The Scarlet Letter* has been noted in Lockhart's *Adam Blair*; see Stephenson and Stephenson ("Adam Blair," 7).

It must be observed that the sympathetic sun of the forest—part of the "wild, heathen Nature of the forest, never subjugated by human law, nor illuminated by higher truth" (1:203)—is distinct from the judgmental noonday sun of the scaffold scenes.

46. Lowes, *Road to Xanadu*, 56, 480 n.

47. The relevant quatrain in "The Church" is:

> I love to hear the glorious swell
>   Of chanted psalm and prayer,
> And the deep organ's bursting heart
>   Throb through the shivering air.

See James Russell Lowell, *A Year's Life* (120).

48. James Russell Lowell's comment on balancing sense and spirit appears in *Conversations on Some of the Old Poets*, 78. His comment on Shelley and physical sensation appears in a letter to Maria Lowell's cousin Eliza Webb Lippitt in *New Letters*, 207. Lowell might have read Shelley's poem "Lines to an Indian Air" in the *Posthumous Poems* of 1824. For variants given by Robert Browning, see his letter to Leigh Hunt, 266–67. The poem is later retitled "The Indian Serenade."

49. Crews, *Sins of the Fathers*, 146 n.

50. Ibid., 145–48.

51. The possibly sexual pun of "organ-pipe" has been mentioned by Michael Davitt Bell, "Arts of Deception," 49; and Pfister, *Production of Personal Life*, 138–39. It should be added that the phrase "organ pipes" appears, without double entendre, in Longfellow, *Kavanagh*, 169.

The argument developed here plainly speaks to a heterosexual love between unrelated partners in Hawthorne's novel, but there have been many other readings of sexuality in *The Scarlet Letter*. Focusing on Chillingworth and Dimmesdale, David Leverenz discusses homosexual rape (*Manhood*, 270–78); and T. Walter Herbert considers masturbation (*Dearest Beloved*, 190–98). Monika Elbert concurs with and elaborates on Leverenz's view ("Hester on the Scaffold," 246–48, 253). Scott S. Derrick ("Curious Subject") and Karen L. Kilcup ("Ourselves Behind Ourself") also comment on homosexuality in the novel, and

Claudia Durst Johnson writes about both impotence and masturbation in that work ("Impotence and Omnipotence"). Considering the ancestral sex scandal in the Manning family, Leslie Fiedler (*Love and Death*, 229–30) and Philip Young (*Hawthorne's Secret*, 115–47) write about incest in *The Scarlet Letter*.

52. David B. Downing is perceptive when he writes that the passage about Dimmesdale's presentation of the Election Sermon "literally throbs with its densely charged presentation of the thematic heart of the novel" ("Swelling Waves," 23). And I agree that the minister's pleasure is complemented by pain—he does feel great guilt for his adultery and his silence. However, I do not agree that Dimmesdale has completely denied his sexual energies and failed to achieve any satisfaction (24). It may be that here Dimmesdale is not so much protected from "intimate contact" with Hester (21) as figuratively permitted it.

53. Briggs offers his judgment of "A Legend of Brittany" in a letter to Lowell, quoted in part in Scudder, *James Russell Lowell*, 1:120. Hawthorne wrote that the conclusion of *The Scarlet Letter* "broke [Sophia's] heart and sent her to bed with a grievous headache—which I look upon as a triumphant success!" (16:311). Sophia Hawthorne later wrote to her sister Mary Mann on 12 February 1850, "[*The Scarlet Letter*] is most powerful, & contains a moral as terrific & stunning as a thunder bolt. It shows that the Law cannot be broken" (16:313 n). Sophia also wrote to Hawthorne's sister, Maria Louisa, on 28 April 1850, "Nathaniel's fame is perfectly prodigious. In Boston I hear the full blast. Some say [*The Scarlet Letter*] is the greatest book that ever was written, & *unqualified* praise comes from the most fastidious highly cultivated & most gifted persons. Mr. Emerson told me the other day that the Introduction was *absolutely* perfect in *wit*, in *life*, in *truth*[,] in *genial spirit & good nature* and that there was nothing equal to it in the language—This was immense commendation from him who is never satisfied." (This passage is published with the permission of the Berg Collection of English and American Literature, The New York Public Library, Astor, Lenox and Tilden Foundations.) And Sophia wrote to her sister Elizabeth Peabody on 21 June 1850, "The questioning of its morality is of all criticisms the funniest—especially the notion some short sighted persons have about the author's opinion of the crime! When the whole book is one great tragic chorus of condemnation—when such horrible retribution follows, when even the retribution lives & breathes in Pearl from beginning to end" (Edwin Haviland Miller, *Salem Is My Dwelling Place*, 302).

54. Colacurcio, "Sense of an Author," 130.

55. Perhaps Hawthorne's repeatedly referring to his wife Sophia as "my Dove" (see, for example, 15: 290, 294, 295, 296, 299, 305, and 320) owes something to the same phrase in The Song of Solomon (2:14, 5:2, and 6:9).

56. Regarding the minister's not being "a disciple of true love," see Ernest Sandeen, "*Scarlet Letter*," 428. On Dimmesdale's not regretting his passion, see 427. On his conscience and pride, and his redeeming his passion, see 433. On his appeal as a lover, see 435. Regarding love as "the deep force" of the novel, see 426.

57. For further treatment of the allusion, see Osborn and Osborn, "Another Look at an Old Tombstone"; Crain, *Story of A*, 202, 265–67 n.

58. Marvell, "The Unfortunate Lover," 27.

59. Male, *Hawthorne's Tragic Vision*, 99. Reinforcing the frequent use in *The Scarlet Letter* of the word "fallen" is the frequent use there of the word "lapse" (1:10, 40, 123, 213, 217, 251, 263) and its variants ("lapsed," 1:204; "elapse," 1:96; and "relapsed," 1:248). Even as "lapse" indicates passage or period (as in "lapse of time"), it also indicates error—indeed, Original Sin—hence the word, applicable to *The Scarlet Letter*, "postlapsarian." For an interesting essay on the Garden of Eden in Hawthorne, see William H. Shurr, "Eve's Bower."

60. Chillingworth may perhaps be identified as one of "the wicked" who "search out iniquities" in others (Psalms 64:2, 6). Hawthorne may have had the sixty-fourth psalm in mind since the Massachusetts Bay Colony is referred to in *The Scarlet Letter* as a place "where iniquity is dragged out into the sunshine" (1:54), a place where "iniquity is searched out" (1:62). I thank my daughter, Emily Kopley, for noting the verbal correspondences. Clearly, Chillingworth's searching out iniquities is providentially permitted.

61. For the second scaffold scene as an inversion of the crucifixion, involving Hester and Pearl as Mary and Mary Magdalene, and Arthur as a resistant Jesus, see Hugh J. Dawson, "Triptych Design," 13. For the third scaffold scene as a version of the Pietà, see Todd, "Magna Mater," 424; Gervais, "Papist among Puritans," 14; Dawson, 13; Newberry, *Hawthorne's Divided Loyalties*, 176; Evans Lansing Smith, "Re-Figuring Revelations," 100; and Gatta, *American Madonna*, 17–18. An interesting speculation on Hawthorne's comparison of Hester to the Madonna is offered by Jessie Ryon Lucke, "Hawthorne's Madonna Image," who notes that the family of a slave mistress and her children in Cuba was referred to as a holy family in the novel *Juanita*, by Sophia Hawthorne's sister Mary Peabody Mann. Lucke suggests that perhaps Sophia, who, like her sister, had visited Cuba, might have mentioned such terminology to her husband. For the fullest study yet of the relationship of Catholicism to Protestantism in nineteenth-century America, see Jenny Franchot's *Roads To Rome*, which features a chapter on *The Scarlet Letter*, "The Hawthornian Confessional," 260–69. For an autobiographical essay with treatment of Catholicism and *The Scarlet Letter*, see Sweeney, "Madonna."

62. It is noteworthy that, living in Salem at 14 Mall Street (near Forrester Street) in 1849 and 1850, the Hawthornes were very close to a Catholic Church, St. Mary's Church (at Mall and Forrester). As he planned and wrote *The Scarlet Letter*, Hawthorne would surely have seen the comings and goings of the St. Mary's parishioners. On 19 August 1849, Sophia Hawthorne wrote from the Mall Street house, "The children are watching the Catholics as they throng to church." (See Sophia Hawthorne to her mother, Mrs. Elizabeth Palmer Peabody. The passage is quoted with the permission of the Berg Collection of English and American Literature, The New York Public Library, Astor, Lenox and Tilden Foundations.) Hawthorne would probably have heard the Catholic congregants, as well: Julian Hawthorne wrote that the Mall Street house was "small and ill-placed in a narrow side-street, with no possibility of shutting out the noise of traffic and domestic alarms" (*Hawthorne and His Circle*, 5–6). Hawthorne would certainly have heard any church bells, too. It is notable that Joseph B. Felt wrote of Salem in 1845, "there are two organs, of small size, in the Crombie street and the Catholic churches" (*Annals of Salem*, 2nd ed., 1:504). Perhaps—especially during summer months when windows would have been open—Hawthorne, like Hester, heard something of the sounds from within the church. For the history of the Catholic Church in Salem, see Louis S. Walsh.

63. For Lowell's report on his conversation with Hawthorne and his own comment on the planned confession of Dimmesdale to a priest, see James Russell Lowell, *Letters*, 1:302.

An interesting issue to pursue with regard to the attitude of Lowell and Hawthorne toward Catholicism is the importance of the views of Lowell's fiancée Maria White and Hawthorne's wife Sophia Hawthorne. Maria White attended Ursuline Convent in Charlestown—indeed, she was one of the Protestant girls who hid and then escaped when the convent was burned by an angry mob (Maria White Lowell, *Poems*, 6–10). The infamous convent burning is well described by a former convent student, Louisa Goddard Whitney, in *Burning of the Convent*, and the event is ably examined by Billington, "The Burning of the Charlestown Convent"; Cohen, "Alvah Kelley's Cow"; Franchot, *Roads to*

Rome, 135–54; and Schultz, *Fire and Roses*. Of particular interest is the fact that the mob suspected that a nun had been buried alive at the convent (Franchot, 139–40, 399 n; see also Schultz, 108) since Maria later wrote a poem, "Legend of the Brown Rosarie," which mentions a nun buried alive (Maria White Lowell, *Poems*, 77), and since James Russell Lowell's source for "A Legend of Brittany," "The Three Red Monks," concerns a young woman's burial alive. Surely Maria conveyed to James both her interest in Catholicism and her extraordinary experience in the besieged convent. Indeed, he alluded to the burning of the convent in *Conversations on Some of the Old Poets* (187).

While Sophia Hawthorne did not have a Catholic education, she did have a sympathy for Catholicism. This is intimated in a 28 February 1869 letter she wrote to her friend Mrs. Mary Hemenway: after describing a moving experience she had had in a Catholic church, she adds, "You need not fear that I shall become a Roman Catholic under all this influence. But I find I can do justice to that faith, instead of feeling above it." (This passage is quoted with the permission of the Phillips Library, Peabody Essex Museum, Salem, Massachusetts.) Sophia must have shared her thoughts about Catholicism with Nathaniel before he wrote *The Scarlet Letter*. It was probably she who placed "the sweet and lovely head of one of Raphael's Madonnas" in Hawthorne's study in the Old Manse (10:5; see also 8:324). Furthermore in a 3 May 1846 letter to Maria Louisa Hawthorne, Sophia refers to "the sweet Madonna who presided over my husband's study in Concord." And in a 2 December 1849 letter to Elizabeth Palmer Peabody, Sophia notes, with regard to another image of the Madonna, that she and her husband saw "a peculiar beauty in the Mother of Christ." (These passages are quoted by permission of the Berg Collection of English and American Literature, The New York Public Library, Astor, Lenox, and Tilden Foundations.) It is interesting to note that Maria Lowell wrote to Sophia Hawthorne of her feelings for the Virgin Mary: "Mary is a type of all women, and I love the Catholic feeling that enshrines and appeals to her. It has its root in the very deepest principle of life," Rose Hawthorne Lathrop, *Memories of Hawthorne*, 119.

64. For further information on the *Boston Miscellany*, see Mott, *History of American Magazines*, 718–20, and Chielens, 70–73. Hawthorne was apparently considered as a possible editor of the magazine in the summer of 1842; see his 20 August 1842 letter to Robert Carter, 15:644–45.

65. James Russell Lowell, "Old English Dramatists," *Boston Miscellany*, April 1842, 145; *Conversations*, 133.

66. For Lowell on "the undying fires," see ibid.; the passage appears, slightly modified, in *Conversations*, 132. Lowell's comment on Wordsworth's Ode appears in *Conversations*, 49–50. Lowell's treatment of the amaranth appears in "Old English Dramatists," April 1842, 146; this passage is included, lightly revised, in *Conversations*, 136–37.

67. James Russell Lowell, *Conversations*, 119.

68. For Lowell on Spenser, see James Russell Lowell, *Writings* 4:299; for Lowell's admiration of Hawthorne, see *New Letters*, 104.

Chronology

1804	Nathaniel Hawthorne is born on July 4 in Salem, Massachusetts, the second of three children of Elizabeth (neé Manning) and Nathaniel Hathorne, a ship's captain.
1808	Hawthorne's father, Nathaniel Hathorne, dies of yellow fever at Suriname (Dutch Guiana). The Hathornes move to the Manning family home on 12 Herbert Street, Salem.
1813	In November, a foot injury causes temporary lameness and keeps Nathaniel from school for fourteen months. He is tutored at home by Joseph Worcester, who will later become the noted lexicographer.
1814	At midyear, a new physician, Dr. Smith of Hanover, prescribes a new form of hydrotherapy and by late August there is some improvement.
1818	In the fall, the Hathorne family moves to Raymond, Maine, which is still a wilderness area. Nathaniel will later idealize his life in Maine, where he hunted, fished, and roamed through the woods at will. During the winter of 1818–1819, he attends school at nearby Stroudwater, under the direction of Reverend Caleb Bradley, a Harvard graduate. He is restless and unhappy here. Nevertheless, he reads a good deal during this time, his two favorite books being Spenser's *Faerie Queene* and Bunyan's *Pilgrim's Progress*.

1819   In the summer, Nathaniel returns to Salem to live with his mother's family, under the guardianship of his uncle Robert Manning. His mother stays in Maine. Here he attends Samuel Archer's school on Marlborough Street. During this time, Hawthorne reads a great deal, including *Waverley*, *The Mysteries of Udolpho*, *Roderick Random*, *The Adventures of Count Fathom*, and the first volume of *The Arabian Nights*.

1820   Prepares for college under Benjamin L. Oliver in Salem, and works part-time as secretary and bookkeeper for his Uncle William in the stagecoach office. Also embarks on a short-lived project as publisher, editor, and author of a newspaper, *The Spectator*, patterned after the famous journal of Addison and Steele. The issues, which are carefully written out by hand, include such essays as "On Wealth," "On Benevolence," and "On Industry." The first issue is dated August 21, 1820 and the last, September 25, 1820.

1821   Writes to his mother informing her that he does not want to become a minister, lawyer, or physician, but, rather, an author. In October, Nathaniel enters Bowdoin College, New Brunswick, Maine. Decides to take his meals at the home of Samuel Newman, a young and competent professor of Greek and Latin. At Bowdoin, he befriends Horatio Bridge, Franklin Pierce, Jonathan Cilley, and Henry Wadsworth Longfellow.

1825   In September, Nathaniel graduates from Bowdoin, 18th in a class of 38. Returns to live with his family in Salem.

1828   Nathaniel adds the "w" to his family name. In October, *Fanshawe* is published anonymously by the Boston publisher, Marsh and Capen. Hawthorne soon realizes that publishing this apprentice work is a mistake, and disposes of as many copies as he can locate.

1829   Plans a second collection of stories, to be called *Provincial Tales*, and submits manuscript to S. G. Goodrich, editor of *The Token*.

1830   From this year forward, Hawthorne's stories and sketches begin appearing anonymously in gift-annuals, newspapers, and magazines—*The Token*, "The Hollow of the Three Hills" in the *Salem Gazette*, the *New-England Magazine*, the *American Monthly Magazine*, and *Youth's Keepsake*.

1831	A fire at the Marsh and Capen store destroys all the unsold copies of *Fanshawe*. Hawthorne releases some tales intended for publication in *The Token*: "The Gentle Boy," "The Wives of the Dead," "Roger Malvin's Burial," and "My Kinsman, Major Molineux." Hawthorne visits the Shaker community in Canterbury, New Hampshire, where he develops a keen interest in their way of life and its literary possibilities.
1832	Hawthorne plans a third collection, to be called "The Story Teller." During September and October he makes extensive journeys in northern New York State, visits Niagara Falls, and travels through the heart of the White Mountains of New Hampshire, Vermont, and Montreal.
1834	During November and December, "The Story Teller, Nos. I and II," is published in *New-England Magazine*.
1835	"Young Goodman Brown" is published in *New-England Magazine*. "The Minister's Black Veil," "The Maypole of Merrymount," and "The Wedding-Knell" are accepted for publication in *The Token*.
1836	In January, Hawthorne makes his entry into the professional literary world when he moves to Boston to edit *American Magazine of Useful and Entertaining Knowledge*. In March, the first issue with Nathaniel's name as editor appears—in May, the magazine goes bankrupt. From May to September, Hawthorne, with the help of Elizabeth Palmer Peabody, writes *Peter Parley's Universal History, on the Basis of Geography* (published in 1837).
1837	*Twice-Told Tales* is published in March. Unbeknownst to Hawthorne, Horatio Bridge has given his financial guarantee to the publisher. In July, Longfellow's highly favorable review of *Twice-Told Tales* appears in the *North American Review*, declaring Hawthorne to be "a new star . . . in the heaven of poetry." In the fall, Hawthorne begins his association with John L. O'Sullivan's *Democratic Review*. Eight Hawthorne pieces appear there in fifteen months. In November, he meets Sophia Amelia Peabody.
1838	From July to September, Hawthorne lives in North Adams, Massachusetts, where he enjoys observing small-town rural life, and makes trips to the Berkshires, upstate New York, Vermont, and Connecticut.

1839	In January, with the help of Sophia's sister, Elizabeth, and as a result of insufficient earnings as a writer, Hawthorne takes on appointment as measurer in the Boston Custom House, a position he will hold for two years. On March 6, he writes the first surviving love letter to Sophia Peabody.
1840	In November, Hawthorn resigns from the Custom House, effective as of January 1, 1841. In December, he publishes *Grandfather's Chair*, a children's history of New England, dated 1841. Late in the year, Hawthorne invests in George Ripley's Brook Farm, an experiment in communal living in West Roxbury, Massachusetts, with the hope that he would find a situation that would support his writing.
1841	During the winter, Hawthorne returns to Salem and publishes *Famous Old People*. In March, *The Liberty Tree* is published. For several months, Hawthorne labors among the transcendental community before giving up his plan of bringing Sophia there after their marriage. In October, he leaves the community for Boston, forfeiting his financial investment. Nevertheless, his experience at Brook Farm will provide the basis for *The Blithedale Romance*.
1842	In January, the second edition of *Twice-Told Tales* is published, with an additional volume containing sixteen more recent tales and sketches together with five that antedate the 1837 collection. On July 9, Hawthorne and Sophia Peabody are married. They move to Concord, Massachusetts, and rent the Old Manse, where they will live until October 1845. Hawthorne completes another children's book, *Biographical Stories for Children*.
1844	On March 3, their daughter Una, named after Spenser's heroine, is born at the Old Manse. From October 1844 to October 1845, Hawthorne lives in Concord. Ralph Waldo Emerson, Henry David Thoreau, and Louisa Alcott are resident in Concord as well.
1845	From January to April, Hawthorne edits Horatio Bridge's *Journal of an African Cruiser*. In October, the Hawthornes move to his mother's house in Salem, as Nathaniel seeks a political appointment to supplement his meager income from writing. It is not until 1847 that the Hawthornes find their own house in Salem.

1846   On April 9, Hawthorne is sworn in as surveyor at Salem Custom House on Derby Street, having been nominated by President Polk. The first two years in the position are not a productive literary period. In June, *Mosses from an Old Manse* is published in two volumes. It is a critical, albeit not a financial, success. On June 22, Julian Hawthorne is born.

1847   *Mosses from an Old Manse* inspires Poe's review "Tale Writing–Nathaniel Hawthorne," published in *Godey's Lady's Book* in November in which he complains of Hawthorne's monotony of style and penchant for allegory.

1848   In November, Hawthorne becomes manager and corresponding secretary of Salem Lyceum, engaging lecturers for the organization's regular programs. He invites Emerson, Thoreau, Theodore Parker, Horace Mann, Charles Sumner, Daniel Webster, and Louis Agassiz to lecture.

1849   On June 8, Hawthorne, a Democrat, is removed from office at the Custom House, following the election of Whig President, Zachary Taylor, in 1848. On July 31, his mother dies. In September, he begins writing *The Scarlet Letter*, which he originally planned as a long short story, and "The Custom House."

1850   In March, *The Scarlet Letter* is published in an edition of 2,500 copies. This is followed by a second edition of 2,500 in April, followed by a third edition of 1,000 copies in September. In June, the Hawthornes move to a small red farmhouse, "Red Cottage," in Lenox, Massachusetts. On August 5, Hawthorne meets Herman Melville at a literary picnic in the Berkshires. In August, he also begins *The House of the Seven Gables*. On August 17 and 24, Melville's flattering and effusive essay, "Hawthorne and His Mosses" appears anonymously in *The Literary World*. In November, *True Stories from History and Biography* (a reissue of *Grandfather's Chair* and *Biographical Stories*) is published, dated 1851.

1851   In March, a third edition of *Twice-Told Tales* is published, with a preface. In April, two printings of *The House of the Seven Gables* are issued, followed by one in May and September. On May 20, Rose Hawthorne is born. In

November, *A Wonder Book for Girls and Boys* is published, dated 1852. In December, *The Snow-Image* is published, dated 1852. Melville dedicates *Moby-Dick* to Hawthorne, "In token for my admiration of his genius."

1852   In May, Hawthorne buys the Alcott House in Concord, naming it "The Wayside." In July, *The Blithedale Romance* is published. In September, Hawthorne publishes *Life of Franklin Pierce*, a campaign biography of the presidential candidate. In November, Franklin Pierce is elected president.

1853   In March, Hawthorne is nominated for the lucrative consulship at Liverpool and Manchester by President Pierce. In July, he embarks on an eleven-day voyage for England with his family aboard the paddle-wheel steamer, the *Niagara*. In September, *Tanglewood Tales*, a volume of children's stories, is published.

1853-7   While working as United States Consul, Hawthorne keeps notebooks in which he records his English experiences and impressions.

1854   Revised edition of *Mosses* is published.

1856   In November, Melville visits Hawthorne in Liverpool on way to the Holy Land. He also meets Hawthorne briefly on return journey in May 1857.

1857   In October, Hawthorne gives up his consulship.

1858   In January, Hawthorne travels to Italy by way of France and takes up residence in Rome. He keeps notebooks on his Italian experiences and begins work on an English romance, never to be completed, but published posthumously as *The Ancestral Footstep*. From May to October, the Hawthornes live in a villa in Florence. He begins work on a romance with an Italian theme.

1859   In June, Hawthorne returns to England, where he rewrites the Italian romance.

1860   In February, *The Transformation* is published in England; in March the romance is published in America with the title *The Marble Faun*. In June, Hawthorne returns to America and settles at "The Wayside," in Concord, where he begins work on a second version of his English romance.

1861   Hawthorne abandons the romance, after making seven studies for the story. The fragment is published as *Dr.*

Grimshawe's Secret. In autumn, Hawthorne begins work on a series of English essays. He begins a new romance on the theme of elixir of life, but abandons this in 1862. Set at the time of the Revolution, the fragment is published posthumously as *Septimius Feiton*.

1862   Hawthorne's health declines and he is deeply troubled by the Civil War. He travels to Washington, D.C., where he meets President Lincoln and tours the battlefields at Manassas and Harpers Ferry, Virginia. Upon his return home, he writes "Chiefly About War Matters," which appears in the *Atlantic Monthly* in July.

1863   In September, *Our Old Home* is published, the collected essays on England, most of which had appeared separately in *Atlantic Monthly*.

1864   On May 19, while on a tour of New England with Franklin Pearce, Hawthorne dies quietly in his sleep in Plymouth, New Hampshire, having written three chapters of another romance about the elixir of life, posthumously published as *The Dolliver Romance*.

Contributors

HAROLD BLOOM is Sterling Professor of the Humanities at Yale University. He is the author of 30 books, including *Shelley's Mythmaking* (1959), *The Visionary Company* (1961), *Blake's Apocalypse* (1963), *Yeats* (1970), *A Map of Misreading* (1975), *Kabbalah and Criticism* (1975), *Agon: Toward a Theory of Revisionism* (1982), *The American Religion* (1992), *The Western Canon* (1994), and *Omens of Millennium: The Gnosis of Angels, Dreams, and Resurrection* (1996). *The Anxiety of Influence* (1973) sets forth Professor Bloom's provocative theory of the literary relationships between the great writers and their predecessors. His most recent books include *Shakespeare: The Invention of the Human* (1998), a 1998 National Book Award finalist, *How to Read and Why* (2000), *Genius: A Mosaic of One Hundred Exemplary Creative Minds* (2002), *Hamlet: Poem Unlimited* (2003), *Where Shall Wisdom Be Found?* (2004), and *Jesus and Yahweh: The Names Divine* (2005). In 1999, Professor Bloom received the prestigious American Academy of Arts and Letters Gold Medal for Criticism. He has also received the International Prize of Catalonia, the Alfonso Reyes Prize of Mexico, and the Hans Christian Andersen Bicentennial Prize of Denmark.

MILLICENT BELL is Professor Emeritus of English at New York University and Boston University. She is the author of *Shakespeare's Tragic Skepticism* (2002), *Meaning in Henry James* (1991) and editor of *The Cambridge Companion to Edith Wharton* (1995).

FREDERICK C. CREWS is a professor emeritus of English at the University of California, Berkeley. He is the author of *Skeptical Engagements* (1986), *The Random House Handbook* (1987), and *Out of My System: Psychoanalysis, Ideology, and Critical Method* (1975).

JANE DONAHUE EBERWEIN has been Distinguished Professor of English at Oakland University, Rochester, MI. She is the author of "His Wayes Disgrac'd Are Grac'd: Edward Taylor's Metrical History of Christianity as Puritan Narrative" (2003), "Art, Nature's Ape: The Challenge to the Puritan Poet" (1997), and editor of *An Emily Dickinson Encyclopedia* (1998).

DAVID C. CODY has been an associate professor of English at Hartwick College. He is the author of "Blood in the Basin: The Civil War in Emily Dickinson's 'The Name of It Is Autumn'" (2003), "'Foot-Prints on the Sea-Shore': Hawthorne as Romantic Rambler" (1989), and "Faulkner, Wells, and the 'End of Man'" (1993).

EDWIN HAVILAND MILLER is a professor emeritus of English at New York University. He is the author of *Melville* (1969), editor of *The Artistic Legacy of Walt Whitman: A Tribute to Gay Wilson Allen* (1970) and *Walt Whitman's Poetry: A Psychological Journey* (1968).

SAMUEL COALE has been a professor of American literature at Wheaton College. He is the author of "Mysteries of Mesmerism: Hawthorne's Haunted House" (2001), "Styron's Disguises: A Provisional Rebel in Christian Masquerade" (1995), and "Spiritualism and Hawthorne's Romance: The *Blithedale* Theatre as False Consciousness" (1994).

MICHAEL DUNNE has been a professor of American literature at Middle Tennessee State University. He is the author of *Metapop: Self-Referentiality in Contemporary American Popular Culture* (1992), *Intertextual Encounters in American Fiction, Film, and Popular Culture* (2001), and *American Film Musical Themes and Forms* (2004).

JOSEPH FLIBBERT was a professor of English at Salem State College and President of the Hawthorne Society (1983-1984). He is the author of *Melville and the Art of Burlesque* (1974) and served on the editorial board of the *Encyclopedia of American Literature of the Sea and the Great Lakes*.

DAN McCALL has been a professor of American studies and English at Cornell University. He is the author of *The Example of Richard Wright* (1969), *The Man Says Yes* (1969), and editor of *Melville's Short Novels: Authoritative Texts, Contexts, Criticism* (2002).

DAVID B. KESTERSON has been professor of English and interim Vice President for Academic Affairs at the University of North Texas. He is the author of *Critical Essays on Hawthorne's "The Scarlet Letter"* (1988), *Bill Nye: The Western Writings* (1976), and *Bill Nye* (1981).

RICHARD KOPLEY has been professor of English at Penn State. He is the editor of Poe's *Pym: Critical Explorations* (1992), *Prospects for the Study of American Literature: A Guide for Scholars and Students* (1997), and the Penguin edition of *The Narrative of Arthur Gordon Pym* (1999).

Bibliography

Abel, Darrell. "The Devil in Boston." *Philological Quarterly* 32 (1953): 366–81.

———. "Hawthorne's Dimmesdale: Fugitive from Wrath." *Nineteenth-Century Fiction* 11 (1956): 81–105.

Anderson, Charles R. *The Magic Circle of Walden*. New York: Holt, Rinehart, and Winston, 1968.

Anderson, Douglas. "Hawthorne's Marriages." In *A House Divided: Domesticity and Community in American Literature*. Cambridge: Cambridge University Press (1990): 97–120.

Baughman, Ernest W. "Public Confession and *The Scarlet Letter*." *New England Quarterly* 40(1967): 532–550.

Bayer, John G. "Narrative Techniques and the Oral Tradition in *The Scarlet Letter. AmericanLiterature* 52 (1980): 250–263.

Baym, Nina. "Nathaniel Hawthorne and His Mother: A Biographical Speculation." *AmericanLiterature* 54 (1982): 1–27.

———. "*The Marble Faun*: Hawthorne's Elegy for Art." *New England Quarterly* 44(1971).

Bell, Millicent. *Hawthorne's View of the Artist*. Albany: State University of New York Press, 1962.

———, ed. *Hawthorne and the Real: Bicentennial Essays*. Columbus: Ohio State University Press, 2005.

Bercovitch, Sacvan. *The Office of "The Scarlet Letter."* Baltimore: Johns Hopkins University Press, 1991.

Blair, Walter. "Hawthorne." In *Eight American Authors: A Review of Research and Criticism*. Edited by James Woodress. Rev. ed. New York: W.W. Norton (1971): 85–128.

Branch, Watson. "From Allegory to Romance: Hawthorne's Transformation of *The Scarlet Letter." Modern Philology* 80 (1982): 145–160.

Brodhead, Richard H. *Hawthorne, Melville, and the Novel*. Chicago: University of Chicago Press, 1976.

Brooke-Rose, Christine. "A for But: The Custom-House in Hawthorne's *The Scarlet Letter." Word and Image* 3 (1987): 143–155.

Budick, Emily Miller. "Hester's Skepticism, Hawthorne's Faith: or, What Does a Woman Doubt? Instituting the American Romance Tradition." *New Literary History* 22 (1991): 199–211.

Carlson, Patricia Ann. *Hawthorne's Functional Settings: A Study of Artistic Method*. Amsterdam: Rodopi, 1977.

Carton, Evan. "'A Daughter of the Puritans' and Her Old Master: Hawthorne, Una, and the Sexuality of Romance." In *Daughters and Fathers*. Edited by Lynda E. Boose and Betty S. Flowers. Baltimore: Johns Hopkins University Press (1989): 208–232.

Chandler, Elizabeth Lathrop. "A Study of the Sources of the Tales and Romances Written by Nathaniel Hawthorne before 1853." *Smith College Studies in Modern Languages* 7 (1926): 1–64.

Charvat, William, et al. *The Centenary Edition of the Works of Nathaniel Hawthorne*. Columbus:Ohio State University Press, 1980.

Coale, Samuel Chase. *Mesmerism and Hawthorne: Mediums of American Romance*. Tuscaloosa: University of Alabama Press, 1998.

———. "The Romance of Mesmerism: Hawthorne's Medium of Romance." In *Studies in the American Renaissance 1994*. Edited by Joel Myerson. Charlottesville: University Press of Virginia (1994): 271–288.

Colacurcio, Michael J., ed. *New Essays on "The Scarlet Letter."* Cambridge: Cambridge University Press. 1985.

———. *Hawthorne and the Historical Romance of New England*. Princeton: Princeton University Press, 1971.

———. "Footsteps of Ann Hutchinson: The Context of *The Scarlet Letter." ELH* 39 (1972): 459–494.

Crain, Patricia. *The Story of A: The Alphabetization of America from "The New England Primer" to "The Scarlet Letter."* Stanford, Calif.: Stanford University Press, 2000.

Crowley, J. Donald, ed. *Hawthorne: The Critical Heritage*. New York: Barnes & Noble, 1970.

Donohue, Agnes McNeill. *Hawthorne: Calvin's Ironic Stepchild*. Kent, Ohio: Kent State University Press, 1985.

Downing, David. "The Swelling Waves: Visuality, Metaphor, and Bodily Reality in *The Scarlet Letter*. *Studies in American Fiction* 12 (1984): 13–28.

Ehrlich, Gloria C. *Family Themes and Hawthorne's Fiction: The Tenacious Web*. New Brunswick, N.J.: Rutgers University Press, 1984.

Elbert, Monika. "Hester on the Scaffold, Dimmesdale in the Closet: Hawthorne's Seven-Year Itch." *Essays in Literature* 16 (1989): 234–255.

Fiedler, Leslie. *Love and Death in the American Novel*. 1960. New York: Anchor, 1992.

Fogle, Richard Harter. "Byron and Nathaniel Hawthorne." In *Romantic and Victorian Studies in Memory of William H. Marshall*. Edited by W. Paul Elledge and Richard L. Hoffman. Rutherford, N.J.: Fairleigh Dickinson University Press (1971): 181–197.

———. *Hawthorne's Fiction: The Light & the Dark*. Norman, OK: University of Oklahoma Press, 1964.

Friedman, Robert S. *Hawthorne's Romances: Social Drama and the Metaphor of Geometry*. Amsterdam: Harwood Academic Publishers, 2000.

Gatta, John. *American Madonna: Images of the Divine Woman in Literary Culture*. New York: Oxford University Press, 1997.

———. "The Apocalyptic End of *The Scarlet Letter*." *Texas Studies in Literature and Language* 32 (1990): 506–521.

Gerber, John C. "Form and Content in *The Scarlet Letter*." *New England Quarterly* 17 (1944): 25–55.

Gollin, Rita. *Portraits of Nathaniel Hawthorne: An Iconography*. DeKalb: Northern Illinois University Press, 1983.

Green, Carlanda. "The Custom-House: Hawthorne's Dark Wood of Error." *New England Quarterly* 53 (1980): 184–195.

Hall, Lawrence Sargent. *Hawthorne, Critic of Society*. New Haven: Yale University Press; London, H. Milford; Oxford University Press, 1944.

Hartman, James D. *Providence Tales and the Birth of American Literature*. Baltimore: Johns Hopkins University Press, 1999.

Idol, John L., Jr. and Buford Jones, eds. *Nathaniel Hawthorne: The Contemporary Reviews*. Cambridge: Cambridge University Press, 1994.

Keil, James C. "Reading, Writing and Recycling: Literary Archaeology and the Shape of Hawthorne's Career." *New England Quarterly* 65 (1992): 238–64.

Kennedy-Andrews, Elmer, ed. *Nathaniel Hawthorne: "The Scarlet Letter."* New York: Columbia University Press, 1999.

Laffrado, Laura. *Hawthorne's Literature for Children*. Athens: University of Georgia Press, 1992.

Lewis, R. W. B. *The American Adam: Innocence, Tragedy, and Tradition in the Nineteenth Century*. Chicago: University of Chicago Press, 1955; reprint, Chicago: University of Chicago Press, 1971.

Luedtke, Luther S. *Nathaniel Hawthorne and the Romance of the Orient*. Bloomington: Indiana University Press, 1989.

Lundblad, Jane. *Nathaniel Hawthorne and the Tradition of Gothic Romance*. Uppsala, Sweden: A.-B. Lundequistska Bokhandeln. 1946.

McFarland, Philip James. *Hawthorne in Concord*. New York: Grove Press, 2004.

McPherson, Hugo. *Hawthorne as Myth-Maker: A Study in Imagination*. Toronto: University of Toronto Press, 1969.

Mellow, James R. *Nathaniel Hawthorne in His Times*. Boston: Houghton Mifflin, 1980.

Mitchell, Thomas R. *Hawthorne's Fuller Mystery*. Amherst: University of Massachusetts Press, 1998.

Moore, Margaret B. *The Salem World of Nathaniel Hawthorne*. Columbia: University of Missouri Press, 1998.

Newberry, Frederick. *Hawthorne's Divided Loyalties: England and America in His Works*. Rutherford, N.J.: Fairleigh Dickinson University Press, 1987.

Person, Leland S., Jr. "Hawthorne's Love Letters: Writing and Relationship." *American Literature* 59 (1987): 211–227.

Reynolds, Larry J. "*The Scarlet Letter* and Revolutions Abroad." *American Literature* 57(1985): 44–67.

Schubert, Leland. *Hawthorne, the Artist: Fine-Art Devices in Fiction*. 1944. New York: Russell & Russell, 1963.

Stanton, Robert. "Hawthorne, Bunyan, and the American Romances." *PMLA* 71 (1956): 155–165.

Stein, William Bysshe. *Hawthorne's Faust: A Study of the Devil Archetype*. Gainesville: University of Florida Press, 1953.

Stokes, Edward, M.A. *Hawthorne's Influence on Dickens and George Eliot*. St. Lucia; New York: University of Queensland Press, 1985.

Turner, Arlin. *Nathaniel Hawthorne: A Biography*. New York: Oxford University Press, 1980.

Van Doren, Mark. *Nathaniel Hawthorne*. New York: Viking, 1949.

Waggoner, Hyatt H. *The Presence of Hawthorne*. Baton Rouge: Louisiana State University Press, 1979.

Walter, James. "The Letter and the Spirit in Hawthorne's Allegory of American Experience." *ESQ* 32 (1986): 36–54.

Warren, Austin. "*The Scarlet Letter*: A Literary Exercise in Moral Theology." *Southern Review* n.s. 1 (1965): 22–45.

White, Paula K. "Puritan Theories of History in Hawthorne's Fiction." *Canadian Review of American Studies* 9 (1978): 135–153.

Wineapple, Brenda. *Hawthorne: A Life*. New York: Alfred A. Knopf, 2003.

Woodberry, George Edward. *Nathaniel Hawthorne*. Introduction by Richard Poirier. New York, New York: Chelsea House, 1980.

Acknowledgments

"The Artists of the Novels: Coverdale, Holgrave, Kenyon" by Millicent Bell. From *Hawthorne's View of the Artist*. New York, N.Y.: University Publishers Inc., (1962): 151–173. © 1962 by the State University of New York. Reprinted by permission.

"Homely Witchcraft" by Frederick C. Crews. From *The Sins of the Fathers: Hawthorne's Psychological Themes*. New York: Oxford University Press (1966): 171–93. © 1966 by Frederick C. Crews. Reprinted by permission.

"'The Scribbler of Bygone Days': Perceptions of Time in Hawthorne's 'Custom House'" by Jane Donahue Eberwein. From *The Nathaniel Hawthorne Journal 1977*. Edited by C.E. Frazer Clark, Jr. Detroit, M.I.: Gale Research (1980): 239–47. © 1980 by Bruccoli Clark Publishers, Inc. Reprinted by permission.

"'The Dead Live Again': Hawthorne's Palingenic Art" by David C. Cody. From *ESQ*, vol. 35, no. 1 (1st Quarter 1989): 23–42. © 1989 by the Board of Regents of Washington State University Press. Reprinted by permission.

"Intercourse with the World: *The Blithedale Romance*" by Edwin Haviland Miller. From *Salem Is My Dwelling Place: A Life of Nathaniel Hawthorne*. Iowa City, Iowa: University of Iowa Press (1991); 366-75-6. © 1991 by the University of Iowa. Reprinted by permission.

"The Romance of Mesmerism: Hawthorne's Medium of Romance" by Samuel Coale. From *Studies in the American Renaissance* (1994): 271–88. © 1994 by Joel Myerson. Reprinted by permission.

"Narrative Transformations of Romanticism" by Michael Dunne. From *Hawthorne's Narrative Strategies*. Jackson, M.S.: University Press of Mississippi (1995): 129–54. © 1995 by the University Press of Mississippi. Reprinted by permission.

"'That Look Beneath': Hawthorne's Portrait of Benevolence in *The House of the Seven Gables*" by Joseph Flibbert. From *Critical Essays on Hawthorne's* The House of the Seven Gables. Edited by Bernard Rosenthal. New York, N.Y.: G.K. Hall & Co. (1995): 114–28. © 1995 by Bernard Rosenthal. Reprinted by permission.

"The Tongue of Flame" by Dan McCall. From *Citizens of Somewhere Else: Nathaniel Hawthorne and Henry James*. Ithaca and London: Cornell University Press (1999): 45–70. © 1999 by Cornell University Press. Reprinted by permission.

"Hawthorne's 'Mad, Merry Stream of Human Life: The Roman Carnival as Apocalypse' in *The Marble Faun*" by David B. Kesterson. From *Value and Vision in American Literature: Literary Essays in Honor of Ray Lewis White*. Edited by Joseph Candido. Athens: Ohio University Press (1999): 95–114. © 1999 by Joseph Candido. Reprinted by permission.

"A Poem by Lowell" by Richard Kopley. From *The Threads of* The Scarlet Letter: *A Study of Hawthorne's Transformative Art*. Newark, D.E.: University of Delaware Press; London: Associated University Presses (2003): 36–63. © 2003 by Rosemont Publishing & Printing Corp. Reprinted by permission.

Every effort has been made to contact the owners of copyrighted material and secure copyright permission. Articles appearing in this volume generally appear much as they did in their original publication—in some cases Greek text has been removed from the original article. Those interested in locating the original source will find bibliographic information in the bibliography and acknowledgments sections of this volume.

Index